INDIANA JONES IN HISTORY

From Pompeii to the Moon

Justin M. Jacobs, Ph.D.

To Rick~

Best wishes,

Pulp Hero Press
The Most Dangerous Books on Earth
www.PulpHeroPress.com

Pulp Hero Press publishes its books in a variety of print and electronic formats. Some content that appears in one format may not appear in another.

Editor: Bob McLain
Layout: Artisanal Text

ISBN 978-1-68390-099-3
Printed in the United States of America

Pulp Hero Press | www.PulpHeroPress.com
Address queries to bob@pulpheropress.com

For Sasha and Lance—
may you, too, turn the wonders of your youth into a lifelong pursuit.

CONTENTS

List of Documentary Episodes

Twenty-one short documentary episodes have been created by the author to further illustrate and expand upon the themes, characters, and events narrated in this book. Each episode is between ten to fifteen minutes long and is available to stream for free at indianajonesinhistory.com. (Alternatively, you can simply enter the episode number and title into any Internet search engine.) The documentary is distinct from the book and may be watched independently of it. But for those who wish to watch the episodes in a way that corresponds to the content of each chapter in this book, a list of the most relevant episodes has been provided at the end of each chapter.

Episode I: Who Was Indiana Jones?

Episode II: Excavating Pompeii

Episode III: Building the Louvre

Episode IV: The Elgin Marbles

Episode V: The Great Belzoni

Episode VI: Egyptology & Egyptomania

Episode VII: The Sultan and the Pasha

Episode VIII: The Trojan War

Episode IX: Tutankhamun

Episode X: The Mummy's Curse

Episode XI: Moses vs. Pharaoh

Episode XII: The Treasures of China

Episode XIII: The Forbidden City

Episode XIV: The Silk Road

Preface

For nearly two hundred years, every adventure began with a secret. Some of them were big, others small. A few of them were heinous; many were harmless.

But they were all secrets.

What was the secret? Quite simply, it was this: that every adventure was merely what it appeared to be. On the contrary, most adventures were a great deal more than what they appeared to be. What they appeared to be was all about science. But more often than not, "science" turned out to be a vague pretext for a whole host of hidden motives—some less savory than others.

This book traces those motives over two centuries of expeditions, excavations, and exploration undertaken by daring scientists and adventurous scholars, all in the name of a higher good. Most of our time will be spent in the Middle East and China, with some brief but notable interludes in Latin America, Africa, and Europe. No matter where we go, however, we will be hot on the trail of Western archaeologists, historians, artists, ambassadors, journalists, anthropologists, geologists, ethnologists, businessmen, philanthropists, museum curators, and idle gentlemen as they invoke the selfless ideals of science for hidden political, financial, or social gain. We begin with the greatest enabler of all—the modern museum—and its rise from the gritty excavations of Pompeii to Napoleon's martial endowment of the Louvre. From there we move on to explore the logic of the "compensations of plunder," without which we cannot understand the underlying barter calculus of nearly every dig prior to World War I. A journey into the popular consumption of Egyptomania and the rise of non-Western discontent with Western archaeologists will round out our time in the nineteenth century, before turning to the tumultuous era of the two world wars. Along the way, we will bump into an Italian circus freak with dreams of becoming a hydrologist and a Jewish refugee with a penchant for jumping out of American airplanes and stealing documents from the French state.

Such a diverse cast of characters and backdrops will be brought together under the iconic shadow cast by Indiana Jones. Of course, the Indiana Jones film franchise is pure Hollywood fiction. But the central dramatic premise of these hugely popular movies—that the future of the human race somehow depends upon the "proper" handling of art and artifacts—is one that would resonate quite deeply with the known ideological dispositions of the real-life historical coun-terparts to Indiana Jones. Unfortunately, claims that this or that archaeologist was "a" (or sometimes "the") real-life Indiana Jones have become a tired cliché of the "adventure biography" genre, casting much confusion and doubt about what the business of archaeology and expeditions was truly all about. Typically, these are marketing ploys that go no further than the dust jacket, with a conventional biography of a single explorer awaiting the reader inside.

This book is different. From the outset, I acknowledge and embrace the unsentimental truth of the matter: that there is no premeditated historical counterpart for the man with the bullwhip. George Lucas and Steven Spielberg may be master filmmakers, but they are not historians. As I discuss in detail in chapter 8, "Hollywood vs. History," the main plotlines and creative inspiration for all four completed films owe little debt to anything recognizable as historical scholarship, either then or today. And yet somehow the filmmakers, despite being largely uninterested in the historical authenticity of their protagonist, still managed to give cinematic voice to some of the enduring themes and controversies of their hero's real-life profession.

It is the evolution of these themes and controversies that form the narrative spine of this book. Since no single person can ever be identified as the inspiration for the fictional Hollywood icon, I waste no time in trying. Far more interest-ing is a history of the very real ideas, events, and institutions that made possible the Western cultural fantasy of a debonair archaeologist with a talent for punching Nazis. In place of a single protagonist seemingly larger than life, we will instead encounter a great many fascinating historical figures in the geopolitical context of their own day and age. These men, most of whom were just as industrious and clever as any character dreamt up by a Hollywood screenwriter (if not quite as handsome), cannot be understood without an examination of the ever-changing ideas, events, and institutions that facilitated their activities. Unlike the Indiana Jones of the silver screen, Indiana Jones in history was only as successful as the historical conditions of the day allowed him to be.

No matter what conditions they faced, however, every adventurous scholar and daring scientist over the past two centuries was convinced of two absolute truths in life. The first was that science is good. The second, which followed naturally from the first, was that "my" science is better than "your" science. From these two unshakeable convictions arose both impressive achievements and dubious perversions, from the laudable preservation of untold aesthetic masterpieces to the nigh unspeakable horrors of the Holocaust. In 1977, Richard Nixon, the disgraced American president, gave voice to one of the most famous distillations of the cognitive dissonance produced by adherence to ostensibly admirable yet ultimately self-serving ideals. Three years after resigning his office on the threat of impeachment, the British journalist David Frost asked Nixon whether or not criminal activity could be justified so long as it was done "in the best interests of the nation." Nixon's response? "Well, when the president does it, that means that it is *not* illegal."

These words are worth bearing in mind over the course of the following chapters. After all, nearly every scholar who removed art and artifacts from one land to another would have subscribed to a slightly revised version of Nixon's famous statement, with the substitution of "archaeologist" (or any profession thought to adhere to scientific standards) for "president," and "illicit" for "illegal." In other words, "when a scientifically trained scholar does it, that means it is *not* illicit." When such a widely accepted truism is combined with the typical conceit every one of us holds toward our own most noble ideals—or those of our collective communities, nations, and empires—it becomes increasingly difficult to see where the beautiful ideal ends and the selfish reality begins.

This book treats in equal measure both the abstract ideal and the messy reality. The historical Indiana Jones was not all about science and duplicity. Much of his time was spent mired in mundane logistics. After all, he had to form productive relationships with the local elites who signed his passport and the local laborers who got their hands dirty on his behalf. How could he get them to render assistance to the foreign explorer? Were they coerced into doing so, or was their participation voluntary? If coerced, who coerced them? If voluntary, what was expected in return? What role did the institution of the modern museum play in all this? Did the people of the Ottoman and Chinese empires know just what the foreigners were up to, or was a measure of deceit involved? Why was the situation in China so different from that in the Middle East? And the most vexing question of all: If it was okay for Europeans to remove artifacts from distant lands in the year 1825, why was it no longer okay to do so in 1925? What changed in those intervening years?

These are all valid and interesting questions, and each will be answered in turn in the pages that follow. At the center of the narrative are the men who invoked lofty ideals in order to accomplish the mundane work of digging, chiseling, pushing, pulling, cutting, mapping, and displaying the forlorn treasures of our world, usually in service to some hidden political, financial, or social agenda. For about a hundred years, the Western archaeologist pretty much had his way, filling his museums back home with the most magnificent collections of art and antiquities the world has ever seen. The first five chapters of this book narrate the major events, people, and themes of this century of privilege. Eventually, however, the Western monopoly proved difficult to maintain, and it was only a matter of time before the discourse of "science" was turned back against its creators by those once excluded from the archaeological enterprise (chapter 6). The ideal of politically disinterested science then further splintered under the weight of two world wars, with scholars on all sides of the conflict invoking similar ideals in pursuit of irreconcilable goals (chapter 7). An eighth and final chapter turns to Indiana Jones in Hollywood, using the knowledge gained in the first seven chapters to test the historical accuracy of the stories told by these iconic films.

These fascinating yet complex developments are described here for the first time in a single continuous narrative. Our time frame is the two hundred years in which the scientific ideal could be invoked to transport cultural treasures across ethnic, cultural, and political boundaries without the taint of blatant hypocrisy. This means that some of the greatest archaeological discoveries of the modern world, such as the Terracotta Army in China, are not discussed in the following chapters. The reason is simple: the Terracotta Army, disentombed in 1974, was found during a time when it was no longer possible for European and American scientists to claim possession of artifacts far from their shores. As a result, the Terracotta Army is fascinating for what it can tell us about the China of 206 B.C. But it is much less interesting for what it can tell us about the China of 1974, other than the fact that it was a strong and stable country perfectly capable of keeping its treasures from leaving its borders. By contrast, the excavation of King Tut's tomb by a British archaeologist five decades earlier—treated in chapters 3 and 6—reveals a great deal about the history of the world during the 1920s.

One of the unique features of this book is that it pays more attention to the ever-changing political and economic conditions that enabled the Western archaeologist than it does to the discoveries themselves. This is not a history of Western civilization as told through the great digs of our time. Rather, it is a history of how those digs came to be in the first place. In other words, it is a history of the world that created Indiana Jones more than it is about Indiana Jones himself.

Continue the journey at indianajonesinhistory.com:

- EPISODE I: Who Was Indiana Jones?

CHAPTER ONE

That Belongs in a Museum

Lying on his deathbed, wracked by severe asthma and pneumonia, Lieutenant Colonel Karl Jakob Weber cut a pathetic figure. On January 11, 1764, in a desperate plea to Ferdinand of Bourbon, King of Naples and Sicily, Weber asked His Majesty to grant "a fortnight of leave in Naples" so that he might recover from a "serious infirmity contracted in the underground excavations" of Resina, the modern-day city built atop the buried ruins of Herculaneum, approximately ten miles northwest of Pompeii. The king, in recognition of Weber's thirteen-year tenure as chief overseer of the excavations for his father, Charles, granted the request, along with fifty ducats to effect a cure. It was all for naught. Just one month later, Weber, aged fifty-two, succumbed to his illness, having found no remedy for the "health I lost in the grottoes" of the buried Roman cities.

Weber, a Swiss military engineer in the Royal Guard, died in pursuit of an idea. In order to understand the significance of this idea, we need to know what preceded it. Before Weber's arrival, the excavations at Resina had been carried out under the eye of Spanish engineer Rocque Joaquin de Alcubierre. In 1738, Alcubierre was entrusted with preparing plans for a new summer palace and pleasure gardens to be built for his king at the seaside town of Portici, about five miles southeast of Naples and well within the shadow of Mt. Vesuvius. This charge brought Alcubierre into contact with the local residents of nearby Resina, who had long managed to squeeze a profit from the archaeological wonderland hidden beneath their town. Every time a farmer dug a new well into the artesian aquifers below, he happened upon some portion of broken marble or cracked statuary, for which any number of wealthy landlords, nobles, or traveling antiquarians were willing to pay good money. Already by the sixteenth century, four marble torsos recovered from underground shafts were on proud display in the courtyard of a local church. Some residents even touted their services as "guides" who could help escort courageous customers down into the hastily burrowed tunnels in search of their own buried treasure.

Alcubierre imposed an order and discipline on the situation in Resina, but he did not challenge the goals or methods of the scavengers who had come before him. He simply wanted to do what they had done, but on a much grander scale—for this time, the customer was the powerful and wealthy Charles of Bourbon, the newly crowned King of Naples and Sicily. Charles, born to a dynasty of French extraction but groomed for a Spanish throne, instructed Alcubierre to "build a few grottoes and see what might be found." Of course, both Charles and Alcubierre, long aware of the ancient goods peddled by the locals, knew what was likely to be found beneath the soil of Resina: a labyrinthine cellar full of complimentary Roman antiquities. Unburdened by rival claims of ownership, each would be fit to decorate the king's new palace at Portici.

Alcubierre had not been trained to dig for antiquities, for no such training yet existed anywhere in the world. Instead, the recovery of buried treasure was a task most often delegated to someone already proficient in the art of digging a deep and stable hole in the ground, one that would not bury its occupants alive—in other words, someone who knew how to manage a mine. In the middle of the eighteenth century, only military engineers were likely to possess such expertise. Men like Alcubierre also evinced the highly desirable skills of an experienced cartographer, with advanced training in mathematics and architecture. Most of the time, they spent their days managing a team of laborers—soldiers, convicts, and local residents—who quarried for suitable geological materials with which to construct military fortifications. It was a relatively simple matter, then, to redirect such talents toward the retrieval of buried antiquities. As one contemporary noted, in selecting a director of the excavations, Charles of Bourbon

Figure 1.1.
Charles of Bourbon, King of Naples and Sicily.

chose Alcubierre "because he professes military architecture." In other words, Alcubierre "knew how to operate an underground excavation in a safe manner and he knew how to make plans of the buildings he would encounter there."

Such plans were a pragmatic means to an end. After all, King Charles viewed the treasures of Pompeii and Herculaneum not through the eyes of an archaeologist or historian, but rather through those of a politician. And politicians have attempted to wrap themselves in the prestige of artistic glory since time immemorial. Whenever they do so, they tend to fetishize the aesthetic and moral qualities of the art they have commissioned or the antiquities they have collected. In eighteenth-century Europe, kings, dukes, earls, and courtiers acquired and displayed an eccentric cornucopia of ancient manuscripts, seals, inscriptions, weapons, statues, paintings, and talismans primarily for the prestige these objects conferred upon them in elite social circles. The objects were arranged in such a way as to narrate in visual form the story of one man's greatness, usually by references to stories told in the Greek, Latin, or Hebrew literary canon. What politicians did *not* do were to craft broad narratives of how this or that aspect of our world came to be. Their collections were private, and the mythologized messages they projected were tailored to accentuate the glory of one man and one man alone. These politicians did not strive to present even the pretense of an objective commentary on the history of art, nature, or society.

Besides politicians, there were antiquarians. Antiquarians differed from politicians in their attempt to extract from their art and antiquities a body of knowledge that was at least nominally independent from the reputation and image of the men and women who owned the objects. Most importantly, they tended to impose some sort of classification system onto their collections in order to make objective sense of what often appeared to be subjective chaos. These classification schemes may seem quirky and bizarre today, but they represented a definite break with the self-referential and grossly mythologized messages projected by the murals, reliefs, and busts decorating any number of royal palaces. The wealthiest and most resourceful antiquarians built collections that were so renowned that a new German word, *wunderkammer* ("cabinet of curiosities"), was coined to describe them. Some antiquarians chose to highlight the natural sciences, while others focused more on art and antiquities. Many *wunderkammer* were little more than status symbols, a place to impress one's colleagues, family, and friends with spectacle rather than scholarship. What antiquarians all had in common, however, was an avowed commitment to an externally imposed classification system that was not beholden to a vainglorious politician.

To our eyes today, the antiquarian's *wunderkammer* often appears just as chaotic and whimsical as the private palace collections of kings and queens. And in practice, the line separating the two was frequently blurred. The Portici Palace, the institutional embodiment of this overlap, was conceived and built with both modes of representation in mind. King Charles wanted to portray himself as an enlightened monarch who patronized bodies of knowledge—the arts and

Figure 1.2. Art as propaganda.
Most private collections of art in Europe were purposely
arranged to overwhelm the visitor with mythical
tales and literary allusions of the owner's grandeur.
Detached analysis of such a spectacle was unlikely.

Figure 1.3. Ole Worm's Wunderkammer.
Though the cabinet of curiosities promised access to an
eclectic body of organized knowledge separate from
the identity of its owner, most guests—by invitation
only—still came for the spectacle, and associated that
spectacle with the personal virtue of its curator.

sciences—separate from his individual persona. But he was also an arrogant politician who wanted nothing more than to stock his palace with as many specimens of art and antiquities as he could, regardless of whether or not any independent body of knowledge was produced by their recovery. The only "knowledge" Charles truly wished to produce was the knowledge that he, more than any other monarch, represented a revival of the glories of ancient Rome. For when a European king associated himself with the Romans, he was attempting to claim political descent from the largest, most powerful, and longest-lasting empire ever to rule over Europe.

In order to claim symbolic descent from the Romans, however, nothing was more important than the ownership and display of antiquities evocative of the Roman era. Above all else, this was the primary motivation behind the early excavations of Pompeii and Herculaneum. Alcubierre was not interested in reconstructing the urban layout of an ancient Roman city or in reinterpreting the history of the Roman empire. These would constitute distinct bodies of knowledge wholly unrelated to King Charles the man. To put it another way, he was not interested in constructing narratives of how anything unconnected to the personal power and reputation of his own political patron came to be. His goal was simple: turn the newly built Portici Palace into something that would leave an indelible impression on all who visited its halls. If successful, Alcubierre would give Charles of Bourbon an antiquarian spectacle unmatched anywhere else in Europe. Of course, some learned men would study the ruins with an eye toward increasing the store of human knowledge about the distant past. But most visitors lucky enough to be invited to the Portici Palace would come away having indulged in a seductively emotional experience, convinced that this was a king worthy of a realm far greater than just Naples and Sicily—much like the Romans themselves.

The goal of the excavations was thus clear. But how to go about it? For a little more than a decade, from 1738 to 1750, Alcubierre was given free rein to devise his own approach to the site. His sole motivation was to obtain rare Roman antiquities as cheaply and efficiently as possible. Everything else

Figure 1.4. Excavating Pompeii.
In an excavation pit in Pompeii, the upper classes and a pet dog look on while the lower classes bend their backs in hard labor. Over the next two hundred years, this scene—dog included— would be repeated over and over again throughout the world, with the substitution of dark-skinned labor for that of white.

was a secondary concern. But there were several important logistical matters requiring Alcubierre's attention before spade could be set to soil. At the top of this list was the question of labor: Who was going to dig? Certainly not Alcubierre, and certainly not anyone who had received an education, title, or inheritance. Such "dirty" work was considered beneath their social station, and most of them openly sneered at it. The stigma of laboring with one's hands was so great that anyone with the means to avoid such work—i.e., wealth and connec- tions—would have leveraged all available resources to do so.

That left the lower classes. Here we get our first glimpse of a tense social dynamic destined to be repeated time and again at nearly every dig or expedition for the next two hundred years. It is a phenomenon familiar to us from the iconic opening scene of *Raiders of the Lost Ark*. Two men enter a site, both intent on working together to remove a valuable antiq- uity, and both expecting to get paid for their efforts. But one man (Indiana Jones) is a learned cosmopolitan scholar, while the other man (Satipo, his Peruvian guide) is an uneducated local. Both are engaged in precisely the same physical activity: the removal of an artifact. But only one man has the education, wealth, and social network necessary to justify his removal of the antiquity as an altruistic act in service to a greater power (i.e., a *wunderkammer*, museum, or other learned organization).

The local guide, handicapped by his lack of education, wealth, and social network, can do little to combat the assumption—cast upon him by his upper-class employer— that his participation is motivated solely by greed and avarice. As happens in the film, it is assumed that someone like Satipo would betray his social "better" the moment his back is turned. After all, the assumption goes, such backstabbing behavior is what passes for "honor" among the lower classes. In the end, the scholar takes all the credit and returns home to pomp and circumstance, while the lower-class laborers fade into anonymity, ritually mocked and maligned for their need to place economic subsistence above scholarly research. This division of labor was reflected in the field, as when T.E. Lawrence ("Lawrence of Arabia") said of the British archaeologist Flinders Petrie that what he wants "is a pedestrian intelligence to do the hackwork for him, while he does the fine things." In *Raiders of the Lost Ark*, Satipo meets with a predictably gruesome death, one clearly meant as recompense for his betrayal of the scholarly hero, who stops to mock his corpse on his way out of the cave.

To be fair, a few of the men who labored for Alcubierre at Resina did conceal an unsavory past. Some were forced laborers, which denoted a mixture of criminals, slaves, and other subjugated unfortunates. In 1743, a visiting Englishman provided a vivid description of twenty galley slaves "chained together, two and two, and guarded by soldiers." Each slave had a "small basket into which they put what they find, and are well searched at their coming out from their work." Military discipline was the order of the day, and even the smallest instance of theft was met with flogging, torture, or exile. But there was another group of laborers as well, one whose participation was largely voluntary. These were the "freemen," and they were compensated for their labor. We will refer to them— and others like them throughout the world—as "subsistence diggers." This useful phrase highlights their own motivation for participating in the excavations: to extricate themselves from chronic poverty by supplementing meager incomes with sideline labor, be it through the actual sweat of their brow or the sale of purloined artifacts on the underground market.

Willingly employed or not, all the laborers under Alcubierre's watch were sent into dangerous and even life-threatening conditions. The perils of the excavations were distinct to each site. Herculaneum, for instance, lay beneath the modern-day town of Resina, which had been built atop the magma-encased ruins of its predecessor. This delicate situation required Alcubierre's men to burrow directly underneath the foundations of private residences and streets, a risky proposition that frequently resulted in cracked walls and sinkholes on the surface. The wealthier and more resourceful of Resina's landowners, mindful of irrecoverable property damages, repeatedly petitioned the king to order Alcubierre's men to stay away from their property, often with success.

Conditions within the tunnels themselves were horrid. The cramped and narrow spaces were poorly ventilated and filled with an insalubrious mix of torch smoke and salty perspiration. Artesian aquifers blended with rainwater run-off to create a cold and damp environment. In most passageways, there was barely enough room for two workers to pass one another by. One contemporary observer concluded that Alcubierre and his engineers had "satisfied themselves with cleaning out the city like a mine, by leaving a number of pillars to support the roof, which otherwise would be in danger of falling." Even the simplest act of entering and leaving Herculaneum was fraught with peril. In a letter to King Charles, Weber once noted "the obvious danger to my life of being lowered on a rope twenty-seven meters into the Pozzo dei Ciceri," something he did "solely out of love for Your Majesty." Weber complained that he was "daily exposed to many unfortunate accidents and events of a different kind," and felt uneasy in committing his life "to the forced laborers who manage the wheel, axle, ropes, pulley, and net."

Alcubierre experimented with various measures to improve working conditions within the tunnels, even going so far as to install a manual air pump whose thirty-six sections of tin tubing extended more than forty meters up to the surface. But no one could escape the ill effects of the toxic subterranean air.

Workers were frequently stricken with tuberculosis, various eye ailments, lung problems of every sort, and pneumonia. Alcubierre once felt compelled to take a four-year leave of absence to recover his health, while Weber succumbed to pneumonia before his fifty-third birthday. As the dangers of Herculaneum become increasingly known, the mothers of Resina began to forbid their sons from working as guides. Small riots were known to break out when news of a freeman fatality circulated around town.

In contrast to the hardened lava tunnels of Herculaneum, Pompeii was mostly one big field of soft volcanic ash, too soft and shifty to allow for anything other than the intermittent cultivation of crops. Though this allowed for excavations to take place in the open air, still there were lurking dangers. The lack of a hardened magma substratum made digging easier, but it also meant that ashy fields could collapse without notice, burying workers alive. Most sinister of all, however, were the pockets of odorless carbon dioxide concealed within the pyroclastic debris. These hidden pockets of poisonous gas, known as *mofeta*, were dreaded as much as any underground horror of Herculaneum. The only warning available to the laborers at Pompeii was if the *mofeta* also contained traces of hydrogen sulfide, in which case it emitted the pungent aroma of rotten eggs. When such came to pass, everyone at the site ran for their lives, in one case creating a work stoppage that lasted for three whole months.

None of these assaults on life and limb, however, were enough to deter Charles of Bourbon, who received daily updates from the comfort of his palace. So long as periodic antiquarian harvests met with the king's approval, the operations at Herculaneum and Pompeii continued to receive his blessing and financial support. King Charles was determined to drape himself in the most authentic revival of Roman regalia yet seen, and only one thing could stand in his way: the depletion of his antiquarian quarry. As such, Alcubierre spared no effort to ensure an unbroken parade of glitzy centerpieces for the royal palace. He focused his excavations on sites closer to the Bay of Naples, hoping to find wealthy Roman seaside villas filled with expensive statuary and paintings. Once an ancient habitation was identified, Alcubierre directed his laborers to tunnel straight into the corners of individual rooms, on the belief that small valuables were more likely to be stored near the walls.

In his wake, Alcubierre left a calculated trail of destruction. By today's standards, his methods are best described as little more than the glorified burglary of an ancient tomb. They were justified at the time, however, through the lofty façade of royal virtue, which inclusion of these antiquities into the king's collection was designed to reinforce. In both Herculaneum and Pompeii, long-buried residences were surgically disemboweled, only to be reburied with backfill once the most valuable possessions of its long-dead owners had been removed. Paintings and murals, preserved in almost pristine condition, were simply cut out of the wall and deposited in the king's storeroom. Most disturbing of all, Alcubierre was ordered to smash and destroy any antiquity or painting deemed too similar to any artifact already housed in Portici Palace. The violent gouge marks of the pickaxe are still visible on some murals today. The goal was not to recover and preserve a complete historical record of the site, but rather to increase the value of what King Charles selectively chose to retain. As such, duplicate antiquities could only serve to dilute the uniqueness of the royal collection.

By the standards of his day, Alcubierre had acquitted himself well. The end more than justified the means: Charles now owned an incomparable antiquarian trove capable of placing him among the foremost patrons of the arts. And that is exactly the image his ministers began to cultivate abroad. In 1750, an English translation of Marquis Don Marcello di Venuti's *Description of the First Discoveries of the Ancient City of Heraclea* appeared in London. The author began by "congratulating our Age, that it has been able, as it were, to look back, and actually see the Customs and Manner of the Ancients." Who was responsible for this remarkable facilitation of antiquarian time travel? "The learned World render their gratefullest Acknowledgements," di Venuti continued, "of the Magnificences of the unparalleled CHARLES King of the Two Sicilies, who, not regarding any Expence, has not only caused these precious Monuments of Antiquity to be dug out of the Bowels of the Earth; but also preserves them with the greatest Care and Diligence." In case his readers still puzzled over the precise relationship between the recovery of ancient Roman artifacts and the present-day virtue of King Charles, di Venuti spelled it out for them. The excavations at Pompeii, he concluded, had provided the world with "a grander Idea of the Roman Magnificence, and a more glorious Remembrance of our invincible King."

Into this self-congratulatory atmosphere stepped the Swiss engineer Karl Jakob Weber. In 1750, the same year that di Venuti's laudatory tract was published in London, Weber, who had long served as an assistant to Alcubierre, was tapped to replace his supervisor as chief director of the excavations. The new director had some radically new ideas about how to run the operations under his charge. Understanding the difference between Alcubierre and Weber is to understand where and when the real-life Indiana Jones enters the historical record. For starters, Weber wanted to end the practice of treating the underground ruins as little more than an antiquarian quarry, in which precious artifacts were stripped from their surroundings without any regard for geological and historical context. After happening upon a beautiful mosaic in a Herculaneum gymnasium, Weber suggested that "the curiosity of the public and of foreigners will find particular satisfaction in seeing some of those mosaic pavements in their proper places and rooms." In other words, not every antiquity had to find its way into Portici Palace or suffer destruction and reburial—some could be left in their original location for the edification of the general public. To put it another way, not everything uncovered at Pompeii had to be viewed solely in light of its ability to glorify the king. Some things could be preserved for their potential contribution to a separate body of knowledge, knowledge that was entirely divorced from the person and reputation of Charles of Bourbon.

Weber's proposals did not stop there. In order to support the idea of a permanent underground (Herculaneum) or open-air (Pompeii) exhibit of Roman antiquities accessible to a wider audience, Weber had to deal with the interconnected problems of backfill and property rights. Alcubierre had long determined that all excavated soil should be returned to its original underground cavity once objects of interest had

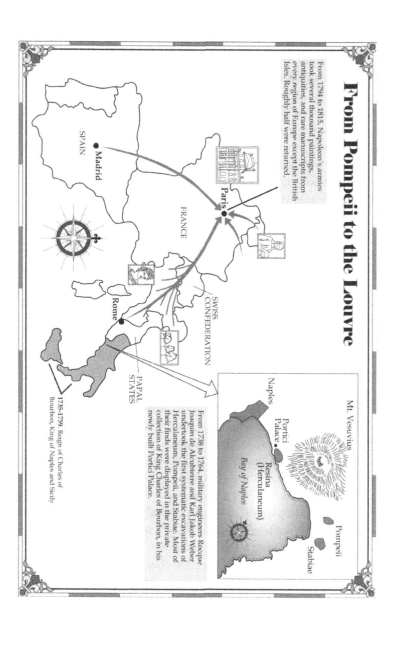

From Pompeii to the Louvre

From 1794 to 1815, Napoleon's armies took several thousand paintings, antiquities, and rare manuscripts from every region of Europe except the British Isles. Roughly half were returned.

SPAIN

● Madrid

FRANCE

Paris ●

SWISS CONFEDERATION

Rome ●

PAPAL STATES

1735-1759, Reign of Charles of Bourbon, King of Naples and Sicily

Mt. Vesuvius

Naples

Portici Palace ●

Resina (Herculaneum)

Bay of Naples

Pompeii

Stabiae

From 1738 to 1764, military engineers Rocque Joaqun de Alcubierre and Karl Jakob Weber undertook the first systematic excavations of Herculaneum, Pompeii, and Stabiae. Most of their finds were displayed in the private collection of King Charles of Bourbon, in his newly built Portici Palace.

been removed or destroyed. Property owners whose fields or residences were impacted by the excavations were invariably compensated for their losses, with the property later restored to its original condition and returned to the owner. Weber, longing to obtain a more comprehensive view of the architectural integrity of the ancient town, experimented with the use of masonry pillars that could support property foundations above ground while ensuring that tunnels below ground could remain clear of backfill—and thus perennially accessible. He also drew up plans to compensate landlords for the permanent appropriation of their property in the event that significant ruins were identified beneath their land.

These proposals were too much for Alcubierre, who warned his former understudy to "put aside the idea that it is the principal concern of your employ to draw the general plan of these ancient cities." According to Alcubierre, "the principal work of the excavators should be inside the habitations, as I have always advised and has been done in the past, since this is where one should hope for the best and most precious treasures." Camillo Paderni, another one of the antiquarians in King Charles' employ, criticized Weber for mounting expenses and lack of portable additions to the gallery at Portici. "With the method of excavating followed by Don Carlo Weber, it is purely by chance that anything is found," Paderni wrote. He further noted that Weber stubbornly focused his efforts on areas where antiquities were known to be scarce, all for the sake of drawing blueprints of the broader urban layout of the ancient cities. Observing that the costs of Weber's approach "mount daily," he lamented the ways in which Weber "is determined to draw a plan of Pompeii and Stabiae and tries to assert with his Swiss logic that these plans are more necessary and have greater merit than the antiquities which might be found."

Weber's ideas were years ahead of their time, and few people in Naples took them seriously. But scholars elsewhere in Europe found much to admire. One such enthusiast was Johann Joachim Winckelmann, a German art historian and amateur archaeologist. In 1758 and again in 1762, Winckelmann made two extended trips to visit the excavations at Herculaneum and Pompeii. What he observed in Weber's approach elicited a profound admiration. "To this intelligent man," Winckelmann observed, referring to Weber, "are owed all the sensible arrangements made. The first of these was to draw up an exact plan of the underground galleries and the excavated buildings in all their dimensions." He described Weber's plans of the underground excavations as "drawn with such incredible exactness" that they facilitated "great insights which, God willing, I will one day bring to light."

Winckelmann's desire to "bring to light" Weber's blueprints stemmed from his adverse reaction to the closely guarded nature of King Charles' operation. Access to the dug-out sites was tightly restricted, and all visitors were supposed to apply for royal permission to enter any part of the excavations. This fact highlights yet another distinctive feature of the antiquarian mindset, both in Europe and elsewhere: the recovery and display of the material past were privately funded affairs, with "finders keepers" the motto of the day. As such, access to the results of any excavation—including the subsequently enriched Portici Palace—was limited to the bankrolling patron and members of his selected social network. Visitors such as Winckelmann were not even allowed to take notes during their tour. The goal was not historical knowledge for all; it was the exaltation of King Charles as the reincarnation of Roman glory. "Everything is guarded with such jealously," Winckelmann later fumed, "that one cannot measure the diameter of a single column even at the temple or forum in Pozzuoli. How much time I wasted at Portici trying to form a clear notion of the ruins!" For now, no one in Naples was interested in implementing any of Weber's or Winckelmann's ideas. For half a century after Weber's death, the buried cities of Mt. Vesuvius continued to be regarded as little more than well-stocked antiquarian quarries. Weber's own plans of the ruins were not published by the Accademia Ercolanese, the privately funded learned body associated with the ruins, until 1797, more than thirty years after his death. The magnificent collection inside Portici Palace—part spectacle, part *wunderkammer*—was adequate to the king's needs, and Charles of Bourbon felt no real compulsion to tout his antiquarian *bona fides* to anyone but other elites.

But Weber had taken the first steps in the implementation of a novel concept: that there was be a higher secular good beyond the reputation of his patron, and that this good could best be served through scientific preservation and public education. Fortunately for Weber, just across the Alps in France, Louis of Bourbon was ready to pick up where Weber had left off. If Weber is to receive credit for embodying the earliest ideals of the modern museum in an outdoor setting, then Louis XV is to receive credit for doing the same indoors. As an institution, the museum will eventually come to constitute the center of gravity around which the entire world of art and antiquities revolves. It will provide Indiana Jones with his classic signature phrase ("That belongs in a museum!") and ensure that audiences know who is the bad guy (the one who keeps the artifact for himself) and who is the good guy (the one who puts the artifact in a museum). Without a museum, a collector of antiquities is little more than a glorified treasure-seeker, much like Alcubierre and King Charles, redeemable only through a transparently self-serving and dubious discourse of gentlemanly virtue. With it, however, he becomes the celebrated guardian of all that is good in science and civilization.

So where and when did this powerful institution come about? In 1750, the same year that Weber took over the reins of the Vesuvius excavations, the Luxembourg Gallery opened its doors in Paris. The origins of this new gallery lay in the royal palace at Versailles, where the burgeoning collection of Louis XV's artwork could no longer fit into the limited space for display. Some of the king's ministers proposed displaying these languishing paintings in such a way so as to educate French artists about what "good" art looked like before they went on to further study in Rome. For nearly thirty years until its closure in 1779, the Luxembourg Gallery shouldered this role. We will view it as a transitional institution, halfway between a cabinet of curiosity and its more famous successor: the Musée du Louvre.

What distinguished the Luxembourg Gallery in its time and place was the obsession of its curators on an adherence to the ideals of science and education. All previous collections of art, the *wunderkammer* included, had attempted to overwhelm their audiences with a claustrophobic assortment of optical delights and marvelous clutter. Critical examination of the collection was of secondary importance, and, when undertaken, lacked both rigor and methodology. It was increasingly believed, however, that the merits of any given work of art lay beyond the reach of the untrained eye. Instead, like the natural world, they could only be unlocked through trained scientific analysis. A true scientific methodology would then in turn produce a pedagogical agenda for the improvement of the people, who, once improved, would prove worthy of the title of "citizen" rather than "subject." Though the Luxembourg Gallery was primarily intended for French artists, interested members of the general public could gain admittance as well. Once inside, they were treated to a carefully prepared exhibition of Enlightenment ideals. In order to mold an accomplished French painter—or simply a generalist connoisseur of painting—science and reason would now be called upon to facilitate the desired transformation of the individual.

Applied to the world of art, "science" and "reason" took the form of a classification scheme shamelessly plagiarized from the natural sciences. Exhibition rooms in the Luxembourg Gallery organized their artwork according to the artistic qualities each group of paintings was believed to embody. Visitors were then encouraged to compare and contrast these collective qualities with other groups of paintings. If you wanted to learn about the art of drawing and expression, examine the work of Guido Reni, but avoid those of Caravaggio. Move on to the next hall to compare ten different paintings each of the Virgin and Child, Passion of the Christ, lives of saints, landscapes, and still life. By such means one might learn the strengths and weaknesses of unique artistic typologies, much as naturalists traced the distinctive traits of each genus and species. Jean-Baptist-Pierre Lebrun, a prominent art dealer and connoisseur, made the connection between art and natural science explicit. "A collection not arranged in that fashion," he observed, "was as ridiculous as a natural history cabinet arranged without regard to genus, class, or family."

The integration of a scientific approach into the first modern museum was not limited to the adaptation of a naturalist classification scheme. Visitors to the Luxembourg Gallery were encouraged to make use of a popular "scorecard" designed by the French painter and art critic Roger de Piles. This scorecard, widely respected and consulted throughout the eighteenth century, assigned a numerical value to an array of artistic criteria, among them composition, color, and light. Gone was the porous subjectivity and narrative chaos of the Portici Palace or the *wunderkammer*. Now it could be established beyond a doubt that Raphael and Rubens were the most overall accomplished painters, because each artist had tied for the most number of points (65) on Roger de Piles' scorecard. If visitors wanted to perfect their appreciation of the use of color, however, they should also take a look at the work of Titian and Rembrandt, who, though falling short in the areas of composition, design, and expression, managed to equal the number of points (17) scored by Raphael and Rubens in color.

NOMS des Peintres les plus connus.	Composition.	Deffein.	Coloris.	Expreffion.
Pouffin.	15	17	6	15
Primatice.	15	14	7	10
R				
Raphaël Santio.	17	18	12	18
Rembrant.	15	6	17	12
Rubens.	18	13	17	17
S				
Fr. Salviati.	13	15	8	8
Le Sueur.	15	15	4	15
T.				
Teniers.	15	12	13	6
Pietre Tefte.	11	15	0	6
Tintoret.	15	14	16	4
Titien.	12	15	18	6
V				
Vanius.	13	15	12	13
Vendeïk.	15	10	17	13

Figure 1.6. Science to the rescue. Roger de Piles' "objective" scorecard for determining the skills of artists.

As should be clear by now, the application of both "science" and "reason" in the Luxembourg Gallery was itself a highly subjective and somewhat arbitrary exercise. Certainly no one today would abide by such mathematically reductive assessments of art. But this use and abuse of "scientific objectivity" need not obscure the larger point. That is, the modern museum is defined by a tripartite commitment to some of the most fundamental values of the Age of Enlightenment: preservation, education, and science. In other words, museums are intended to showcase man's ability to control and impose order upon the natural world. Paintings and artifacts are subject to the natural processes of decay, but museum curators preserve them in a timeless vacuum exempt from the travails of daily existence. The museum then arranges its collections into a didactic display meant to educate its visitors with a sense of their collective cultural identity as members of a civilized society. Finally, both of these agendas—preservation and education—are pursued in accordance with the ostensibly objective principles of science, be they in the form of a scorecard or the latest advances in fabric restoration.

The only thing absent from the Luxembourg Gallery was an explicit targeting of the common people—as opposed to artists—as the intended recipients of the message contained within. This was what the Louvre provided for the first time, thus setting a precedent soon to be followed by all other museums. When the Luxembourg Gallery shut its doors in 1779 to serve as the Paris residence of Louis XVI's younger brother, preparations were already in motion for an even grander museum to replace it. The site that eventually came to house the Louvre's earliest collections was originally a restricted military building that displayed 127 scale models of fortified towns and harbors of France. Now it would serve as the preeminent stage to broadcast the scientific and moral enlightenment of the country's beleaguered monarch. Part and parcel of the Louvre's educational mission was the cultivation of an appreciation and veneration for the person most responsible for allowing the museum to open its doors in the first place. In this case, that person was supposed to be Louis XVI, but numerous delays and a stubborn guillotine prevented him from attending its inauguration. (One critic later claimed that if the Louvre had opened its doors on time, the revolution would not have occurred!)

Regardless of who ruled France, however, the ideological function of the museum remained the same. That is, for the first time, a public institution provided a visible platform for those at the top of the social hierarchy to communicate a secular, scientific message of progressive enlightenment to those at the bottom. This message was conveyed through the medium of art and antiquities, which together represented the cultural identity and heritage of an abstract—and largely imagined—community: the nation. The reason we refer to the nation as an abstract and imagined entity is because most people throughout history tend to identify not with their social "betters" or "inferiors," but rather with their social "equals." In other words, we regard people who talk, eat, dress, and act like ourselves as comprising the members of the most relevant and tangible community in our daily lives. But the members of different economic classes and different geographic regions do not talk, eat, dress, or act like one another, even within regions that we today regard as part of the same state.

The concept of the nation is a powerful one, and once it exists, it can be mobilized to undertake projects unprecedented in both scale and results, for both good and evil. But the important point here is that the nation is something that needs to be brought into existence. It does not form naturally in human societies. People need to be convinced that they belong to the same nation. They need to be convinced that a person living a thousand miles away from them—a person whom they will never meet and with whom they likely evince no common standard of speech—shares some core element of their identity in common with them. It is thus no coincidence that the earliest and most substantive nations in world history were those created through public education initiatives that targeted everyone in society, from wealthy elites all the way down to poor peasants. For education, above all, is the ideological tool of choice for telling people who they are and what they should believe in.

With this in mind, we now are able to comprehend fully the awesome power of the modern museum. When Louis XVI agreed to finance the creation of the Louvre, he was doing much more than simply broadcasting his own personal moral and scientific enlightenment to the world. Instead, by inviting the common French citizen into its exhibit halls, he was positioning himself as the foremost benefactor of the entire French nation. He was telling his people that they shared a common cultural heritage both with him and with one another, and that he was committed to the mutual prosperity of that nation celebrated within its halls. The cultural identity cultivated within the Louvre was akin to a watered-down version of the cosmopolitan ethos long prevalent in elite circles. That is to say, visitors to the Louvre were not encouraged to cultivate pride for a narrowly conceived ethnic French identity, but rather toward a broadly cosmopolitan French standard of culture. After all, most of the masterpieces on display in the Louvre were not produced by artists born and raised in France, but instead came from all over Europe. To subscribe to the cultural identity peddled by the Louvre was to re-create a uniquely French view of core civilized values through works of art that best embodied and expressed those values—in the estimation of the French—wherever in Europe they might be found.

Of course, every museum is beholden to a powerful patron who believes that his identity and his nation are superior to all others. If the Louvre had opened its doors during the reign of Louis XVI, it would have communicated a cultural identity for the French people that was uniquely royalist. As it turned out, the opening of the Louvre ended up being entrusted to a revolutionary committee determined to eradicate the old royalist order. On August 19, 1792, just nine days after the Tuileries Palace was overrun and King Louis taken prisoner, the new National Assembly issued its first decrees regarding the Louvre. The king's museum would now become a cultural symbol "worthy of a free people" and be counted among "the most powerful illustrations of the French Republic." That the new government turned its earnest attention to the accelerated opening of a museum in the midst of a bloody civil war stands as testament to how powerful an ideological and educational tool the Louvre was considered to be.

On August 10, 1793, the Louvre officially opened its doors for the first time. On display were a total of 537 paintings, plus 124 assorted marble and bronze sculptures, precious marbles, pieces of porcelain, clocks, and "other objects." The museum was open to all for the education of all, primarily through the refrain of "liberty" and the "regeneration" of the people. One Republican journalist recounted the touching scene of a "young soldier escorting his father, his mother, and his sister" through the halls of the Louvre. These were "good village people who had never before left their community, and who apparently had never seen paintings other than the sign of the local inn or the smoke-covered daub above the altar." Despite the fact that they "could never tell the difference between a Poussin and a Watteau," they were "all proud to be there." According to this journalist, the son, in particular, was "all the more proud to be leading them, [and] seemed to be saying 'it is I that conquered many of these pictures.'" This emotive vignette illustrates precisely the sort of vertical identification among different economic classes and geographic regions that the museum— and public education in general—was designed to achieve.

The self-appointed stewards of Republican values in revolutionary France still faced a problem, however. In May 1794, Casimir Varon, spokesman for the Conservatoire, a body responsible for determining the disposition of the museum's collections, put it best when he observed that nearly all of the artwork in the Louvre bore "the marks of superstition, flattery, and debauchery." These "playthings of folly and vanity" did not succeed in recounting "the noble lessons that a regenerated people adores: it does nothing for liberty." What Varon is referring to here is a fundamental contradiction inherent to nearly every museum. In brief, a museum is supposed to speak to the masses of people who make up the citizenry of the nation at large, most of whom have yet to benefit from the wealth and education characteristic of the upper classes. And yet the upper classes were largely responsible for the commissioning, financing, and preservation of nearly all of the artwork showcased within the museum. How is a museum curator supposed to tell an uneducated peasant that the "playthings" of the rich and famous constitute an important part of his or her core identity?

Figure 1.7. The Grand Gallery of the Louvre, 1796.
Science, preservation, and education: the tripartite gospel of
the Enlightenment on free display for the French masses.

This thorny task was accomplished in two ways. First, in a clever rhetorical trick later to be adopted in museums throughout the world, the former possessions of the elite were reconfigured as the products of plebeian sweat and blood. After all, few satin-robed aristocrats had actually sewn their own robes. Someone else further down the social hierarchy had done it for them. The fact that the tailor had been compensated for his labor was beside the point. The relationship between noble and commoner was now imagined to have been one of exploitation by the former over the latter. "Those treasures which were previously visible to only a privileged few," one French Republican explained, "will henceforth afford pleasure to all: statues, paintings, and books are charged with the sweat of the people. The property of the people will be returned to them." For most people who have not grown up in luxury and privilege, this is a very seductive message, and it is one that museums have long based their legitimacy upon. No matter how lavish and opulent the holdings of a museum may be, their preservation and display is justified through the idea that they no longer serve the avaricious interests of a closed group of selfish elites. Instead, the museum now holds them in trust as an altruistic gift back to the people whose resources—taxes, labor, etc.—were responsible for their creation in the first place.

Second, the material trappings of the affluent ranks of society were further robbed of their mystical powers through the interconnected processes of "desacralization" and "artifaction." These fancy multisyllabic words describe what is, in essence, a very simple process: the act of removing an object from its original context and placing it into a new context, where it then acquires new meanings and uses. It was marshaled to justify the inclusion of ornate religious art into the secular environment of the Louvre, on the pretext that an altarpiece depicting the merits of kings and queens loses much of its intended message when removed from the church and placed in the cloistered sterility of a museum. Thus Republican intellectuals did not feel overly troubled by the inclusion of religious artwork that commemorated the elites of the old order, for they recognized that such art underwent a process of desacralization the moment it was removed from the drawing room.

For those of us who are not French revolutionaries fixated on the royalist residue of religious art, however, this process is more accurately captured through the ecclesiastically neutral idea of "artifaction." In other words, *all* antiquities and *all* artwork lose their original social functions when transported to the museum. They then take on new lives as curated objects of detached contemplation by people who never saw them in their original context. As a result, these people are free to project new meanings onto them. Museum curators ensured that these new messages were communicated via the classification techniques of the natural sciences. Though the mathematical scorecard of Roger de Piles was long gone, the desire to arrange a collection of artwork according to artificially imposed schools and temporalities remained. The Louvre was the first museum to organize its paintings through the now familiar schema of regional groups of artists marked by the development of a distinctive artistic trait. These retroactively imposed boundaries were then further reinterpreted through placement on a chronological timescale that illustrates the evolution of human ingenuity and intellectual progress. The end result is an artifact that no longer serves the complex social values and economic context it was once created for, but instead tells a sanitized and tidy tale of human progress over the millennia, consumed by people wholly unfamiliar with the past lives of the artifact before them.

A useful analogy is to think of museums and zoos as serving basically the same function, one for the humanities and the other for the natural sciences. Artifaction enables the museum to transform inanimate objects in the same way that the zoo transforms wild animals: both museum objects and zoo animals become permanently divorced from the social or biological context they once inhabited. They then take on new roles and new meanings unimagined by those who interacted with them in their original context. For the first three hundred years of its existence, for instance, the Mona Lisa was a well-regarded but relatively unknown specimen of Renaissance portraiture, familiar only to the kings who flaunted it and the artists who studied it. Since its inclusion in the inaugural collection of the Louvre, however, it has accrued a level of commercial fame and layers of interpretation inconceivable by those who first owned it. The same process occurs in zoos, which turn animals (such as the panda bear) once viewed in utilitarian relation to their natural environment—e.g., predator, prey, or economic resource—into commercially lucrative wards of urban conservation movements.

The ability to create a new context for works of art in the Louvre would prove immensely useful during the Revolutionary (1792–1802) and Napoleonic (1803–15) wars. In these wars, the localized conflict between revolutionaries and royalists eventually blossomed into a conflagration involving nearly every state in Europe. Between 1796 and 1798, French armies led by Napoleon managed to occupy lands in present-day Italy, Austria, Belgium, and Germany. The spoils of war soon flowed into the Louvre. Such blatantly imperialist methods of acquisition, however, could not be justified in the same way that acquisitions from the old French nobility had been justified. For this was no longer a conflict within a single nation, imagined or otherwise. It involved multiple states and multiple nations, each of which was ruled by its own group of proud and jealous elites. If the Louvre was originally established as a public educational trust for the French nation, then how was Napoleon to justify the integration of art and antiquities from outside that nation? This was not simply a question of explaining why Dutch and Italian artwork previously owned by French aristocrats was displayed in a museum designed for the French nation. Now the curators of the Louvre had to explain why Dutch and Italian art *seized* from foreign nobles *in* foreign lands was also in their possession.

This brings us to the final stage in the development of a major metropolitan museum. When political elites embark on distant conquests of foreign lands, museums back home are called upon to reflect, valorize, and justify the expansion of the state whose nation (or nations) it represents. This is done by claiming to represent not only a standard of civilized good taste and civic values to which one nation—the French— should aspire to emulate, but rather a new standard to which all civilized peoples everywhere should rightfully aspire. The ugly corollary to this idea, of course, is that all competing conceptions of what constitutes "civilization" and good taste are necessarily inferior by definition. In 1794, the French soldier-turned-painter Luc Barbier put it well when he declared that "the fruits of genius are the patrimony of liberty." Thus defined, only the French deserve to own "the fruits of genius"—wherever in Europe these might be found—because only the French foster and maintain "liberty." It follows by such logic, then, that any masterpiece found outside the French state had been "soiled by the gaze of servitude." The only way to restore and display the "legacy of great men," Barbier proclaimed, is to deliver them "to the home of the arts and of genius, the land of liberty and equality, the French Republic."

If the French were the only people in the world who believed themselves civilized, such a narcissistic platform would constitute little more than a self-fulfilling prophecy. The problem, however, is that the French were not alone in claiming the mantle of most civilized nation. In fact, most other European monarchs made similar claims for their own nations, for which they, too, were now beginning to construct institutions of public indoctrination like the Louvre. Not only that, emperors beyond the seas—such as the Ottoman and Chinese—also claimed this coveted title, despite the absence of public museums in their states (a fact the Europeans would later exploit). We will refer to this phenomenon as that of "rival cosmopolitanisms." Each showcase museum of the Western world, be it in Paris, London, St. Petersburg, or Berlin, vied with one another to transmit a benevolent cultural message that cast its state's imperial conquests in the most benevolent possible light.

The underlying geopolitical realities, however, never strayed far from the dictates of *realpolitik*: the benevolent French discourse of "liberty" and "regeneration" was based in part upon collections of art and antiquities seized abroad and displayed in Paris, and Paris alone. In 1798, when a major convoy of artwork taken in Belgium and Italy entered Paris, a song written for the occasion declared that "Rome is no more in Rome; / Every Hero, every Great Man / Has changed country: / Rome is no more in Rome, / It is all in Paris." A petition of leading French artists of the day echoed this sentiment when it drew parallels between the Roman appropriation of Greek culture and the French appropriation of other European cultures. "The Romans, once an uncultivated people, became civilized by transplanting to Rome the works of conquered Greece. ... The French Republic, by its strength and superiority of its enlightenment and its artists, is the only country in the world which can give a safe home to these masterpieces. All other Nations must come to borrow from our art as they once imitated our frivolity."

We can safely assume that European rivals of the French— particularly the British—took issue with this sentiment, but not because they believed that Rome was still in Rome. Rather, the British believed that Rome was now in London, because their own geopolitical context demanded that it be so. All this suggests the following: when Indiana Jones proclaims that a coveted artifact "belongs in a museum," he is being slightly disingenuous. What he really means is that it belongs not in *a* museum, but in *his* museum—presumably one located in a major metropolitan area of his own state (the United States)

Figure 1.8. The Imperialist Louvre.
An imaginative rendering of the triumphal procession
of Napoleon's loot into Paris, 1798.

and capable of disseminating an inspiring vision of science, civilization, and modernity refracted through the lens of his own specific culture.

By the end of the eighteenth century, nearly all the elements of the historical Indiana Jones necessary to understand the pop culture icon had already evolved in Europe. First and foremost, the historical Dr. Jones was an educated elite who was either personally wealthy himself (Charles or Louis of Bourbon) or worked for a wealthy patron (Alcubierre and Weber). This meant that he held a position of authority and wielded a measure of power over those around him. He used his access to wealth and power to organize and manage a group of economically and socially disadvantaged people—peasants, slaves, and convicts in Pompeii and soldiers in France—who located and acquired art and antiquities on his behalf. If he spent any time in the field himself, then Indiana Jones was likely a lower elite who had mastered a technical body of knowledge in order to make himself useful to his wealthy patron. In the case of Alcubierre and Weber, their trade was military engineering, which required expertise in geology, cartography, and mathematics.

What most separates Indiana Jones from his predecessors, however, is his avowed commitment to a rigorous scientific methodology, one that marks him out as a progressive agent of modernity and the ideals of the Enlightenment. His commitment may be disingenuous and his methodologies may not stand the test of time, but the sincerity of these commitments is asserted nonetheless. This is what separated Weber from Alcubierre, and it is also what separated the Louvre from the *wunderkammer* and other palace collections of European dukes and princes. In the case of Weber, a commitment to "science" took the form of recording the original context and stratigraphy of the ruined cities of Vesuvius, even if it came at the expense of his king's vainglorious and indulgent desire to exploit an antiquarian quarry. Instead of simply burnishing the reputation of King Charles with the noble yet vague notion of classical virtue associated with a Roman statue, Weber would endeavor to understand how a Roman city was built, how it operated on a daily basis, and how it perished—knowledge that did nothing to burnish the reputation of his king. In so doing, he would produce a new narrative of change over time and the progress of human civilization, both novel concepts in his day.

In the case of the Louvre—and, to a lesser extent, the Luxembourg Gallery—this commitment to science took the forms of preservation, desacralization, and artifaction. In other words, man demonstrated his mastery over nature by removing art and antiquities from their original social or biological contexts. He then arrested the natural process of decay in a man-made vacuum of time and space. Once incubated, the newly created artifact takes on new meanings designed to support the political and cultural agendas of the museum's benefactors. From these calculated efforts emerges a program of public education intended to unite the common citizen into a shared recognition of their identity as members of the same modern nation. If successful, the museum curator will have convinced his audience that they are all the proud and rightful heirs to a national standard of civilized values without peer anywhere else in the world.

In the event that our hypothetical state grows stronger and expands beyond its core ethnic and cultural boundaries, both the museum's collections and its ideological pretensions will grow to encompass, reflect, and justify the new empire. These will be put forth as proof that the national standard of civilized taste—British, French, German, etc.—is truly universal. To see how such claims played out in practice, we turn now to the first acquisitions of art and antiquities to occur outside of Europe. The backdrop is the Ottoman Empire, where military competition between the British and French would soon spill over into the cultural realm.

Continue the journey at indianajonesinhistory.com:

- EPISODE II: Excavating Pompeii
- EPISODE III: Building the Louvre

CHAPTER TWO

The Compensations of Plunder

In 1831, during the twilight of his life, Thomas Bruce, the seventh Earl of Elgin, reflected on the curious twists of fate that had befallen him. With his face disfigured by syphilis, his career and reputation in ruins, his finances beset by creditors, and his domestic life plagued by scandal and mental illness, still the earl found cause to rejoice. Three decades after their removal from Athens to London, the Parthenon marbles—to which Elgin had eponymously lent his name—continued to serve as vindication for his travails. According to the earl, the divisive marbles, taken with the ostensible aim of improving the arts and national taste of Great Britain, had accomplished everything for which he had dared to hope. "My success, to the vast extent that it was effected," Elgin wrote, "will never cease to be a matter of the utmost gratification to me." Ten years later, he breathed his last in Paris, the French capital having long served as Elgin's preferred refuge from crushing debts back home.

Much like Karl Weber, the Swiss excavator of Herculaneum and Pompeii, Thomas Bruce was ruined by the pursuit of an idea. This idea ultimately derailed one of the most promising careers of early nineteenth-century Britain. Born in 1766 to an ancient and distinguished family, Thomas inherited his earldom when he was only five years old. Educated in typical cosmopolitan style across both France and England, he later entered the military and found himself promoted to lieutenant-colonel before his thirtieth birthday. Success in politics followed soon afterward: his election to the House of Lords as a Scottish peer helped launch a career in international diplomacy, first as Envoy Extraordinary to Vienna and Brussels and later as Minister Plenipotentiary to the Court of Prussia. With his future bright, the Earl decided to make it even brighter by walking down the aisle with Mary Nisbet, a twenty-one year-old beauty of Edinburgh high society who stood to inherit a considerable fortune.

The newly married couple had scarcely moved into Elgin's newly constructed mansion at Broomhall when the opportunity of a lifetime presented itself. In the summer of 1798, Napoleon Bonaparte, flush with the success of his continental campaigns, landed a French fleet on the northern coast of Egypt and took the city of Cairo. The British, well aware that Napoleon was more interested in cutting off its trade routes to India and imposing naval dominion over the Mediterranean than he was in ruling Egypt itself, were quick to engage the French on both desert and sea. The ensuing melee, which dragged on in one form or another for several more years, prompted the Foreign Office to consider for the first time the deputation of a permanent ambassador to the Ottoman Empire, under whose suzerainty Egypt was then still nominally subject. In November 1798, Elgin, advised to seek warmer climes for the benefit of his health, wrote to the foreign secretary in London to place his name under consideration.

He got his wish. Before long, Elgin was named Ambassador Extraordinaire and Minister Plenipotentiary of His Britannic Majesty to the Sublime Porte of Selim III, Sultan of the Ottoman Empire. His destination was Constantinople, the political, cultural, and economic center of gravity for the eastern Mediterranean for well over a millennium. (The Ottoman state itself was often referred to in

Figure 2.1. Thomas Bruce, 7th Earl of Elgin.

European circles as the "Sublime Porte," a poetic shorthand derived from the name of a ceremonial gate at the foot of the road to Topkapi Palace, residence of the sultan.) When word of the appointment got out, Thomas Harrison, the architect then putting the finishing touches on the earl's estate at Broomhall, planted the fateful seed in Elgin's mind. It was now acknowledged, Harrison told Elgin, that the best models of classical sculpture and architecture were to be found in Greece, not in Rome. But the only way most students of the arts in Great Britain could study the Greek forms at that time was to consult two-dimensional drawings and engravings reproduced in travelogues. What was needed more than anything else, Harrison suggested, were three-dimensional plaster casts taken directly from the sculptures themselves. On the possibility of removing the originals and bringing them back to Britain, Harrison said nothing.

Elgin loved the idea. With characteristic zeal (and at his own expense), he set about assembling a team of artists and architects to accompany him on the voyage. Their mission, according to the earl, was described in variously lofty terms. They were to stimulate "the progress of the Fine Arts in Great Britain," bestow "some benefit on the progress of taste in England," and improve "circumstances towards the advancement of literature and the arts." These statements suggest that Elgin intended to build the foundations of a British version of the Luxembourg Gallery, which Louis XV had sponsored in hopes of improving the talents of French artists before their pilgrimage to Rome. In other words, the fruits of Elgin's labors in Greece were primarily designed to benefit British artists and the elites they served. If Elgin imagined that any advantages might accrue to the poor common folk of Britain, it could only have been through an indirect trickle-down effect: improve the taste and morals of British elites, and they will in turn improve the taste and morals of the plebeian subjects under their charge.

In November 1799, exactly one year after submitting his name for consideration to the post, Lord Elgin and his wife arrived in Constantinople. His team of painters, draughtsmen, plaster casters, and architects would assemble one year later at Athens, with orders to proceed with their work while Elgin attended to his diplomatic duties across the Aegean Sea. In the Ottoman capital, the British ambassador was treated as the most important person in the sultan's realm. Elgin was showered with attention, from lavish banquets and exclusive audiences to expensive gifts and special privileges. The reason was simple: the French had invaded Egypt, a longstanding colony of the Ottoman Empire, and the British were fighting the French. Of course, everyone knew that motives were selfish on all sides. The French, while claiming to suppress an anti-Ottoman rebellion within Egypt with the altruistic intent of restoring the sultan's rule, were really just trying to supplant British influence in the Near East. For their part, the British, while similarly claiming to restore Ottoman suzerainty over Egypt by kicking out Napoleon, had few goals other than bringing about the reversal of French gains in the eastern Mediterranean.

As for the Ottomans? They just wanted Egypt back. And for the time being, an alliance with the British appeared to offer the best hope of attaining that goal. If the Ottomans had the military capabilities to defeat the French themselves, they surely would have done so. No monarch would voluntarily become indebted to another empire by accepting a subordinate position in an alliance unless he could see no better option of achieving his desired ends. Thus the Ottomans actively encouraged Britain's campaigns against the French in Egypt, in full knowledge that the former were likely to preserve the previous state of affairs while the latter were intent on disrupting it. Part and parcel of this arrangement, of course, was the favorable treatment of Britain's man in Constantinople: Lord Elgin. The fact that the Ottomans were so dependent upon British military assistance to expel the French from their Egyptian province meant that Elgin could ask for pretty much anything he wanted from the Sublime Porte.

Fortunately for the sultan, the earl did not ask for much. In fact, all he wanted was a *firman*. This coveted piece of paper, signed and sealed by an Ottoman official, conveyed to local governors and other imperial functionaries in the provinces that the bearer of such a document was entitled to certain permissions and privileges, and that to obstruct the realization of these favors was to place one's career in jeopardy. In other words, a *firman*'s writ could only be overruled by local officials if the specter of a major geopolitical crisis warranted it. The reason Elgin wanted a *firman* in the first place was because his team of artists and architects had experienced a less-than-welcoming reception in Athens. Since their arrival in August 1800, Elgin's men had been refused access to the Acropolis—the rocky hillside on which the Parthenon and other ancient sculptures and monuments lay—on two grounds. First, as the local governor accurately informed them, the entire citadel area, which afforded incomparable views of the Aegean Sea, was a restricted military site, one stocked with artillery units and numerous ammunition magazines. Second, they were told that access to the Acropolis would allow for similarly incomparable views of Turkish women undressing in the residences below.

Clearly, someone would have to intervene with the local governor if Elgin's men were to commence their task of "improving the national taste" of Great Britain. In May 1801, after nine months of complaints from his men in Athens, Elgin applied

Figure 2.2. View of the Parthenon from the Acropolis, 1821.
Note the architectural clutter, including private residences, that surrounded the Parthenon in the days before they were cleared away in order to facilitate the projection of European fantasies about ancient Greek architecture.

for a *firman*. His timing could not have been better. Just two months earlier, a British fleet of 17,000 soldiers dropped anchor off the Egyptian coast and began to inflict severe losses on the French forces. Amid such a turn of events, it is little wonder that Elgin got exactly what he asked for. Though the text of this first *firman* has long been lost to posterity, correspondence between Elgin and his team in Athens gives us a good idea of what it likely contained: permission to enter the Acropolis, erect scaffolding, complete drawings, make plaster casts, and remove any loose sculpture or inscriptions lying about the premises.

Unfortunately for Elgin's team of artists and architects in Athens, another geopolitical crisis arose just as the *firman* reached its destination. The French fleet was again on the move, and the local governor feared that this time Athens might be targeted by Napoleon's navy. Thus the Acropolis was again put on lockdown, and the sultan's writ denied. Hearing of these developments across the sea, Elgin went back to his desk and applied for a second *firman*, one capable of forestalling any possible obstruction by the local governor, regardless of military exigencies. His timing was again remarkable. On June 17, 1801, the French formally surrendered the city of Cairo to the British, thereby assuring the eventual return of Egypt to Constantinople. Three weeks later, on July 6, Elgin got his second *firman*, a copy of which survives today in Italian translation, then the *lingua franca* of the eastern Mediterranean.

The two events were intimately connected with one another. From the Ottoman perspective, the *firman*—and the removal of any antiquities it entailed—was just another form of diplomatic capital, one that could be spent in any number of strategic ways. We might gloss such transactions as the "compensations of plunder," a useful concept that does much to explain how and why so many antiquities from less-developed parts of the world ended up in the museums of the more developed. In short, the ruler of a state that lacks sufficient resources to achieve its most pressing goals—be they military, economic, or political—will tend to view antiquities as an inexpensive form of leverage capable of enabling the fulfillment of previously unattainable objectives. The Ottomans could not bring about the return of Egypt from French control by their own efforts alone. But the British could. In a very real sense, then, the Elgin marbles were a form of collateral compensation for the recovery of an Ottoman colony. To the sultan, the beauty of such an arrangement was the actual market value of the antiquities in question: nothing. It did not matter that the Parthenon marbles might fetch a small fortune in Europe. As long as they remained in the Ottoman Empire, among local elites who did not yet celebrate classical Greek architecture and were not yet attuned to the ideological potential of the modern museum, they were about as valuable as an untapped oil well. The real question thus becomes: Why *wouldn't* the sultan trade something that was cheap and plentiful (ancient Greek sculpture) for something that was expensive and scarce (military resources to defeat the French)?

There is, however, one further wrinkle to this story. Recall that Elgin did not originally intend to remove any sculptures from the monuments on the Acropolis. He had merely planned to procure three-dimensional plaster casts of the originals, and he continued to profess such limited goals even as he was handed a second, more permissive *firman* in July. The wording of this later *firman* authorized Elgin's team to enter the Acropolis and do pretty much anything his men desired, with the sole exception of removing any antiquity still fused to a monument. The reason for this caveat appears not to have been born out of any concern for the artistic integrity of the site, but rather due to the fear that such removals might compromise the structural integrity of the military installations sheltered within the monuments. (In 1687, an attacking Venetian fleet scored a direct hit on one of the gunpowder magazines stored within, blowing the Parthenon roof to kingdom come.) Even this prohibition was diluted via additional permissions granted to Elgin's architects that they be allowed to dig below the soil to search for buried sculptures and inscriptions, all of which they were permitted to remove.

So how then did the Elgin marbles, which would eventually comprise a collection of friezes, metopes, and pediment, end up in Elgin's possession? The answer is to be found in a peculiar concatenation of events produced by the clash of imperial and local politics in Athens. In July 1801, Elgin handed the second *firman* to Reverend Philip Hunt, a chaplain engaged for the voyage when it first set out from England. On July 22, just two weeks later, Hunt arrived in Athens with both the *firman* and letters of introduction from the Ottoman government commending him to any local authorities he might encounter. Even more valuable, however, was the presence of Rachid Aga, a senior Ottoman official sent to accompany Hunt to Athens. Most likely Rachid's job was twofold: ensure that the local governor did not again flout the provisions of the *firman*, and make sure the British were not monitoring Ottoman military arrangements on the Acropolis.

When Hunt arrived in Athens, he wasted no time in calling upon the Ottoman governor of the city, a man known as the *voivode*. After showing him the text of the second *firman*, Hunt complained about the ill treatment his team had received in all their previous attempts to work in the Acropolis. The *voivode*, cognizant of the presence of Rachid Aga, the sultan's envoy,

Figure 2.3. The Elgin Marbles.
A lifelike battle between a centaur and a Lapith
adorns this metope, now in the British Museum.

claimed that he was mortified to hear of such ill treatment. He then sent for the *disdar*, the local military commander in charge of day-to-day operations on the Acropolis. In a dark twist of fate, the *disdar* himself had fallen terminally ill, so his son—who hoped to inherit his father's lucrative post—was summoned instead. When the son finally appeared, it was the emissary from the Sublime Porte who did all the talking. Effective immediately, the *disdar*'s son was to be sent into exile from Athens. At this moment, for whatever reason, Reverend Hunt intervened and obtained a pardon for him. But the parting words of the envoy from Constantinople were clear: if any more complaints reached his ears, the *disdar*'s son would be sent as a slave to the galleys. As Hunt summarized in a letter to Elgin a few days later, "the death of the old disdar, which happened a few days ago, facilitated our operations because the son who hopes to succeed him in the office ... feels how much reason you have to oppose his views and is now submissive to all our views in hopes of your speaking favourably for him to the Porte."

Just ten days later, the Parthenon marbles were gone, taken down by a team of twenty local Greek laborers on behalf of Reverend Hunt, who had asked the chastened *disdar* for permission to do so. He promptly received it. Long an overly elaborate adornment to an Ottoman military base, the targeted statuary was about to become the "Elgin marbles," complete with a new context and identity realized via the process of artifaction. In this new context, the Elgin marbles assumed fresh significance as cultural emblems of the imperial rivalry between Britain and France. "These admirable specimens of Greek sculpture," Hunt wrote Elgin, had been "repeatedly refused to the gold and influence of France in the zenith of her power." Whichever empire owned the rarest and most authentic classical antiquities could lay claim to representing a revival of Greek and Roman civilization in modern guise. Once apprised of Hunt's successful attempt to exceed the permissions granted in the *firman*, Elgin wasted no time in drawing an explicit connection between his marbles and the cultural and political competition between Britain and France. Regarding the removal of the marbles to London as "a very essential service to the Arts in England," the earl also made sure to point out that "Bonaparte has not got such a thing from all his thefts in Italy."

Of course, Elgin did not view his precious marbles as the result of theft. As far as he was concerned, his men had expended much time, labor, and money to rescue a neglected masterpiece of the ancient world, one in danger of imminent destruction at the hands of the Ottomans. "It grieved me to the heart," Reverend Hunt wrote as the first of the marbles was taken down, "to see the destruction made daily by the Janizaries of the fortress. They break up the finest bas-reliefs and sculptures in search of the morsels of lead that unite them to the buildings after which they are broken with wanton barbarity." Not only that, Elgin later claimed, "the Turks have been continually defacing the heads. In some instances they have actually acknowledged to me that they have pounded down the statues to convert them into mortar." Of use to Elgin in justifying his acquisition of the marbles was the absence in Ottoman lands of any public institution dedicated to preserving art and antiquities for the benefit of the people. This enabled him to claim that the Ottomans did not value or respect the lofty ideals of the ancient Greeks, as embodied through their art and architecture. As a result, the mantle of cultural steward-ship, imagined to have been forfeited by the Ottomans, could now be claimed by the British. This noble task obliged the British not only to preserve the Elgin marbles in accordance with the latest scientific advances, but also to display them for the edification and education of the British public.

This Lord Elgin was prepared to do, and at considerable addi-tional expense to himself. Already by 1803, the earl estimated his personal debt incurred on behalf of the procurement of the marbles at £27,000, a princely sum in his day. Now he would spend even more to build a temporary housing shed in Piccadilly to allow artists, antiquarians, and other educated elites in London to browse the contents of the fifty cases and more than one hundred and twenty tons of ancient Greek statuary he had brought back from Athens. In June 1807, Elgin opened the doors to his own humble version of the Luxembourg Gallery in London, one that, like its counterpart in Paris, was designed to educate native artists on the basis of widely admired models.

Lord Elgin and the Great Belzoni

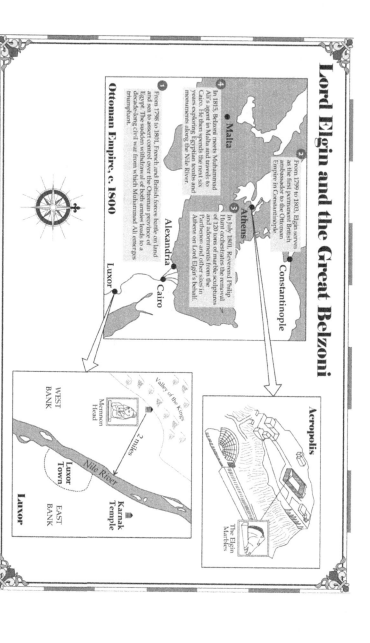

Ottoman Empire, c. 1800

1 From 1798 to 1801, French and British forces battle on land and sea to assert control over the Ottoman province of Egypt. The sudden withdrawal of both armies leads to a decade-long civil war from which Muhammad Ali emerges triumphant.

2 From 1799 to 1803, Elgin serves as the first permanent British ambassador to the Ottoman Empire in Constantinople.

3 In July 1801, Reverend Philip Hunt orchestrates the removal of 120 tons of marble sculptures and adornments from the Parthenon and other sites in Athens on Lord Elgin's behalf.

4 In 1815, Belzoni meets Muhammad Ali's agent in Malta and travels to Cairo. He then spends the next six years exploring Egyptian tombs and monuments along the Nile River.

- Malta
- Athens
- Constantinople
- Alexandria
- Cairo
- Luxor

Luxor

Nile River

Valley of the Kings

WEST BANK

Memnon Head

2 miles

Luxor Town

EAST BANK

Karnak Temple

Acropolis

The Elgin Marbles

His exhibit created such a sensation that Elgin soon found it necessary to implement a rationing system for visitor permits. Among those artists who came to study the Elgin marbles was the young painter Benjamin Robert Haydon, who later wrote:

> The first thing I fixed my eyes on was the wrist of a figure in one of the female groups, in which were visible, though in a feminine form, the radius and the ulna. I was astonished, for I had never seen them hinted at in any female wrist in the antique. ... The combination of nature and idea, which I had felt was so much wanting for high art, was here displayed to midday conviction. My heart beat! If I had seen nothing else I had beheld sufficient to keep me to nature for the rest of my life.

Just four years after his return to England, Elgin could already claim to have fulfilled his mission of improving the national taste of Britain, as embodied through the revolving door of awestruck artists who visited his shed at Piccadilly. Now he needed to turn his attention to his rapidly mounting debts. Happily for the earl, this was a problem whose resolution could be interpreted as a selfless act done in service to the British nation at large. In other words, he could sell the marbles to the British government, which would then bequeath them to the British Museum in the name of the people, a precedent already established by France and the Louvre. Unhappily for Elgin, the British government was not prepared to pay more than a third of the estimated expenses (£90,000 by 1811) now appearing in the earl's account books. These frightening ledgers were the result of ten years of transporting, exhibiting, and preserving the marbles, in addition to accrued interest from several large unpaid loans. As a result, Elgin refused to sell, and the marbles were moved to another storage site in London while their owner pondered his next move.

Events on the continent, however, soon brought the marbles back into the spotlight, though not as Elgin might have wished. In April 1814, the forced abdication and exile of Napoleon brought to a temporary reprieve the near constant warfare occasioned by his rise in France some twenty years earlier. Though Napoleon would famously escape from his island prison of Elba and return to the battlefield at Waterloo, the complex process of repatriating the art and antiquities looted by French armies throughout Europe was already well underway. Thus when Elgin took advantage of this brief cessation of hostilities—and sudden availability of public funds—to renew the government's interest in purchasing his marbles, he found that the legal niceties of ownership were very much on Parliament's mind. No politician in Britain wanted to open himself up to accusations of having acted in a manner similar to that of the hated Napoleon. The director of the Louvre, in an attempt to discredit British proposals to parcel out the collection under his charge to the victors of Waterloo, criticized the British government for its consideration of the Elgin marbles, which he described as having been "plundered" from the "Temple of Athens."

This set the stage for an extraordinary series of meetings and debates in Parliament regarding the circumstances surrounding Elgin's removal of the Parthenon marbles. The question on everyone's mind was whether or not Lord Elgin was guilty of any improprieties during his acquisition of the marbles. In order to satisfy his inquisitors, Elgin needed to alleviate any misgivings they may have had regarding his past interactions with Ottoman officials and their Greek subjects. First to come under scrutiny was the legality of his actions. In other words, had Elgin done anything which was forbidden by Ottoman law? Because the Ottomans had not yet explicitly addressed the treatment of cultural artifacts in their legal statutes, this question could only be answered by reference to the *firman* procured by Elgin in July 1801. As noted above, the *firman* only granted permission to draw, make plaster casts, and remove any loose sculpture or inscriptions that were unearthed in the course of shallow digging. It did not address the removal of the marbles one way or the other, for Elgin had never formally requested such permission.

In the absence of an explicit prohibition communicated by Constantinople, the British Parliament was forced to consider the disposition of the Ottoman government and officials during and after the removal of the marbles. Here Elgin found himself on solid ground. His men had asked the local *disdar* and *voivode* for permission to remove the marbles, and that permission had been granted. Yes, they had exceeded the terms of the *firman*, but this had been done with the full knowledge and cooperation of Ottoman representatives on the ground. As Hunt wrote to Elgin at the time:

> During the whole of my residence in Athens, I am happy to inform your Lordship that there was not an individual, either among the Officers of the Porte, or the Greeks of the city, who did not seem to vie with each other in gratifying your wishes, particularly the *voivode*, the archbishop, and our agent Logotheti, who conjointly possess all the power of the place.

Furthermore, Rachid Aga, the envoy from Constantinople who had participated in the conversations with the *disdar* and *voivode*, had remained in Athens the entire time and had presumably witnessed the removal of the marbles with his very own eyes. After all, the chief purpose of his visit was to keep an eye on what Elgin's men were doing in the Acropolis. Nor was Rachid the only emissary from Constantinople to visit Athens while Elgin's men were engaged in their work, only to allow the work to continue. Finally, in the summer of 1802, just as Elgin was getting ready to leave his post and return to England, he received a series of letters from the Ottoman government which retroactively acknowledged and condoned all the work his men had done in Athens. Without such papers, the marbles—all fifty crates and one hundred twenty tons of them—never could have transited through successive Mediterranean ports.

As a result, there seemed to be no legal hurdles in the way of recognizing Lord Elgin's claim to ownership over the marbles. Everything Elgin and his men did had been authorized or approved by the Ottoman government in one form or another, and nothing was done in secret without the knowledge of relevant authorities. Not only that, nearly every member of Parliament was sympathetic to Elgin's claims that he had rescued the marbles from Ottoman neglect, indifference, and physical destruction. But it was not enough simply to confirm the legality of Elgin's actions. No one disputed that he was now the *legal* owner of the marbles. But was he also the *rightful* owner? That is to say, in an ideal world, did the

Parthenon marbles *belong* in Lord Elgin's possession, or did they belong somewhere else?

This was a judgment call, and not one that could be resolved by reference to a *firman* or an Ottoman customs stamp. The complication that arises with this line of thinking, however, is that it depends upon a subjective interpretation of ideals. And ideals—much like the ideas they are based upon—change over both time and space. Elgin's great misfortune (or at least one of them) was that his acquisition of the marbles was interpreted in a time and place where new ideas incompatible with his conduct had begun to emerge. These ideas were embodied by the Romantic idea of the eternal nation, a concept that, when applied to the realm of geopolitics, lent emotional force to theories about the desirability of "nation-states."

In short, this is the idea, increasingly popular among European intellectuals and artists over the course of the nineteenth century, that the civilized world is made up of distinct national communities defined by empirically tested criteria in areas such as language, culture, physiognomy, economy, and territory. On the assumption that such identities stretch back unaltered into the primordial mists of time, diluted only by miscegenation or the yoke of barbarian rule, it was considered a noble task to "restore" the natural "rights" of nations to live in a state of their own creation and administration. This ideal of the "nation-state" has accrued far more mileage in the minds of its enthusiasts—romantic poets and ambitious politicians, mainly—than it has ever achieved on the ground. Despite untold (and mostly disastrous) attempts to bring nation and state into perfect alignment over the last two hundred years, precious few nation-states worthy of the name have ever been created. Language, culture, economy, physiognomy, and territory are all in constant flux, and attempts to fix any one of them in time or space are destined to fail. The stubborn mutability of mankind, however, has done little to dampen enthusiasm for the ideal itself, and the concept of the nation-state is one still valorized today.

What has all this got to do with Lord Elgin and his marbles? In short, less than a decade after the earl returned to Britain, Greece became the subject of Europe's first national fantasy projected abroad, a development given further impetus by the outbreak of the 1821 Greek war of independence against Ottoman rule. The chief progenitors of this fantasy in Europe were Romantic poets who saw in Greece the melancholy ruins of Western civilization itself, now spoiled through the degenerate rule of culturally alien overlords: the Turks. It was the job of progressive Europeans to help restore the Greeks to their former glory. This they could do by preserving and displaying their ancient heritage and working to bring about independence from Ottoman rule. Lord Byron, one of the most influential of the Romantic poets, did both, famously giving his life in support of the Greek revolution. (He died in 1824 from a fever contracted in Greece.) In 1812, Byron published "Childe Harold's Pilgrimage," destined to become one of his most famous poems. In it, Byron first praises ancient Greece and laments the depths to which its descendants have sunk by virtue of miscegenation and the weight of barbarian yoke. He then singles out Lord Elgin for one of the most scathing and damning indictments yet seen in verse:

> Dull is the eye that will not weep to see
> Thy walls defac'd, thy mouldering shrines remov'd
> By British hands, which it had best behov'd
> To guard those relics ne'er to be restor'd.
> Curst be the hour when from their isle they rov'd,
> And once again thy hapless bosom gor'd,
> And snatch'd thy shrinking Gods to northern climes
> abhorr'd!

As if this was not bad enough, just a few years later Byron also circulated another poem, "The Curse of Minerva," in which Elgin's facial disfigurement, divorce, professional setbacks, and mentally ill child were all invoked as the deserved punishment of the gods for his actions at the Parthenon. Instead of helping the Greeks rediscover their former glory and break the bonds of their current enslavement, Elgin had instead deprived them of an artistic masterpiece essential to the fulfillment of their national destiny.

A literary attack such as this, premised as it was on the ideal of eternal nations, was difficult to refute. The deceptively simple correlation of ancient and modern Greece carried an emotive force to which few people educated in the Greek and Roman classics were immune. It would have been futile for Lord Elgin to try and point out that the Greece of 1812 bore almost no cultural, religious, political, or linguistic resemblance to the Greece of Homer and Aristotle—or at least no more than is the case for any two cultures separated by twenty-five hundred years. In Elgin and Byron's time, the majority of people who would have identified as "Greeks" professed the Eastern Orthodox Christian faith and lived outside the borders of what would eventually become the modern Greek state. As for the Parthenon itself, it had never before served as a cultural symbol of a unified Greek nation. Quite the contrary: it was a temple originally built in homage to the goddess of a single city-state, and likely constituted a humiliating reminder to all "Greeks" living outside of Athens of that city's brutal—and fleeting—hegemony over them. Over the course of its history, the Parthenon had spent far more time as a Christian church, Muslim mosque, and Ottoman military fortress than it had ever spent as a symbol of local Athenian pride. Furthermore, prior to the nineteenth century, it had not served as a symbol of "Greek" pride across the Aegean for even a single second.

To anyone seduced by the national ideal, though, none of this mattered. The "true" Greeks were those who bequeathed science, democracy, and philosophy to Western Europe, and anything that might have happened in Greece since the death of Alexander the Great merely represented the dilution of the original Greek spirit. This spirit could only be cleansed and revitalized by those who currently venerated and internalized the virtues of ancient Greek culture in the present day: the Europeans. Anything that contradicted the fervently desired equation of ancient and modern Greece could be explained away through the discourse of stagnation or degeneration brought about through intercourse with peoples imagined to be less civilized than the original Greeks themselves. This made it easy to dismiss the widely observed phenomenon of local Athenians showing little regard for the monuments in their midst. Of course they treated their monuments like trash: they had already lost the ability to appreciate the genius of their illustrious ancestors, a deplorable state of affairs to be blamed chiefly on the Turks.

European enthusiasts of the Greek romantic fantasy now had another person to blame: Lord Elgin. We might say that the earl was the first cosmopolitan savant of an imperial power to be felled by the national ideal. But he would not be the last. The literary attacks of Lord Byron, read by every subsequent Grand Tour visitor to Athens, succeeded in turning popular opinion against Elgin. On June 7, 1816, when Parliament finally voted to authorize the woefully inadequate sum of £35,000 to purchase the marbles, the measure passed by only the slimmest of margins (82-80). Elgin found it impossible to pay off his debts, a burden his own descendants struggled to meet for many decades to come. The irony, of course, is that in spite of Elgin's own professional and personal ruin, it did not take long for his marbles to become the single most popular and visited artifact in the entire British Museum. And they are likely to stay there. Without any solid legal claim to the Elgin marbles, the only way Greece is likely to get them back is by a reversal of the "compensations of plunder" arrangement used by Elgin to get them to London in the first place. In other words, the real value of the Elgin marbles was not the £90,000 detailed in the earl's account books nor the £35,000 paid by Parliament. In fact, the real price was not a dollar figure at all. It was the defeat of a foreign army and return of an imperial colony to an allied empire. As a result, until the present Greek state—with access to far fewer resources than the Ottoman Empire before it—can find a diplomatic gift to the British comparable to that originally paid in 1801, the marbles are unlikely to find their way back to Athens.

Of course, had the sultan known just how fleeting the gift-wrapped return of Egypt would be, he might not have been so eager to sign off on Elgin's *firman*. After the French retreat from Cairo in 1801, the British army also withdrew from Egypt, content to leave the fate of the land to loosely allied Ottoman combatants. This power vacuum was quickly filled by an Albanian military general named Muhammad Ali. Ali, a member of the eastern Mediterranean cosmopolitan elite whose ranks dominated the upper echelons of the Ottoman state, was sent to Egypt by Constantinople to help the British drive out the French. With the departure of the Europeans, Ali suddenly found himself at the head of the most powerful remaining army in Egypt. Aware that his own central government lacked the ability to restore the sultan's writ in Egypt, Ali moved quickly to quash his local rivals and style himself a *pasha*. Constantinople could only look on with anxiety and dread, hoping that Muhammad Ali would choose to remain loyal to the Sublime Porte and not secede from the empire.

The *pasha* turned out to be a shrewd politician. Over the next five decades until his death in 1849, Muhammad Ali continued to rule Egypt as an Ottoman province in name, while accruing near dictatorial powers to himself on the ground—with little to no input from his nominal overlords in Constantinople. In one form or another, Ali's descendants would remain in power in Cairo until 1952, when they were finally toppled by a military coup. Despite his Albanian origins and complete lack of cultural, ethnic, and linguistic affinities with his mostly Arab subjects, Muhammad Ali is often credited today with having brought Egypt into the modern world. He was acutely aware of

Figure 2.5. Muhammad Ali, the pasha of Egypt, 1841.

the fact that Ottoman forces, long dominant throughout the Middle East and Mediterranean, could no longer compete with the Europeans. As remedy, Ali devoted considerable effort to modernization initiatives designed to bring the products of European science and industry to Egypt.

As we have already seen, one of the simplest and most affordable ways for rulers in less-developed parts of the world to obtain the fruits of the European industrial revolution was to exchange that which was cheap and plentiful for that which was rare and expensive. In the case of Egypt, this meant the sand-buried antiquities of the Pharaonic age in exchange for European technical advice and machinery. Throughout the reign of Muhammad Ali and those of many of his successors, the Arab, Coptic (Egyptian Christian), and Turkish inhabitants of Egypt did not identify in any meaningful way with the art, monuments, or beliefs of the pharaohs. If anything, the ancient Egyptians were religious apostates, condemned to eternal Muslim or Christian hell for their infamous rejection of Moses and his God, a scriptural anecdote revered by both traditions (see chapter 4). In economic terms, this meant that the material relics of the Pharaonic age, much like the Elgin marbles, held no intrinsic monetary value so long as they remained in Egypt. Much like the Acropolis in Athens, Egyptian pyramids and temples were quarried by local peasants and military authorities, used as trash dumps and makeshift homes by the itinerant poor, and openly vandalized by passersby of every sort.

This was the Egypt that greeted Italian sojourner Giovanni Belzoni. Belzoni, a 6'6" native of Padua who was educated in Rome, is perhaps the most colorful and interesting of all the historical Indiana Joneses. To him falls the distinction of being the first European collector of antiquities to undertake a solitary field expedition deep into the interior of a culturally and religiously alien land. Born in 1778 to a family of modest means, Belzoni managed to escape the conscription quotas of Napoleon's invading army by taking refuge in a Roman monastery. This gave him his first great business idea, and for several years afterward he wandered through Italy selling Catholic talismans and ritual implements. At some point, Belzoni acquired an interest in and familiarity with hydraulics, the art of manipulating water to power a mechanical device without the aid of human muscle. Confident that the fast developing cities of northern Europe would value his newly acquired skill, Belzoni went first to Holland in 1801, where he failed to find employment. Next up was England, where his towering physique found him ready employment not as a hydraulics expert, but rather as a theater circus act. With his herculean frame, the former monk was soon billed as the "Great Belzoni," capable of hoisting up to ten adult men on a carefully crafted shoulder and neck brace as fountains of water danced all around him. For the next twelve years, Belzoni and his rope-dancing wife toured across Europe and the Mediterranean, alternately using his hydraulic skills to re-create naval battles on stage or smearing his face with coal and advertising himself as the "Patagonian Sampson."

Figure 2.6. Giovanni Belzoni in Muslim garb.

In the spring of 1815, Belzoni and his wife decided to take their act to Constantinople, the theatrical Mecca of the eastern Mediterranean. En route to the Sublime Porte, however, they stopped over on the tiny island of Malta. In a startling twist of fate, it was there that Belzoni met a man who introduced himself as Ishmael Gibraltar and claimed to be a commercial agent of Muhammad Ali, the *pasha* of Egypt. Interested only in Belzoni's hydraulic talents, Ishmael told him that Ali was keen on modernizing Egypt along European lines and could use a man of Belzoni's talents. Would he therefore be interested in traveling to Cairo to give the *pasha* a personal demonstration of a device that could pump water up from the Nile, thus enabling more efficient irrigation? Belzoni, thrilled to find a patron who might value his brain over his brawn, changed course and set sail for Alexandria.

Belzoni was impressed with the Albanian ruler of Egypt. "He is constantly inquiring after something new," he later wrote, "and is delighted with any thing strange to his imagination." Most impressive to Belzoni was his willingness to allow the royal fingers to be shocked by a machine that produced an electrical charge. While Belzoni labored for weeks on end in Cairo to build a device that could pump water from the Nile to nearby fields without the assistance of man or beast, he also took time to visit the Pharaonic ruins of Lower Egypt. He climbed to the top of the great pyramids of Giza, got stuck in a tunnel leading to one of the interior tombs, and gazed in admiration at the Sphinx, then still covered to its shoulders in accumulated sand. He also chatted with European travelers in Cairo, a few of whom told him about a marvelous seven-ton granite head buried in the sand at Luxor, some four hundred miles upriver. It was carved with such grace and elegance that the Europeans who had seen it did not believe it possible to have been sculpted by a person trained outside of the Western artistic tradition, as it was then envisioned. So they gave the head a name that connected it to the ancient Greeks: Memnon, an Ethiopian king in Greek heroic literature said to have participated in the Battle of Troy. Unlike the pyramids and the Sphinx, the relocation of such an object just might be within the realm of the possible—that is, for someone with enough engineering and hydraulic expertise to devise a way to drag seven tons of rock over the baking sand to the banks of the Nile, and then float it by barge to a Mediterranean port.

Back at the *pasha*'s court, Muhammad Ali was not impressed with Belzoni's water-pumping device. It was too expensive, too fragile, and only marginally more efficient than traditional reliance on the human labor readily available all year round. With that, Belzoni's economic prospects in Egypt appeared to dry up. He was now faced with a stark choice. He could resume his voyage to Constantinople and return to the stage as an exotic freak-show act, a routine of which he had long tired. Or he could sail upriver to Luxor, draw upon his knowledge and experience with hydraulics, and see whether or not the Memnon Head might budge. The decision was made easier by the fortuitous arrival in Cairo of Henry Salt, an amateur traveler and artist sent by London to take up the post of British consul to the court of Muhammad Ali. Salt knew nothing about Egyptian antiquities, but he did know that the French were interested in acquiring them for the Louvre. In fact, when Napoleon first invaded Egypt in 1798, he had brought with him a hundred and sixty French scholars tasked with the mission of studying the lands, peoples, and histories of the region. Even as these French savants retreated back to Paris with their army in 1801, they were replaced by a new wave of French consuls, travelers, and scholars who took up residence in Cairo and proceeded to fan out across the land.

Having won on the battlefield, the British could not afford to lose in their museums. That the French appeared to value the monuments, artifacts, and inscriptions of the Pharaonic age was more than enough reason for the British to go after them, too, even if no one in London or Paris was quite yet prepared to say why they should be valued. (Not until the unlocking of the hieroglyphs in 1822—a development treated in chapter 3—did the mysteries of ancient Egypt begin to be unraveled in Europe.) Upon his arrival in Cairo, Salt soon became acquainted with Bernardino Drovetti, the former French consul who now devoted his time to collecting Egyptian antiquities for the Louvre. Drovetti was about as much a Frenchman as Belzoni was English: both men were born and raised in Italy.

But whereas Belzoni had managed to escape conscription into Napoleon's army, Drovetti had voluntarily enlisted and later chose to adopt French citizenship. Now the fate of Egypt's antiquities would be determined by two Italians committed to serve on opposite ends of one of Europe's greatest imperial rivalries. Both men wanted the Memnon Head, and both men now had deep pockets to draw from: Drovetti from the Louvre, and Belzoni from Salt, who hoped—but had not yet formally arranged—to sell it to the British Museum.

Once contracted by Salt, Belzoni made his way to Upper Egypt and began to search for antiquities. In his possession was a *firman* obtained by Salt from Muhammad Ali in Cairo—and not, as was the case with Elgin in subjugated Greece, from the sultan's men in Constantinople—along with detailed instructions from the consul regarding his task in Luxor. Belzoni was to "spare no expense or trouble" in transporting the Memnon Head as speedily as possible to Alexandria. The head itself was described as being "of large dimensions," with "the face being quite perfect, and very beautiful," and the surface colored by a mix of "blackish and reddish granite, and covered with hieroglyphics on its shoulders." Salt further instructed Belzoni to confirm its identity by looking for a "hole bored artificially, supposed to have been made by the French for separating the fragment of the body." Though it is impossible to know if Drovetti was in fact responsible for this minor mutilation, Salt's attribution of the blemish to the French fit perfectly with the image he wished to project. Because only the British refrained from wanton mutilation of Egypt's past, it naturally followed that only the British were qualified to exert their political and economic influence in the Egypt of Salt's day.

In Belzoni's own account of the expedition, published in 1820, he describes how he succeeded in removing the Memnon Head only over the strenuous objections and machinations of Drovetti, who bribed local officials in hopes of sabotaging his recruitment of laborers. Surely Drovetti has his own version of the story to tell. All we know for certain is that Belzoni did indeed emerge the victor, and all seven tons of the Memnon Head arrived safely intact in London two years later without any further mishaps. In stark contrast to the Elgin Marbles, no controversy accompanied the Memnon Head back on its voyage to Britain. Unlike with Greece, Egypt did not yet figure prominently in the European historical imagination, and neither its ancient Pharaonic past nor its current Muslim inhabitants were familiar enough for anybody to contemplate the "revitalization" of the latter on the basis of the former. Belzoni, unique in his day for the passion with which he promoted the genius of Egypt's ancient arts, was certain that the brilliance of old had long since departed the land. He later wrote:

> On looking at an edifice of such magnitude, workmanship, and antiquity, inhabited by a half savage people, whose huts are stuck against it, not unlike wasps' nests, and to contrast their filthy clothes with these sacred images, that once were so highly venerated, makes one strongly feel the difference [between] the ancient and modern state[s] of Egypt.

As a result, even the Memnon Head itself was imagined to rejoice at its removal to a more civilized land. In one of the most famously self-serving passages in the annals of the historical Indiana Jones, Belzoni described his first encounter with the half-buried granite head in near comically anthropomorphist

Figure 2.7. The removal of the Memnon Head from Luxor.

terms. According to him, he "found it near the remains of its body and chair, with its face upwards, and apparently smiling on me, at the thought of being taken to England."

To be fair, we should note that Belzoni was largely correct in his assessment of the general apathy and indifference shown by the populace of Egypt toward his and Drovetti's activities. Neither man encountered much difficulty in procuring his *firman*, nor did either man meet with any sort of principled opposition to his removal of an antiquity from Egypt. And what opposition there was bore little resemblance to the nationalist logic of our own day and age, so often retroactively applied. Local Egyptian officials and Arab peasants, both in Luxor and elsewhere, did occasionally balk at rendering assistance to the European explorer, but not because they believed their country had a natural or inherent right to the antiquity in question. Almost always, such opposition was based upon the pragmatic and wholly rational desire to reap as much economic benefit from the enterprise as the European himself was imagined to derive. One of the most common sources of friction stemmed from a request on the part of the village headman, or *sheikh*, to funnel all wages through his own hands before they reached the laborers. Because such practices tended to end in graft, with a concomitant decrease in both wages and morale for the laborers, the foreigner almost always refused, leading to an acrimonious test of wills. At a bare minimum, *firman* or not, local officials would rarely lift a finger until they had been placated with prestigious gifts of European manufacture—watches, tinned goods, pistols, etc.—and assured a cut of any gold or other precious metals commonly believed to be hidden inside or nearby the antiquity.

As for the local peasants, both in Egypt and elsewhere, so long as they could overcome the prevalent fear of malevolent spirits trapped within, there was hardly a statue, tomb, or monument they wouldn't help excavate in exchange for an honest day's wages. The letters of Flinders Petrie, a British archaeologist active in Egypt for nearly four decades beginning in the 1880s, reveal the extent to which the local residents regarded the foreign excavator in economic rather than cultural terms. In 1883, while excavating a site at Tanis in the Nile Delta, Petrie noted how "the shekhs tried to stop the people from working, because they did not get the money through their hands." But the Egyptian peasants, Petrie continued, "are so glad to get regular pay without any deduction that they say they intend to work, shekhs or no shekhs, as long as there is pay to be had." As a result, so long as they are "paid regularly," Petrie concluded, the peasants "defy anything short of open violence to stop them." On average, those who volunteered to do manual labor for Petrie tended to make about twice as much as they would in their usual occupations. In fact, there was such an abundance of eager hands that Petrie once admitted to "discharging for laziness freely," as "there are so many applicants for work."

Another way to think of all this is to say that Petrie, Elgin, Salt, Belzoni, and Drovetti were each able to get what they wanted from Ottoman Greece and Egypt because they were able to take advantage of a favorable exchange rate in the market of antiquities. Their homelands in Europe—or, in the case of Belzoni and Drovetti, the adopted European empires that employed them—had a significant head start in the construction of the modern museum. By virtue of the socio-political value that museums confer upon the governments and wealthy elites that finance them, both the Louvre and the British Museum were able to bestow a hefty monetary value upon those antiquities that lacked any intrinsic financial worth in their current state abroad. Because the Parthenon marbles and Memnon Head represented a known (if subjective) value in London, but were essentially worthless in Athens and Luxor, European collectors could and did manipulate the market "exchange" rate with regard to labor, transportation, and purchase.

The locals, not yet initiated into the world of museum politics, were largely unaware of the economic, political, cultural, and social value such antiquities would magically assume once transported to Europe. As a result, both the sultan in Constantinople and the Arab peasant in Luxor were generally content with the "compensations of plunder" that they received. In this sense, the *firman* was more like a receipt for payment in non-monetary form. After all, from the perspective of anyone who lived in a world without museums, antiquities that lacked an obvious religious or cultural utility to the communities surrounding them held no inherent value for those communities beyond what they could induce from the Europeans in exchange for their removal. As a result, *any* form of compensation was considered to be a good deal, from the expulsion of the French army in Egypt to a day's wages laboring under the desert sun during the agricultural off-season. In fact, both parties to the exchange believed they were getting something for practically nothing. Not only that, the locals, unable to fathom a world in which an impractical institution like the museum could suddenly confer monetary value upon seven tons of malevolent granite, were convinced that Indiana Jones was out of his mind.

Indiana Jones was not out of his mind, nor was anyone with whom he dealt anywhere in the Ottoman Empire. Until Egypt built its own museums and schools and told its own citizens that the Pharaonic past was an integral part of their present identities—a very artificial and unnatural idea—the Memnon Head, perched in the sand on the western shore of the Nile at Luxor, was for all intents and purposes worthless to every Egyptian. The fact of the matter is that both the European explorer and the Egyptian native were making sound calculations based on a rational assessment of the exchange rate for antiquities in whichever social, political, or economic market they happened to make their livelihood. In this chapter, we have seen how the European office of ambassador or consul was most favorably positioned to manipulate these various markets. For they alone saw both ends of the spectrum: on the one hand, wealthy European elites and the politically charged museums they financed; on the other, impoverished frontiers of a beleaguered rival empire and the unprotected antiquities that lay inside.

Lord Elgin had faced sharp criticism in the British Parliament for having acted in "the character of merchants." But he was merely the first to do so, and by no means the last. No matter how much Elgin might speak of improving the national taste of Britain or Belzoni about his "researches" in Egypt—for such was the word he used to lend scholarly respectability to his actions—both men were engaged in what were essentially economic transactions obscured through lofty words. It did not take long for those locals living on the frontier end of these expeditions to realize just how flourishing a trade European consuls were now managing. A Chinese official stationed along the ancient routes of the Silk Road once observed that the European consulate only purported to represent a benign institution of diplomacy. "In reality," he continued, "they are a base from which a monopoly on all commercial transactions is forcibly imposed." If we think of the trade in antiquities as consisting of economic transactions conducted through non-monetary means, it becomes clear just how pivotal a role ambassadors and consuls could play in the relocation of so many antiquities to European and American museums over the next hundred years. Due in large part to the efforts of Elgin and Salt in Greece and Egypt, by the early nineteenth century the collection of antiquities in the Ottoman Empire had become big business in Europe.

And with the unlocking of the hieroglyphs and extension of Grand Tour itineraries to Egypt, it was about to get even bigger.

Continue the journey at indianajonesinhistory.com:
- EPISODE IV: The Elgin Marbles
- EPISODE V: The Great Belzoni

CHAPTER THREE

Consuming Indiana Jones

In 1819, three years after its removal from the west bank of the Nile at Luxor, Belzoni's seven-ton head of granite—baptized the "Younger Memnon" so as to invoke a respectable Greek pedigree—was gently mounted upon its new resting place: a marble pedestal in the Townley Gallery of the British Museum. The grey fog of London was a world away from the desert rays of the Egyptian sun that had long baked its serene visage. More importantly, the Memnon's colossal size and alien contours left it poorly served by the classical décor of its new home. The hallways of the British Museum had been designed to showcase the flowing and comparatively petite forms of Greek and Roman art, not those of the monolithic and more angular Egyptian. In fact, during Belzoni's time most European collectors did not even consider Egyptian antiquities to be a form of "art" at all. In a letter to Henry Salt, the British consul in Cairo who had sponsored Belzoni's labors in the field, Joseph Banks, the director of the British Museum, described the Memnon Head as unfit to be placed alongside Greek and Roman "Fine Art." Instead, it was showcased in a separate "Egyptian Room," effectively cordoned off from the acknowledged artistic forbears of Western civilization. "Whether any statue that has been found in Egypt," Banks continued, "can be brought into competition with the grand works of the Townley Gallery remains to be proved."

Banks was putting it gently. By 1819, the weight of seven decades of scholarly disapproval rested heavily upon the shoulders of the Younger Memnon. In 1753, when the British Museum first opened its doors, an eclectic assortment of mummies, sarcophagi, statuary, and ritual talismans from

Egypt already decorated its halls. Among the mostly upper class and cosmopolitan patrons of the museum, however, such familiarity seems only to have bred contempt. Jan van Rymsdyk, the author of a 1778 guidebook to the "Museum Britannicum," declared his intention not "to put myself in Perspiration concerning any of the Hieroglyphic Emblems, or Monstrosities of the Egyptians, for it is all Labour in vain, or washing a Blackamore white." In another guidebook from the previous year, Alexander Thomas contrasted the antiquities of Greece and Italy, "where all the polite arts were carried to the highest perfection" and "where wit and elegance resided," to the unfortunate specimens from Egypt, "where a deity was represented with the head of a dog" and "a lion was the most respectable inhabitant of one city."

Figure 3.1. The animal gods of ancient Egypt. Anubis (with a dog's head) and Nephthys (with the body of a hawk) prepare a corpse for the afterlife.

The most damning indictment of all, however, was delivered in 1786 by John Woodward, a well-known physician and collector. "There never appears one single figure that shews any thing of art or good work," he concluded. "Their limbs are stiff, and ill-proportioned; their bodies awkward, shapeless, and far inferior to the life. ... No people living had ever so enormous and perverse a fancy as they appear to have had. They really aimed at something that was hideous, deformed, and monstrous; a beast, or a fowl, with the head and face of a man; the head of a dog, or some other brute, of an hawk, or the like, upon an human figure." Once again, the impossible standard against which Woodward insisted on judging the ancient Egyptians was that represented by the Greco-Roman tradition. "They seem to have affected what was ugly and irregular, as much as the Greeks, the Romans, and others, who had something of spirit and a genteel fancy, did what was handsome, well-proportioned, beautiful, and like nature." At best, the works of the pharaohs were regarded as "wondrous curiosities." At worst, they were "monstrous curiosities." Either way, they were mere oddities, unfit to be judged alongside the transcendent artistic productions of what were then regarded as the boundaries of Western civilization.

Boundaries, however, can change. Sometimes they are changed by the fortunes of the battlefield. But just as often they are transformed through advances in knowledge. More than anything else, it was this glaring lack of knowledge about the Pharaonic era among European scholars that helped to reinforce its "curious" qualities and ensure its continued separation from the Greeks and Romans. As late as 1819, the year of the Memnon installation, Egyptian hieroglyphs remained as impenetrable as ever. Everyone could see that the pantheon of Pharaonic gods included dogs and birds, but no one knew why. Until the unfamiliar Egyptian spirits, rites, and mummies could be placed into some sort of socio-political or historical context, no self-respecting European gentleman was prepared to claim a hybrid dog-god as part of his own cultural heritage. As a result, most people who took an active interest in Egyptian antiquities and other Pharaonic *miscellanea* did so on the presumption that they offered a conduit to

the mystical wisdom of the occult. The underground trade in
mummies is a case in point: though superstitious ship captains
often refused to set sail from Alexandria if they learned of
a mummy onboard, once in Europe, these desiccated corpses
were quickly ground into a fine powder and sold as a potent
remedy for various ailments.

A wondrous curiosity indeed! For as long as anyone could
remember, Egypt had been synonymous with the dark alleys
of the occult, not the splendid plinths of the leisured classes.
Slowly but surely, Belzoni began to change all that. In 1821,
still smarting over the lack of recognition and compensation once expected to derive from his exploits in Egypt,
the Paduan giant undertook his most ambitious project yet.
Hoping to cash in on tales of his strength, daring, and hydraulic ingenuity along the Nile, Belzoni organized a life-size
reconstruction of Pharaonic tombs and artwork for an indoor
display in London. Opened to the general public in 1821,
the exhibition contained a virtual reproduction of the tomb
of Seti I, complete with decorated walls and scale models.
Visitors were mesmerized. One man saw in the exhibition
"the most gratifying consequence of exploring the remains
of ancient Egypt" and delighted in the memory of sitting "in
them as in the realities themselves," among "the presence
of objects that fill the mind with pleasing wonder." Another
visitor described "the vivid colours and extraordinary figures
on the walls and ceilings, the mummies scattered in various
places, the statues of fine earth." The inevitable result was
the cultivation of an emotion "of grand and poetical nature;
fed as the imagination is by the strangeness and stillness of
the scene, and the partly ascertained, and partly unknown
nature of the objects."

Belzoni's exhibition provided a feast for the senses, not for
the mind. What he succeeded in doing was to package the pharaohs into a capitalist commodity for paying consumers. We
will refer to this phenomenon as "Egyptomania." Though consumers of Egyptomania may end up learning something about
ancient Egypt, such knowledge is an incidental by-product
of the chief intended experience: a visual and exotic delight
for the senses. Belzoni, having failed to make the pharaohs

palatable to educated European elites, marketed them instead to the general public. As the self-proclaimed sophisticate continued to sneer at the Memnon Head in the halls of the British Museum, thousands of Londoners proved more than willing to part with a shilling for the opportunity to gawk at Belzoni's indoor panorama. Admittedly, the line separating these two audiences was porously drawn. Contemporary drawings of Belzoni's reconstructed tomb show well-groomed gentlemen in top hats and coattails, flanked by respectable ladies weighted down by flower bonnets twice the size of their heads. As long as the pharaohs remained outside the hallowed grounds of the British Museum, it seems, even a stodgy sophisticate could indulge in a modest helping of Egyptomania from time to time.

Belzoni's ambitions, however, had never been modest. In order to drum up enthusiasm for his London exhibition, he pursued a variety of promotional initiatives among both highborn and low. The London *Times* carried advance notice of the exhibition, while the publisher John Murray arranged for the publication of Belzoni's personal narrative of the expedition to coincide with the opening of his panorama (editions in French, Italian, and German followed soon thereafter). For those who wished to imagine themselves by Belzoni's side, waist deep in the scalding sands of Egypt, a separate folio volume containing forty-five lavishly illustrated color plates was also put on sale. With much of London abuzz, Belzoni then made the shrewd acquaintance of Thomas "Mummy" Pettigrew, an enterprising physician with a penchant for hosting morbid "unwrapping" parties. When Belzoni offered one of his Egyptian mummies for a promotional undressing—"the most perfect mummy known in Europe, entire in all its limbs and the hair visible on its head," according to a later catalogue—Pettigrew readily obliged. Then, as the London exhibition stretched into the early months of 1822, Belzoni tried to maintain public interest by publishing two additional volumes of plates, one of which was presented as a gift to the Duke of Sussex.

After twelve months of healthy ticket sales, the exhibition finally closed its doors. Less successful incarnations soon

*Figure 3.2.
Egyptomania in
London.*
A re-creation of
the Abu Simbel
colossi for the
Egyptian Court
in the Crystal
Palace exhibition
of 1854. The
origins of this
and every other
international
showcase of
ancient Egypt
can trace their
origins back to
Belzoni's 1821
indoor panorama
of the tomb of
Seti I in London.

followed, first in Paris, then back in London. Despite these
diminishing returns, Belzoni's indoor panoramas left an institutional legacy that far outlived their creator. For the rest of the
nineteenth century, the discovery of any previously unknown
ancient civilization would be packaged and sold to the general
public in ways that were strikingly similar to the commercial
models first pioneered by Belzoni. In 1839, John Stephens and
Frederick Catherwood embarked on an expedition to Central
America in order to investigate early rumors of what would
eventually be identified as the ruins of the Mayan civilization.
Upon their return, Catherwood painstakingly re-created water-
color scenes of the jungle ruins, which were offered for sale as
lithographs. Catherwood was also an accomplished painter of
indoor panoramas, with a resumé of exhibits in London, New
York, Boston, Baltimore, and Philadelphia. A decade later,

London hosted the first "world's fair," sparking a host of imitators over the next fifty years, from Paris to Philadelphia. These visually indulgent spectacles displayed the diversity of the world in ways that both delighted and instructed the general public, most often by resorting to familiar stereotypes of dynamic Westerners and stagnant Orientals. Exhibits on European and North American nations, for example, highlighted progress in science and industry. Exhibits for places like Egypt and China, however, invariably took their cues from Belzoni's original London panorama, highlighting the "wondrous curiosities" of an ancient civilization whose descendants had fallen from grace.

Egyptomania—along with all the other "manias" spawned by its success—was what the masses consumed. The true European sophisticate would seldom admit to being enchanted by such "monstrous curiosities," even if he, too, could not entirely resist their exotic allure. In general, though, social elites tended to echo the sentiments of a 1774 guidebook to London, which cast a dim view on the intellectual capacity of those "idle men and women" who wandered into the British Museum, only to "return neither wiser nor better," their "understandings being as much darkened as their memories are unretentive." For them, only the fleeting and superficial experience of Egyptomania was deemed suitable. The self-appointed guardians of scholarly and cultural standards needed their own, more respectable means of interaction with the pharaohs, one not premised upon the vulgar novelty of visual stimuli.

In 1822, the French scholar Jean-François Champollion rose to the occasion. Based upon a comparative analysis of the trilingual Rosetta Stone and hieroglyphs etched into an obelisk transported to England by Belzoni, Champollion advanced his now celebrated claim regarding the nature of Egyptian hieroglyphs. Long viewed as the inscrutable signs of an arcane priesthood, the hieroglyphs were now shown to be anything but. According to Champollion, the ancient Egyptian script was governed by phonetic values much like any other script. The individual graphs didn't represent profound ideas or abstract concepts. Rather, they represented mundane consonants and vowels, which were then strung together to spell similarly mundane words.

In short, the hieroglyphs were useful, not mystical. Though they could and did record the exploits of gods and kings—often in tedious detail—they were also used to record the number of oxen in a stable and a list of groceries to buy. For many Egyptomania enthusiasts, this was a disappointment, to say the least. But for scholars, collectors, and other social and cultural luminaries throughout Europe, Champollion had unlocked a whole new mode of engagement with Egypt: Egyptology. The land of mummies now had a recorded history—thirty-six centuries of it, in fact. Thomas Young, one of the first to attempt a translation of the Rosetta Stone, had given up the pursuit after all his early glosses seemed only to reveal details of "ridiculous rites and ceremonies." He claimed to see "nothing that looks like history." But Champollion had managed to give to Young and every other European scholar a respectably boring list of the names of kings, temples, and wars in ancient Egypt, one sure to keep the fickle crowd at bay.

Yet the poor benighted masses were not the only people the Egyptologists wanted to keep at bay. So, too, were the modern-day inhabitants of Ottoman Egypt—mostly Arabs, Copts, and Turks—excluded from the newly fashioned cultural identity imposed upon the country by Egyptologists. Though they had managed to recover more than three millennia of previously unknown dates, names, and battles, the Egyptologists had not done so for the edification of their contemporaries in Egypt. On the contrary, all the information yielded by the hieroglyphs was interpreted as an additional commentary on the origins of Western civilization. In other words, no European scholar responded to the unlocking of the hieroglyphs by humbly conceding the august pedigree of a rival Oriental civilization. Instead, they portrayed the pharaohs as the earliest progenitors of their own civilization—one defined, in suitably vague terms, as "Western." This shift can be traced in one of the first guidebooks for the British Museum to be published after Champollion's linguistic coup. "The object of the present work," its author noted, "is to publish a Selection of the Choicest Monuments existing in the National Collection of this country. It commences with those of Egypt, from the high authenticated antiquity of many of them, and from their being the source from which the arts of Sculpture and of Painting, and perhaps even the Sciences, were handed to the Greeks—and from the Greeks to us. They are the Alpha of the history of Art."

With the Pharaohs now reimagined as the cultural ancestors to the Greeks, there was no longer any need to invent outlandish, speculative identities for the artifacts of ancient Egypt. The Memnon Head was the first to experience this transformation. With the hieroglyphs now deciphered, it was no longer possible to claim that this represented the head of Memnon, an Ethiopian king alleged by Homer to have participated in the equally legendary battle of Troy. The hieroglyphs were clear and unequivocal: the head belonged to Ramses II (1303–1213 B.C.), one of the most powerful pharaohs ever to rule over a Nile kingdom. On first glance, however, by stripping Europe's most famous "wondrous curiosity" of its literary associations with a celebrated Greek battlefield, the Egyptologists had appeared to bring about a dramatic devaluation of Belzoni's prize find. But a second glance reveals quite the opposite. For if the death of King Memnon, "lone Trojan warrior," is followed by the birth of King Ramses, "grandfather of all Greeks," then we need not wonder at the lack of anxiety among Egyptologists toward the replacement of one cultural ancestor (Memnon) with another (ancient Egypt). To put it another way, the cracking of the hieroglyphic code enabled European scholars and politicians alike to broaden their horizons far beyond individually prized works of art like the Memnon Head and instead to claim all of Egypt as their inheritance—to the exclusion of anyone imagined to be outside the ever-shifting boundaries of Western civilization.

Egyptology and Egyptomania were born and raised in Europe, not Egypt. Both traced their origins to the 1820s, and each bore the cultural DNA of its father: one given life by a lowborn Italian circus freak eager to please the masses, the other by a cerebral bookworm whose life's work could only be appreciated by a tiny sliver of humankind. Belzoni died in 1823, Champollion in 1832, both tragically young. Scarcely had they breathed their last, however, before the intellectual and commercial enterprises they pioneered began to spread beyond the boundaries of Europe. Ironically, the first expansion was

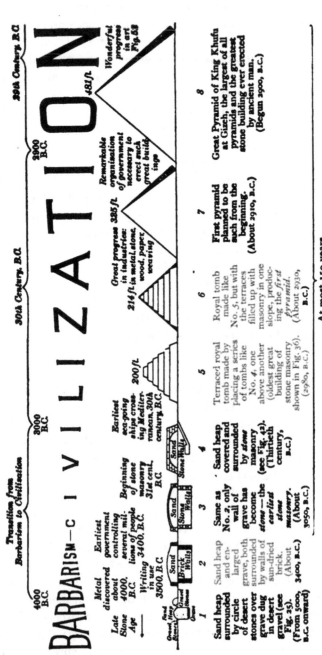

BARBARISM—CIVILIZATION

Transition from Barbarism to Civilization

4000 B.C. 3000 B.C. 30th Century, B.C. 39th Century, B.C.

Late Stone Age

Metal discovered about 4000 B.C. Writing in use 3500 B.C.

Earliest government controlling several millions of people about 3400 B.C.

Beginning of stone masonry 31st cent. B.C.

Earliest sea-going ships crossing Mediterranean, 30th century, B.C.

Great progress in industries: in metal, stone, wood, paper, weaving.

Remarkable organization of government necessary to erect such great buildings

Wonderful progress in art Fig. 53

200 ft. 214 ft. 385 ft. 481 ft.

1
Sand heap surrounded by circle of desert stones over grave dug in desert gravel (see Fig. 23). (From 5000, B.C. onward)

2
Sand heap and enlarged grave, both surrounded by walls of sun-dried brick. (About 3400, B.C.)

3
Same as No. 2, only wall of grave has become stone — the earliest stone masonry. (About 3050, B.C.)

4
Sand heap covered and surrounded by stone masonry (see Fig. 42). (Thirtieth century, B.C.)

5
Terraced royal tomb made by placing a series of tombs like No. 4, one above another (oldest great building of stone masonry shown in Fig. 36). (2980, B.C.)

6
Royal tomb made like No. 5, but with the terraces filled up with masonry in one slope, producing the first pyramid. (About 2950, B.C.)

7
First pyramid planned to be such from the beginning. (About 2900, B.C.)

8
Great Pyramid of King Khufu at Gizeh, the largest of all pyramids and the greatest stone building ever erected by ancient man. (Begun 2900, B.C.)

At most 150 years
(from earliest stone masonry to the Great Pyramid)

into Egypt itself. Europeans brought their baggage—both literal and metaphorical—back into Egypt by rail and steam: two modes of transport that simultaneously embodied and enabled the growing reach of European empires. In September 1830, the first commercial steam engine line began to transport passengers by rail from Liverpool to Manchester. By the end of the decade, steamships could ferry a growing number of modestly moneyed travelers from any number of ports in Europe to Alexandria, Jerusalem, or Constantinople in about two weeks—less than half the time it had taken previous generations to make the same trip by wind and sail.

Their arrival in Egypt gave rise to a tourist industry that catered exclusively to the needs of the burgeoning leisured classes of Europe and North America. By the middle of the nineteenth century, a modestly successful Englishman could book a month-long vacation to Egypt via a London-based travel agency; stay in comfortable Victorian-style lodgings in Cairo; interpret everything he saw through an English-language guidebook indebted to the cultural prisms of Egyptology and Egyptomania; speak, eat, and dress exactly as he might do back home; trace the itineraries of famous European and American poets, novelists, and princes who had carved their name in various monuments on previous trips; and return home with affordable souvenirs manufactured to foreign tastes. The superficial contours of Egypt became so well known that a review of one travelogue in 1863 declared "that Egypt as a place for descriptions of travel is almost exhausted; the Nile entirely so. The river is as familiar as the Thames, and the traveller, unless he has something new to say ... might as well publish an itinerary of his journey from Calais to Rome." No European who went to Egypt as a tourist was obliged to learn a single word of Arabic unless already inclined, nor

Figure 3.3 (Opposite). From barbarism to (Western) civilization. In his widely adopted textbook on the history of Western civilization, first published in 1914, American Egyptologist James Breasted equates ancient Egypt with the monumental tombs of its elite classes, and portrays them as marking the transition from barbarism to civilization.

conform to Muslim sensibilities in matters of dress, custom, or habit. (By contrast, Belzoni and all previous generations of Western travelers in Egypt and the Near East had invariably donned turbans for men and veils for women, in conformance with local customs.) With the possible exception of his local *dragoman*, or guide—contracted through a Western-owned travel agency or hotel—the European could in fact now spend months and even years in Egypt without ever having engaged in a single substantive interaction or discussion with someone who was actually born and raised in Egypt.

The ideological influence of Egyptology and Egyptomania is readily apparent in the letters of Lucie Duff-Gordon, an Englishwoman who lived in Egypt for seven years in the middle of the nineteenth century. In 1865, she published for public consumption many of her letters to family and friends back home. In them, we can see how an educated European with the means to travel to Egypt made sense of the land and people around her. According to the book's preface, Lady Duff was inspired by "the wretched condition of the Arabs" in Egypt to publish her letters and thus bring attention to their

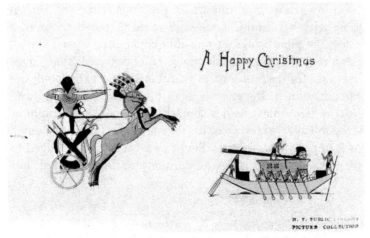

Figure 3.4. Merry Christmas from the Pharaohs.
A tourist postcard from Egypt fuses the cultural preferences
of Western visitors—Christianity and the pharaohs—
into an anachronistic but profitable commodity.

plight. Though she saw in them "the relics of a most ancient and noble race, once the possessor of a high and distinct form of civilization," they had long since been "crushed under the same barbarian force which destroyed the last remnants of the civilization of Greece." Who were these so-called barbarians? Why, the Turks, of course, who dominated the Ottoman bureaucracy. For most Europeans, the Turks were the original "Oriental despots," whose rise to power ushered in an era of widespread stagnation across the eastern Mediterranean and Near East. As a result, it fell to selfless men like Lord Elgin to venture into the lands of the barbarians and rescue whatever remained of the ancestral civilizations now struggling under the yoke of the Turks.

Because the Orient was synonymous with the Ottomans, and because the Ottomans were synonymous with stagnation, Lady Duff regarded the present-day inhabitants of Egypt with a mixture of pity and contempt. She referred to her Arab servants as "dear, good, lazy fellows, or rather, children; their ways amuse me infinitely." In another passage she assures the recipient of her letter that "you would like the people, poor things! They are complete children, but amiable children." In evaluating these "children," Lady Duff deployed an early version of the "nature vs. nurture" argument. Anything deemed unpleasant among the Egyptians was said to be due to the corrupting influence of their figurative "parents"—the Turks. Anything worthy of praise, however, was chalked up to a miraculous biological inheritance from their figurative "ancestors"—the forbears of Western civilization, among which the pharaohs were now included. In this vein, one local man was described by Lady Duff as having "walked straight out of a hieroglyph." Another was said to look "so much like Father Abraham" that "I felt quite as if my wish to live a little a few thousand years ago had been fulfilled." She variously described Egypt as an embodiment of "the real Arabian Nights," the setting for "a passage in the Old Testament," or a country in which "all is so scriptural."

Consuming Indiana Jones, 1821-1912

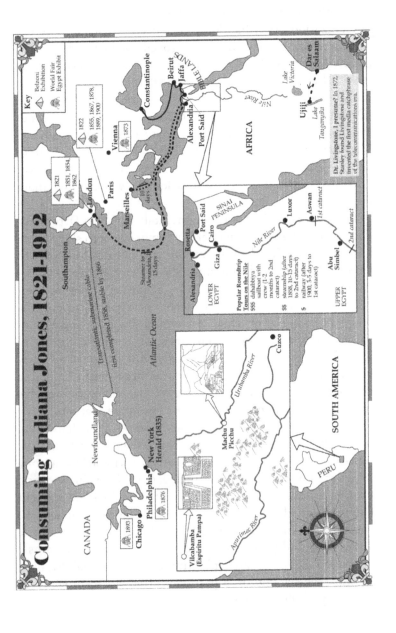

For Lady Duff as for most Europeans and Americans, the history of Egypt began with the pharaohs and ended with Islam. Anything that fell outside these chronological parameters was simply not worth discussing. Within these parameters, however, two topics towered above all others. The first, noted above, was the ways in which the civilization of the pharaohs was imagined to have laid a foundation for the rise of the Greeks. The second was less ambitious, but far more pedantic: biblical archaeology. This field of study shared much in common with its cousins on the Nile. Much like Egyptologists, those who scoured the Near East for evidence of the peoples, places, and events mentioned in the Old Testament took their work very seriously, and imagined it to carry momentous implications for the history of Western civilization. Conversely, much like those who indulged in Egyptomania, the ranks of biblical "archaeologists" also included a substantial number of amateur enthusiasts who cared little for the big questions of history. Instead, they devoted themselves to a narrow and sensationalist pursuit of unexplained "mysteries" and "wonders" recorded in the Judeo-Christian canon.

Just as with Egyptology and Egyptomania, proponents of both modes of engagement with the so-called "Bible lands" often found themselves forced to share the same space. Their cumulative efforts are best represented by the activities of the London-based Palestine Exploration Fund, founded in 1865 to promote scientific research capable of shedding light on the history of Egypt, the Near East, and the Levant as alluded to in the scriptures. Not just any scripture, however: only events, peoples, and places mentioned in the Hebrew and Christian Bibles were deemed suitable for archaeological investigation. This overt and unabashed bias permeated the pages of the Fund's hugely popular *Quarterly Statement*, first issued in 1869 and still in operation today. Much ink was spilled in an attempt to identify all the place names mentioned in the Old and New Testaments, and then to mark them on a map overlaid with their latter-day Arabic-language equivalents. As in Egypt, the present-day inhabitants of the region were regarded with a mixture of pity and contempt. If the people of Palestine were of any interest at all, it was only to shed light on the ancient Hebrew and Christian societies that had somehow survived within the unconscious recesses of their minds. In 1858, the popular John Murray guidebook even went so far as to tell its readers that "the Bible is the best handbook for Palestine; the present work is intended to be a companion to it." Unfortunately, the Bible may have brought the tourists, but the tourists made it harder to find traces of the Bible. "Many of the ancient and peculiar customs of Palestine are fast vanishing before the increasing tide of Western manners," the founders of the Fund claimed upon its establishment, "and in a short time the exact meaning of many things which find their correspondences in the Bible will have perished."

Correspondences with the Judeo-Christian scriptures were what mattered. To biblical archaeologists and their attentive audiences, it was of little consequence that toponyms such as "Iraq" had existed within Muslim societies for more than a millennium. The region was instead habitually referred to as "Mesopotamia," an archaic Greek phrase meaning "between the rivers" (the Tigris and Euphrates). Much as the appellation of "Memnon" was chosen to suggest a respectable Greek pedigree for a work of Egyptian sculpture, "Mesopotamia" was deliberately invoked to erase the presence of any society, language, or religion to arise in the region since the spread of Islam. Western interest in the Islamic identity of the Near East ebbed so low that a 1892 advertisement in the pages of the *Quarterly Statement* for a book entitled *Palestine Under the Moslems: A Description of Syria and the Holy Land from A.D. 650 to 1500* was forced to promote it as a "novelty" product. The sale of such a book was justified on grounds that "hardly anything has been done ... in English" and that "no attempt has ever been made to systematize, compare, and annotate" Western knowledge about Muslim societies in the Bible lands.

The practice and consumption of Egyptology, Egyptomania, and biblical archaeology was so pervasive within Euro-American communities—both at home and abroad—that all but the most educated of its members would be hard pressed to say anything about the lands and peoples of the Middle East that was not derived from the ideological agendas of these three phenomena. This was still the case up until very recently, when the exportation of radical Islamist terrorist organizations into Europe and America finally forced many Westerners to confront the present-day political and cultural complexities of the Middle East for the first time. For confirmation of the lingering sway Egyptology, Egyptomania, and biblical archaeology continue to hold in our own times, however, we need to look no further than Hollywood. Indeed, two of the plot lines for the first three Indiana Jones films focus on the adventures of a Western archaeologist (Egyptology) who spends the majority of his time in Muslim lands, yet is concerned solely with "wondrous curiosities" (Egyptomania) mentioned in the Hebrew and Christian bibles (biblical archaeology). (As a brief aside, I can still recall my giddy selection of Egypt as the subject of a "country study" assignment in the sixth grade—only to discover, much to my dismay, just how little the encyclopedia entry for "Egypt" resembled the Egypt of my imagination. After pleading with my teacher, I received permission to ignore the Egypt of today in favor of the Egypt of yesterday. My class presentation on "Egypt"—how to disembowel and preserve a mummy—earned an "A"!)

Figure 3.6. A parody of a parody of a parody.
At Legoland California, a popular children's toy is used to re-create the Luxor Hotel in Las Vegas, itself a re-creation of common Egyptomania motifs first popularized by Belzoni in 1821.

What can account for such a consistent aversion to the cultures, customs, and lore of the Muslim Middle East? The answer is simple: humans are biologically wired to be enamored with themselves. Apply this principle to a larger group of humans—a city, nation, religion, or culture—and we can expect to find entire groups of people to be more favorably disposed toward the customs, habits, appearance, and language of their own group than toward those of others. We can think of this tendency in terms of what we will refer to as a preference for one's own ethnic or cultural "avatar," either real or perceived. Simply put, an avatar is the embodiment of one person or idea in the shape of another person. In the present context, the original person—or idea—is "the West" (or "Westerners"), however loosely defined. The "avatar" then becomes the person who embodies or represents this Western identity to an audience back home while he or she lives and travels outside Western lands. The creation of an avatar can be premised upon perceived ethnic traits (skin color, physique, hair), perceived cultural traits (language, food, religion, dress), or both. It helps explain why a terrorist attack responsible for the deaths of a hundred people in Paris, for instance, is far more likely to elicit the sustained emotional investment of the Western public than the tragic demise of tens of thousands of culturally and ethnically unfamiliar people in distant Syria.

Throughout the entirety of the time span covered by this book, light-skinned men of European descent and Christian faith served as the most common ethnic and cultural avatars for a Euro-American audience back home. Few people in London, Paris, or New York were interested in hearing about the travails of Belzoni's Arab porters, for the simple reason that it was difficult to imagine oneself in their skin. But with someone like Belzoni, they all had a definite impression of his Italian background, possibly shared or were at least sympathetic to his Catholic faith—at least when contrasted with Islam—and knew that in most habits of daily life he resembled them more than either of them resembled the Egyptians. As a result, an increasing number of literate consumers proved willing to part with a few coins for the opportunity to read about the marvelous adventures of their own cultural or ethnic avatars in lands they would likely never visit themselves.

In the United States, some of the first profitable ventures in this vein were the aforementioned expeditions of John Stephens and Frederick Catherwood to Central America. Between 1839 to 1843, Stephens and Catherwood undertook two separate expeditions to Mesoamerica and produced three beautifully illustrated sets of their archaeological travel accounts. Priced within range of the American middle-class consumer, the first double-volume set sold more than twenty thousand copies within the first three months of its printing. This was no homage to the Mayan peoples whose ruins were chronicled within its pages, however. For at the top of Stephens and Catherwood's agenda was a scarcely concealed desire to claim an indigenous antiquity in the Americas equal to that of the Old World, one worthy of U.S. patronage. Outlandish theories about the migration of ancient Egyptians to Mesoamerica were debunked and replaced with a theory of indigenous construction by civilized peoples whose ancestors had degenerated under the weight of Spanish despotism. (Note the exact parallel to the role ascribed by Europeans to the Turks, who were said to have debased the once glorious races of the Near East.) Significantly, the great Mayan ruins of Mesoamerica were said to have been built by peoples who migrated southward from North America, where the less spectacular archaeological finds of Native American burial mounds were said to presage the more impressive ruins further south.

With all Spanish influence in the Americas deemed corrosive and the pre-Columbian indigenes said to have originated in North America, Stephens and Catherwood were now free to claim the great monumental ruins of Mesoamerica— said to rival those of the Old World—for the United States alone. "The casts of the Parthenon are regarded as precious memorials in the British Museum," Stephens wrote, "and casts of Copan would be the same in New-York." Because they belonged by "right to us," Stephens "resolved that ours they should be." Just like the Arabs of the Near East, the latter-day descendants of the Mayans and other indigenous peoples were also of little concern, having forsaken any and all claims to the ruins in their midst by their alleged indifference to Western science, preservation, and education. No wonder the American reading public devoured Stephens and Catherwood's books with such gusto: here they learned that they were the one and only heirs to an indigenous American antiquity equal to, but not derivative of, the pyramids and monuments of Europe and the Middle East. We might think of this as "the Mayan mirage."

By the second half of the nineteenth century, the vicarious thrills of Western avatars like Stephens and Catherwood were about to become even bigger business. In 1858, the first submarine telegraph cable was laid across the Atlantic Ocean, connecting the westernmost tip of Ireland with the easternmost tip of Newfoundland. In 1866, after eight years of setbacks and repairs, the "trans-Atlantic cable" was deemed stable. Messages that used to take ten days or more to cross the ocean by ship could now be transmitted in less than twenty-four hours by wire. This technological breakthrough initiated a sea change in the popular consumption of the historical Indiana Jones. Previously, any profits yielded by the commodification of Egyptomania, biblical archaeology, or the Mayan mirage (beyond the tourist industry, that is) came in the form of public exhibitions or the sale of lengthy travelogues. These were random and contingent affairs, profitable only for the duration of the exhibit or print run of the book.

But with the newfound ability to transmit the written word across the globe within a mere day or two, the exploits of adventurous and daring Western avatars could now be packaged and serialized in newspapers and periodicals on a regular and affordable basis. This made available an audience far larger than had ever been tapped before, giving rise to a new business model dominated by what legal scholar Tim Wu refers to as the "attention merchants." Mostly newspaper editors and other media magnates, these bold entrepreneurs published written and visual content sure to capture the attention of a wide swathe of the reading public, then resold the attention of their audiences to advertisers eager to pitch their products to captivated consumers.

But how could they capture the attention of an audience large enough to bring in the most lucrative advertisers? Salacious accounts of homicides and other criminal activity—adapted from police reports and interviews—were the first resort of the attention merchant, both then and today. But for those who could afford to underwrite more ambitious narratives, culled far beyond the local police precinct, Belzoni and his Egyptomania business model offered an endless store of commercial possibilities. The first man to exploit this potential to its fullest capacity was James Bennett, Jr., owner of the *New York Herald*. By the time the trans-Atlantic cable was complete, the *New York Herald* had already amassed a daily circulation of 84,000 readers, reputed to be the highest of any newspaper in the world. Like Belzoni, Bennett had a knack for showmanship. He once famously claimed that the purpose of his newspaper was "not to instruct but to startle and amuse." Entranced readers were treated to page after page of sensationalized news, gossip, rumors, and hoaxes, all justified on the basis of being "in the public interest." From our perspective, the *New York Herald* was the literary embodiment of the "wondrous" and "monstrous curiosities" brought to Europe from Egypt by Belzoni a half century earlier, now made cheaply available on a daily basis to all literate men and women from the comfort of their homes.

In 1869, three years after the stabilization of the trans-Atlantic cable, Bennett decided to exploit its potential to its fullest capacity. During a meeting in Paris, he met and contracted the itinerant American traveler and writer Henry Stanley for an ambitious assignment: lead an expedition through East Africa with the intent of locating and reporting upon the whereabouts of David Livingstone. Livingstone, a Scottish Congregationalist with the London Missionary Society, had spent most of the past several decades attempting to convert the native peoples of central Africa and to track the source of the Nile. He failed on both accounts. Far more successful, however, was a travelogue he penned in 1857 entitled *Missionary Travels*. In it, Livingstone portrayed himself as a manly Christian explorer waging a moral crusade against the Arab-run slave trade in Africa. The book and its various sequels brought Livingstone both fame and wealth, neither of which deterred him from returning to his favorite haunts in east-central Africa. Before long, however, news of Livingstone's activities slowed to a trickle. Eventually, he vanished entirely, giving rise to speculation of an untimely demise somewhere in an African jungle. By the time Bennett met Stanley in 1869, no one had heard from Livingstone in nearly four years.

Bennett, however, did not commission an expedition from Stanley because he was genuinely concerned about Livingstone's welfare. He did so because he wanted to profit from the serialized reports of a fearless Western explorer trekking among lions, snakes, and cannibals in search of the world's most famous Christian missionary. All the ingredients for a blockbuster scoop were in place: not just one but two Western avatars, each drawn from one side of the Atlantic, beset on all sides by dark-skinned savages and immoral Muslims, and fed to an avid public in endlessly profitable doses, all without the lengthy lag time associated with the book publishing industry. For two full years, from 1870 to 1871, Stanley's riveting accounts of his movements from Dar es Salaam to the shores

Figure 3.7. Stanley Meets Livingstone.
An imaginative rendering of the first "reality" expedition
made profitable by the trans-Atlantic cable, as serialized for
Western audiences in the pages of the *New York Herald.*

of Lake Tanganyika filled the pages of the *New York Herald*. A bestselling book, *How I Found Livingstone*, followed in 1872. In it, Stanley dedicated his labors to Bennett, whose "generosity" and "liberality" were said to have "originated, sustained, and crowned the enterprise." No longer were archaeologists and explorers confined to the patronage of kings, dukes, and earls. The trans-Atlantic cable had enabled a new species of capitalist entrepreneur—the print media tycoon—to usurp the role of cultural and social trendsetter once reserved for the titled elite.

Stanley knew that Bennett's readers were interested only in him and Livingstone, not Africa or the Africans. In justifying his frequent use of the first person pronoun, Stanley observed that he was "writing a narrative of my own adventures and travels, and that until I meet Livingstone, I presume the greatest interest is attached to myself, my marches, my troubles, my thoughts, and my impressions." He presumed correctly. The "*New York Herald* Expedition" (for such it was called) brought lifelong and posthumous fame to both Stanley and Livingstone. But why? Unlike Belzoni, neither man discovered anything that was yet unknown to their audiences back home. And though Livingstone had garnered some minor fame for his tirades against the Arab-run slave trade in Africa, everything else he set his hand to had ended in abject failure. For his part, Stanley was a competent writer and occasional journalist, but he, too, had accomplished very little worth capturing the attention of future historians. So why has everyone in the Anglophone world heard of Stanley and Livingstone?

The answer is simple. Together, Stanley and Bennett created the world's first media catchphrase. The words "Dr. Livingstone, I presume?" are familiar to nearly every literate person in the English-speaking world. This despite the fact that very few of them actually know who spoke it; when, where, or why it was spoken; who Livingstone was; or why they should care. In order to satisfy the "public interest"—as Bennett would have phrased it—the uninspiring answers are, in order: Henry Stanley; 1871 in the town of Ujiji, as a greeting to Livingstone; a failed missionary and explorer; and you shouldn't care one bit. The whole expedition was a media stunt, designed to sell advertising space in the *New*

York Herald. And it worked. Readers found the phrase so memorable and hilarious—who else but another white man could
possibly merit such a gentlemanly greeting in the wilds of
Africa?—that Stanley managed to profit off of its reproduction
for years to come, even going so far as to perform it in staged
reenactments before captive audiences.

So Stanley found Livingstone. That was the story. It did not
matter that Livingstone had never been "lost" in the first place.
In fact, he had been living in peace and comfort along the shores
of Lake Tanganyika for years, surrounded by local peoples with
whom he was on friendly terms. Nor did Livingstone return
with Stanley to Western civilization. All Stanley came back
with was a signed letter from Livingstone attesting to the fact
that Stanley had reached Ujiji and the two of them had met and
conversed. That letter legitimized what can only be described
as a very expensive and elaborate media stunt—the first of its
kind. We might say that the significance of the *New York Herald*
Expedition of 1870–71 lies in the fact that it was completely
insignificant in every conceivable way other than the profitable
spectacle it created for itself. In other words, it was famous
for having made itself famous, like any number of celebrities
and reality television contestants of our own day and age.
The new era of print journalism enabled by the trans-Atlantic
cable meant that spectacles, in and of themselves, staged or
unstaged, could generate an endlessly reproducible profit for
any attention merchant capable of packaging and transmitting
them to audiences throughout the world.

Not every trade lent itself to such spectacles. The business
of archaeologists and explorers, however, did. From this point
forward, many of them would grapple with the dilemma of
how to balance their scholarly credentials against the prospect
of lucrative profits awaiting them in the realm of the attention merchants. In fact, those best known to us today usually
achieved their fame as a direct result of publicity generated
from a profitable partnership with one of the titans of print
media. This was certainly the case with Hiram Bingham, who
is often credited with the "discovery" of Machu Picchu. A closer
look, however, reveals that Bingham's fame derives less from
any scholarly feat—of which he could claim few—than from

his ability to exploit the two winning features of Belzoni's business model: Western avatars and wondrous curiosities.

In 1875, just three years after Stanley published *How I Found Livingstone*, an austere missionary family in Hawaii welcomed Bingham into their lives. After escaping stateside to obtain graduate degrees at Berkeley and Harvard, Bingham found his interest in Latin America piqued by the 1898 Spanish-American War. A series of exploratory trips to Venezuela and Bolivia followed, mostly in search of historical records concerning Simón Bolívar, the "founding father" of several South American countries. Still unable to secure anything other than an adjunct teaching position at Yale, Bingham returned to South America in 1908 as his university's representative to the Pan-American Scientific Congress. A trek through the mountains of Chile and Peru followed, leading to Bingham's first glimpse of the monumental ruins of the Incas, all dated to the fifteenth and sixteenth centuries. Bingham saw in the Incan ruins the architectural legacy of a people who had fought the Spaniards long before Theodore Roosevelt or Simón Bolívar had done so.

Excited at the prospect of making his mark in a virgin field, Bingham returned to Yale and began his search for a suitably compelling research question. The one he chose, if successfully answered, was sure to turn heads: Where was Vilcabamba, the final refuge of the last Incan king on the eve of its destruction by Spanish soldiers? In order to find it, Bingham needed to return to Cuzco, a mountaintop town in southeastern Peru that once served as the capital of the Incan empire. Now it was the launching point for any trek into the surrounding peaks and valleys, where Bingham hoped to find the ruins of Incan civilization. Bingham struggled to find financial backing for his expedition, with Yale contributing its name ("The Yale Peruvian Expedition") but little else. In an early display of his proclivity for showmanship, Bingham managed to raise some of the money by contracting a series of articles for *Harper's Magazine*, with the promise of far more to come for any editor beguiled by his tales of the "lost cities" of the Incas.

On July 19, 1911, Bingham set off from Cuzco in search of Vilcabamba. Just five days later, he found Machu Picchu instead. Actually, the word "found" is a bit misleading.

Everyone from the Peruvian subprefect of Cuzco to a drunken merchant outfitter of the expedition clear on down to the Indian porters carrying his luggage all knew about the ruins already. In fact, the only reason Bingham even bothered to climb the peak in the first place was because local informants had tipped him off to some "old ruins" at Huayna Picchu ("Young Peak"), surmised perhaps to contain a link to Vilcabamba. In fact, the ruins were atop Machu Picchu ("Old Peak"), just over the ridge. After a mere five hours at the site, Bingham left the ruins at Machu Picchu and continued his search for Vilcabamba. One month later, he "found" it, too, nestled in the thick jungle amongst a smattering of unimpressive ruins. Though the historical identity and importance of either site was not immediately obvious, numerous clues suggested that the ruins on Machu Picchu were not those of Vilcabamba, the last refuge of the besieged Incas. The clearest testimony of this came from the lips of Bingham's own native guide, who repeatedly referred to the jungle floor ruins—not Machu Picchu—as "Vilcapampa."

Bingham had a decision to make. He had been led to two different Incan ruins, and had every reason to believe that one of them—that of Machu Picchu—was certainly not "the lost city of the Incas." But the more likely candidate, Vilcabamba, lacked the aesthetic allure of a mist-enshrouded mountaintop site. Machu Picchu was undeniably beautiful. Vilcabamba, buried in a forbidding tangle of jungle undergrowth, was an Incan encampment built in haste and bereft of splendid architecture and romantic beauty. Moreover, built as it was toward the end of the Incan empire, after a full century of contact with the Spaniards, Vilcabamba also revealed extensive use of red tiles in the construction of its buildings. To Bingham, the lost city of the Incas should evince pure Incan ingenuity, not cultural exchange with Europeans. Seen in this light, Machu Picchu was a much more attractive candidate for Bingham's "lost city," even if he already knew that it could not be the last refuge of the Incas. (It would later be determined that Machu Picchu represented a much earlier Incan site, built prior to contact with the Spanish, and served as a ritual retreat for the king.)

There was just one problem. During the brief five hours Bingham had spent atop Machu Picchu, he had already managed to spot the name of a potential rival, etched in charcoal on the walls of one of the temples: "Lizarraga 1902." Who was Lizarraga? Before he could tout his "discovery" of Machu Picchu as the "lost city of the Incas," Bingham had to make sure that no other Western avatar had beaten him to the site. According to notes scribbled in his journal while in the field, Bingham appears to have resigned himself to the likelihood of defeat. "Augustin Lizarraga is discoverer of Machu Picchu," he wrote after having learned the full name of his predecessor, "and lives at San Miguel Bridge just before passing." Later, however, Bingham decided to pay a quick visit to the Lizarraga abode in person, just to make sure. When a man with much darker skin than himself answered the door, Bingham knew that Machu Picchu was now his. Though the man turned out to be Augustín's brother, Bingham already had all the information he needed to know that only he could serve as an acceptable Western avatar to audiences back home. For the Lizarragas were, as Bingham himself later put it, "half-castes." No one in New York, Paris, or London would pay money for the vicarious thrill of being put in Augustín Lizarraga's shoes.

With that, Bingham returned home to regale the American press with tales of the lost city of the Incas: Machu Picchu. Following the same model of reporting that made Stanley and Livingstone famous, journalists from all the major New York papers lapped up Bingham's evocative description of Machu Picchu. Bingham became an overnight sensation, even earning a meeting with President Taft. Funding, too, was now much easier to come by. Not only did Yale finally open its checkbook, but the National Geographic Society also proved eager to associate itself with Bingham. At the invitation of Gilbert Grosvenor, the editor of *National Geographic Magazine*, Bingham lectured to an audience of 1,200 at the Masonic Temple in Washington, D.C. Before long, Bingham was able to organize the "Peruvian Expedition of 1912 under the Auspices of Yale University and the National Geographic Society." One year after he had spent a mere five hours at the site, Bingham returned to Machu Picchu with a formidable crew at his disposal. This time he cleared away the ubiquitous overgrowth, washed off the charcoal graffiti (including "Lizarraga 1902"!), dug up the graves, and took hundreds of pictures.

The end result was the next installment in the Egyptomania craze, this time featuring the Incas. As evidence that Bingham was far more interested in popularizing a romantic image of an ancient civilization for mass consumption than he was in crafting a responsible scholarly narrative, we need look no further than the title of the *National Geographic* article he penned upon his return in 1913: "In the Wonderland of Peru—Rediscovering Machu Picchu." If the evocation of Belzoni's "wondrous curiosities" in the title was not proof enough, just consider the sheer number of Bingham's own photographs that were published alongside the article: a whopping 250! With just over ten thousand words in the entire article, this is approximately one photogenic image of Machu Picchu and its environs for every forty words of text. Or, to put it another way, one photo for every single sentence or two! This was a visual smorgasbord for the eyes, not for the brain, and it was transmitted to 140,000 subscribers across the globe. With the prospect of endless fame and fortune now before him, Bingham stuck to his preferred version of Machu Picchu until the day he died. In 1948, he exploited the manufactured romance and mystery of the site one last time with the publication of a predictably titled book, *Lost City of the Incas*, now considered a "classic" of the genre.

That genre is the genre of Indiana Jones, long before Harrison Ford took up the role. Not the historical Indiana Jones, of course, but the consumed Indiana Jones. The consumed Indiana Jones invites the leisured classes of the world to tag along vicariously on expeditions into the unknown corners of the world, confident in their ability to tramp through jungles and deserts, ward off hostile natives (or Nazis), rescue damsels in distress (an aloof missionary in Africa will also do), and return home laden with treasures.

One of the last men to invoke the glamour of the archaeological hunt was Howard Carter, whose discovery of the tomb of Tutankhamun will be treated more fully in chapter 6. Here it will suffice to note that, upon discovery of the tomb in 1922,

Figure 3.8. Avocados from Peru.
The exotic allure of Machu Picchu, first popularized by Hiram
Bingham in the pages of *National Geographic Magazine*, is
still used to market any number of products—including
avocados—to Western consumers eager to embrace the
escapist fantasies of the age of exploration. Copyright
and courtesy of the Peruvian Avocado Commission.

Carter and his wealthy patron, the Earl of Carnarvon, managed
to transition almost instantaneously from the exclusive and
profitless world of Egyptology into the inclusive and profitable
world of Egyptomania. Within weeks of the discovery, the Earl
of Carnarvon contracted with the London *Times* for a monopoly
on access to the site, and began to showcase the tomb to friends,
business associates, and anyone else he wished to impress.
Before long, a chaotic circus atmosphere enveloped the tomb.

Although Carter himself may have been an Egyptologist,
the tomb was sold to the public as Egyptomania. The socially
reticent Carter found the earl's theatrics irritating, to be sure,
but still he performed his expected role as obliging host. Nor
was Carter himself numb to the financial opportunities yielded
by his discovery of the tomb. Much as with James Bennett, Jr.
and the *"New York Herald* Expedition" a half century earlier,
Carter knew how to package his discovery for the general
public. In his own account of the initial discovery—of which
there are several versions—Carter re-created the alleged dialogue between himself and Lord Carnarvon as he obtained his
first glimpse by candlelight of the treasures in the tomb:

At first I could see nothing, the hot air escaping from the chamber causing the candle flame to flicker, but presently, as my eyes grew accustomed to the light, details of the room within emerged slowly from the mist, strange animals, statues, and gold—everywhere the glint of gold. For the moment—an eternity it must have seemed to the others standing by—I was struck dumb with amazement, and when Lord Carnarvon, unable to stand the suspense any longer, inquired anxiously, "Can you see anything?" it was all I could do to get out the words, "Yes, wonderful things."

Here we see Carter making use of all the literary conventions of Egyptomania that have made it so predictably profitable for nearly two hundred years: mist-enshrouded ruins, strange animals, and the glint of gold, all of which cause the viewer to be "struck dumb with amazement." The most telling words of all, however, are saved for the end: "wonderful things"! There are few words more consistently evocative of the commercial allure first tapped by Belzoni a century before. It is thus little wonder that "wonderful things" has entered the popular lexicon as an easily recognized phrase, nearly on par with "Dr. Livingstone, I presume?" As with Belzoni—not to mention Bennett, Stanley, and Bingham—Carter had a very specific audience in mind when he wrote these words. In the passage quoted above, Carter makes reference to "others standing by," all of whom are named in the preceding pages: Lord Carnarvon, Lady Evelyn, and Arthur Callender. They are named because each one is a *somebody*: Carter's friends, patrons, or colleagues. Compare this passage with one that appears just seven pages earlier, when he describes a moment just after the discovery of the outermost gate of the tomb, prior to the notification of the outside world:

It was a thrilling moment for an excavator. Alone, save for my native workmen, I found myself, after years of comparatively unproductive labour, on the threshold of what might prove to be a magnificent discovery.

Note the carefully phrased oxymoron in the second sentence: "alone, save for my native workmen." The phrase contradicts itself. Yet from Carter's perspective—and likely that of his readers, too—to be surrounded by natives *was* to be alone. After all, none of them was a somebody. They were all nobodies. Or, to put it somewhat more delicately—and to resurrect the parlance of this chapter—*they were not Western avatars*. At any given time, Belzoni, Stanley, Bingham, and Carter moved in the company of ten, twenty, sometimes even upward of one hundred local officials, guides, escorts, porters, servants, diggers, cooks, and surveyors. Most of these people had long been familiar with the sculptures, tombs, and ruins that the foreign explorer wished to visit, and had long viewed these things through their own unique interpretive prism. In most cases, the foreign explorer would not—and could not—have found it without their assistance. For example, the first stairs leading down to Tutankhamun's tomb were found by Carter's Arab waterboy. But this detail is carefully elided in Carter's narrative by his resort to the passive voice: "a step cut in the rock had been discovered," he writes. Behind the façade of public narratives, however, the historian can gain an occasional glimpse of the complex tensions that must have run through excavations like these. In 1907, Aurel Stein, who gained global fame through his expeditions on the Silk Road (see chapters 5 and 6), got into a heated debate with one of his Indian assistants, Ram Singh. In the private refuge of his unpublished diary, Stein was forced to acknowledge Singh's "bitter feelings about work supposed to have been done for others' credit."

Unfortunately for Ram Singh and every other hired hand to accompany an expedition, none of them could fulfill the exacting conditions imposed upon anyone who wished to profit from the commercial identity of a Western avatar: light, preferably white skin; spoken and written proficiency in a major European language; immersion in, and sympathy for, Judeo-Christian theology; and knowledge of the dominant historical narrative of Western civilization (Egypt to Greece to Rome to modern Europe) through which any new discovery was expected to be contextualized. As a result, though Euro-American explorers and archaeologists were rarely the first to "find" anything, they were usually the first to "discover" what had already been found by others. To say that they "discovered" an artifact or site is to say that they were the first to bring them to the attention of audiences back home in such a way so as to highlight the ideological conventions expected of any Western avatar (white, Christian, and educated) in non-Western lands. Once fulfilled, these ideological conventions could then be commodified and sold for a profit. In the case of scholars, this usually meant the acquisition of a plush university post, a new academic title, an increase in salary or research funds, or the prestige of an endowed chair. In the case of those willing and able to cross the line from "-ology" to "-mania," this meant the acquisition of celebrity fame and perhaps even fortune.

Either way, the consumed Indiana Jones offered nothing but bit roles for the "natives." True, they might prove useful or obstructive on occasion. But the dramatic tensions and productive engines of any expedition account were invariably reserved for Western avatars. For about a hundred years, from Belzoni to Carter, published narratives of this sort, based at least in part on actual experiences on the ground, flourished in the West. After Howard Carter and the tomb of King Tut, however, the daring exploits of intrepid Western avatars trekking through exotic lands were relegated to the fictional world of novels and film—and there they stayed. Why? The answer is simple. As it turns out, the *consumed Indiana Jones* bore very little resemblance to the *historical Indiana Jones*. The former has existed continuously from Belzoni down to the present day. The latter, however, was undisputed master of his domain for only the briefest stretch of time, and eventually exited the historical stage entirely. How the "natives," "half-castes," and "Orientals" of the non-Western world first began to push him off that stage is told in the next chapter.

Continue the journey at indianajonesinhistory.com:

- EPISODE VI: Egyptology & Egyptomania
- EPISODE XVII: The Mayan Mirage
- EPISODE XVIII: Machu Picchu

CHAPTER FOUR

The Age of Discontent

Once upon a time, everybody was happy. European diplomats, travelers, and hydrologists-turned-circus performers came to Egypt in search of wondrous curiosities, and wondrous curiosities they found. The people who lived in and around these objects and structures, both commoner and highborn, were generally indifferent to their fate. If they thought about them at all, they tended to do so in strictly utilitarian terms, regarding them as a source of fertilizer to be tapped or an abode of malevolent spirits to be avoided. When they began to see white men from distant lands spend an inordinate amount of time, energy, and money in repeated attempts to remove these items, many locals began to suspect that they might contain gold or other precious metals inside. For why else would the Europeans treat such intrinsically worthless ruins with so much care and respect? When gold failed to emerge, most of the locals proved eager and willing to grab their fair share of the foreigner's purse. For the peasants, this meant the provision of labor—digging, hauling, carrying, and sifting—in exchange for market, or sometimes higher-than-market wages. For local elites, this meant the receipt of various exotic luxury goods (e.g., pistols, watches, liquor) along with a certain measure of social prestige derived from his duties as host to a "great"—i.e., resourceful—man from distant lands.

As for the Europeans? They were happiest of all. And well they should be. For in these early years, they almost always got what they had come for: aesthetically imposing adornments for museums and mansions back home. Of course, it wasn't always as rosy as portrayed here. Wages for the local peasants could be lower than market rate, and disappeared entirely if the local official decided to invoke the obligations of corvée labor instead. And the foreign explorer himself could sometimes be a nuisance, be it through unreasonable demands for logistical accommodations, an insistence on wandering into strategically sensitive areas, or unwelcome meddling—conscious or otherwise—into local concerns of every sort. Occasionally, too, the attitudes of the locals toward an appropriated artifact went far beyond belief in a harmless sprite or devil trapped inside. Sometimes they rose to the level of associating its removal with a devastating curse, one that stopped the rain or brought locusts to the fields. And if the result was famine or any other sort of hardship, then the foreigner had best tuck tail and run.

On the whole, however, most expeditions and excavations were successful precisely because they offered what was regarded at the time as a fair and equal exchange, in which benefits for both sides outweighed the negatives. In other words, items that held little value to one party but great value to another were taken by the latter in exchange for something the former valued far more than what had been taken. We first encountered this concept in chapter 2, through reference to the so-called "compensations of plunder" that aptly characterized the activities of Elgin in Athens and Belzoni in Egypt. From the perspective of the historical Indiana Jones, then, we might posit the existence of something called the Age of Content. The Age of Content comes about when the following three conditions have been met. First, the local inhabitants of any given place must exhibit a perceived cultural disconnect toward the ruins and antiquities in their midst. In other words, they must not regard these things as so sacred or precious that the loss of them would constitute a grievous blow to their core group identity. Second, there must be another group of people who perceive these same ruins and antiquities in exactly the opposite way, that is, as representative of some core value or idea integral to their own cultural identity. Third, and most important, the group that wants to remove these objects must be able and willing to compensate the locals, both elite and commoner, for any hardships, inconveniences, or curses that may result from their removal.

When all three of these conditions are met, each party to the transaction will tend to view their involvement in a favorable light, with a minimum of tensions. With the exception of China, to be discussed in chapter 5, the earliest archaeological expeditions carried out by Europeans almost always met these three conditions. As we have seen, European intellectuals since the Renaissance had posited a direct cultural link between themselves and the Greeks and Romans. This meant that when Lord Elgin went to Athens, he perceived a direct cultural link between himself and the civilization represented by the Parthenon marbles. Just as important as Elgin's perception of cultural continuity with the Greeks, however, was the Ottoman perception of cultural discontinuity with the same. Had Elgin attempted to remove a similar object from the façade of an ancient Islamic mosque, he would have been thwarted at every turn. This is because the artifact in question would have been perceived by the locals as culturally continuous with the core precepts of their group identity, and thus unsuitable for any form of compensation.

The Age of Content, then, requires that one party to the archaeological transaction—generally the one with deeper pockets—perceives a legacy of cultural continuity with the object to be removed, while the other party—often poor and desirous of improving its material livelihood—perceives a legacy of cultural discontinuity. This will ensure the absence of volatile ideological frictions, leaving only pragmatic and logistical concerns to be addressed, usually through financial or diplomatic inducements. Conversely, the Age of Discontent comes about when two or more parties to the transaction both perceive in the object to be removed a legacy of cultural continuity with themselves, one felt so strongly as to negate the allure of any form of compensation. The result will be ideological friction, with both sides digging in their heels in response to a perceived existential threat to their most cherished group identity.

So when and how did such ideological frictions arise in the Ottoman Empire, where the majority of European excavations took place? As noted in the previous chapter, once the hieroglyphs were unlocked, ancient Egypt was invited into the club of Western civilization, as forbears to the Greeks. Even before that, though, some measure of fraternal awe and respect for those who built the pyramids had inspired many Europeans and Americans to lay claim to the stone monuments of the pharaohs, irrespective of any imagined association with the Greeks. And so long as the contemporary inhabitants of Egypt subscribed to a different set of views toward the civilization of the pharaohs than did the Westerners, the Age of Content would continue. After all, neither side posed an existential threat to the other. But the moment anyone in Egypt began to share the Western view of the pharaohs, one of the three conditions noted above would cease to obtain. At that point, the Age of Discontent begins.

So what *did* the modern Egyptians think about the ancient Egyptians? After all, we cannot determine when *content* turned to *discontent* unless we know what the people of the Ottoman Empire thought about the antiquities in their midst before the Europeans came along. Of course, we already know that they often believed such things to be haunted by local sprites, devils, and *jinns* (genies), be they in Athens or in Luxor. (Recall, too, that many Europeans during this time also believed in the miraculous healing powers of ground-up mummy dust!) But there was more than just mere superstition. Throughout Muslims lands, by far the most widely digested discourse regarding the ancient Egyptians was that of "Moses versus Pharaoh." This story, integral to the scriptural traditions of Jews, Christians, and Muslims alike, constituted the one and only ideological lens through which most subjects of the Ottoman Empire would have viewed the pyramids, obelisks, and ruins of the pharaohs.

In the Quran, the encounter between Moses and Pharaoh is narrated in much the same way as it appears in the Hebrew and Christian bibles. Moses is sent by God to secure the release of the Israelites from Egypt. "Pharaoh," who remains unnamed and thus representative of all pharaohs, dismisses the signs of God as mere magic and sorcery, and insists on his own divinity instead. "I am not aware of any other lord of yours but myself," he tells Moses. After God sends down a series of devastating plagues upon Pharaoh and his subjects, he at last relents and grants the Israelites their freedom, before once again changing his mind and pursuing them to the Red Sea. With God's help, Moses parts the sea for the Israelites and sends it crashing back down upon Pharaoh and the Egyptians. The moral of the story? Pharaoh is a uniquely Egyptian example of the arrogance of one who rejects God's sovereignty. By extension, the Pharaonic ruins stand as testament to the fate of those who defy God when He reveals Himself. For most Muslims, then, Pharaoh was the embodiment of what was known as *jahiliyya*: the pre-Islamic age of ignorance, paganism, tribalism, hedonism, and indulgence. In other words, to look upon the material ruins of the pharaohs with favor was to pass a positive judgment upon one who defies God.

Figure 4.1. Moses vs. Pharaoh. In this sixteenth-century illustrated Persian manuscript, the staff of Moses is turned into a dragon that devours Pharaoh's men, as a demonstration of God's power.

Any Muslim who had ever attended services at a mosque or listened to his elders preach the Islamic gospel would have been familiar with this story, be they male or female, rich or poor, literate or illiterate. It is hard to imagine any association more negative than that conjured up by the willfully repeated heresies of Pharaoh. That the word "pharaoh" came to be virtually synonymous with that of "heathen" is apparent in the preface to one of the oldest surviving Arabic manuscripts of the *Arabian Nights*, dated to fourteenth-century Syria. Before Princess Shahrazad tells even a single one of her famous tales, the reader is regaled with a heartfelt prayer to Allah:

> Praise be to God, the Beneficent King, the Creator of the world and man, who raised the heavens without pillars and spread out the earth as a place of rest and erected the mountains as props and made the water flow from the hard rock and destroyed the race of Thamud, 'Ad, and Pharaoh of the vast domain. I praise Him the Supreme Lord for His guidance, and I thank Him for His infinite grace.

This is not the *Arabian Nights* of Lady Duff's imagination, as seen in the previous chapter. The Syrian version, filled with shocking violence and raunchy sex, is made pious and respectable through a ritual condemnation of three of the most famous unbelievers in the Islamic world: two blasphemous tribes from the Arabian peninsula (Thamud and 'Ad)—and Pharaoh.

The biblical story of Moses versus Pharaoh was what the Muslim masses consumed. If they knew only one thing about the pyramids and obelisks—or indeed, about any pre-Islamic ruin or artifact—that was it: the men who built them were pagan heretics who had defied God. As such, there was only one lesson to be gained from contemplation of their ruins: the dire fate which awaits all unbelievers. Though literate Muslim elites put some more meat on these rhetorical bones, occasionally adding an element of awe and wonder, they did not alter the basic message. In 1251, Jamal al-Din al-Idrisi, a traveler from the Abbasid Caliphate, offered praise to God for creating "those imposing signs"—the pyramids—that, "even if silent, speak with the worthiest lessons for consideration." What lessons might those be? That Muslims "must travel the Earth and see what happened to those who disbelieved." Al-Idrisi was convinced that the pyramids existed for a reason. After all, had not the Companions of the Prophet seen fit to spare them during the Muslim conquest of the Middle East? They must have done so deliberately, "as a sign to teach a lesson to those who would consider, and a reminder to every seeker of knowledge."

To every pious Muslim, the pre-Islamic ruins were a warning. And so long as Muslims of every class and stripe believed this to be true, there was little chance of ideological conflict between themselves and the Europeans, who viewed them either as wondrous curiosities or as a prelude to the Greeks. This was the Age of Content. The Age of Discontent began when Ottoman elites exchanged Moses vs. Pharaoh for the narrative of Western civilization peddled by European elites. In the process, both parties left the Muslim masses—who continued to subsist on Moses vs. Pharaoh—behind. The shift in ideological tectonics began in 1835. For it was in that year that Muhammad Ali, the *pasha* of Egypt who had once shown such keen interest in Belzoni's hydraulic pump, issued a momentous decree. "Foreigners are destroying ancient edifices, extracting stones and other worked objects, and transporting them to foreign countries," he proclaimed. "If this continues, it is clear that soon no more ancient monuments will remain in Egypt." Aware that European countries had museums in which to preserve and display such objects, Ali promised to do the same in Egypt. "The government has judged it appropriate to forbid the export abroad of antiquities found in the ancient edifices of Egypt and to designate in the capital a place to serve as a depot. It has decided to display them for travelers who visit the country, to forbid the destruction of ancient edifices in Upper Egypt, and to spend the greatest possible care on their safekeeping."

These were grand words, and they yielded an even grander promise: antiquity laws on paper and museums on the ground. Yet neither promise was fulfilled during Muhammad Ali's lifetime. Why? There are two main reasons. First, the Egyptian masses continued to view the ancient monuments through the lens of pragmatic neutrality or Quranic hostility, and they would do so for many decades to come. This meant that they had very little incentive to obey the *pasha*'s decree. Yusuf Hekekyan, an Armenian advisor born in Constantinople but educated in Europe, lamented the "accumulated dust and filth of [Egypt's] modern inhabitants," who "build their miserable huts" on the "spacious roofs" of the ruins. Second, Europeans and Americans continued to pay top dollar to anyone willing to assist them in the removal of antiquities from Egypt. And since Egypt was a relatively poor agrarian country whose leaders desired above all to industrialize along European lines, this created an incentive to trade one thing for the other. And so they did, as part of the continuing saga of the compensations of plunder. For the remainder of the century, obelisk after obelisk would be gifted by the *pasha* and his descendants to various Western powers, in hopes of currying diplomatic favor that could later be spent on wars, loans, or infrastructure.

In light of all this, the 1835 decree represented less a sincere conviction in the Western view of the Egyptian past and more a cynical manipulation of Western discourse for other, less obvious purposes. Muhammad Ali wanted the Europeans to think that he shared their "enlightened" views on history and culture, but he was still at heart a politician in search of wealth

Figure 4.2. An obelisk in Central Park.
In 1877, in a classic example of the continued allure of the "compensations of plunder," Ismail Pasha, hoping to receive valuable diplomatic capital in return, willingly gifted one of three "Cleopatra's Needles" from its millennia-long perch in Alexandria to the United States of America.

and power. Wealth and power, however, were not born out of museums; museums were born out of wealth and power. To someone like Ali, intent on keeping foreign armies at bay and struggling to squeeze every ounce of productivity out of his agricultural economic base, the construction of a museum must have seemed an unimaginable luxury to underwrite. Instead, lip service to the contrary notwithstanding, the *pasha* authorized the construction of eighteen saltpeter factories to be built in the vicinity of ruins, with the ninth pylon of a temple at Karnak dynamited to obtain blocks for one of the factories. Ali even oversaw the quarrying of some of the casing stones on one of the Giza pyramids in order to build a portion of his Alabaster Mosque in Cairo. Hekekyan, writing in his diary in the years after the 1835 decree, lamented the complete and utter lack of enforcement throughout the country. "Would to God every temple could be transported to England and France by some fairy enchanter," he wrote, "and some stringent measures taken to preserve them in Egypt."

So the first substitution of a Western discourse for Moses vs. Pharaoh proved little more than window dressing. While the *pasha* may have been curious about the discipline of Egyptology and its associated institutions, he was not a committed believer. And yet, cynically or not, Muhammad Ali had planted a seed—and future generations of Ottoman officials would do much more to bring it to fruition. In 1858, less than ten years after Ali's death, his son, Said, who had gone to school in Paris and received the bulk of his education in French, oversaw the establishment of an Antiquities Service in Cairo. He then hired a Frenchman, Auguste Mariette, to run it. Mariette and the Antiquities Service were granted exclusive excavation rights throughout Egypt, a steamboat, and the right to mobilize up to seven thousand men for corvée labor on any dig—all on behalf of the government. One French observer, however, was skeptical of Mariette's status. "For better or for worse," he wrote, "Mariette Bey is part of the vice-regal household, on a level with the head of the stables and the chief black eunuque. One has an Egyptologist in the way that one's forbears had an astrologist, a master of parades, awkwardly placed between the fool and the physician."

Were Mariette and the Egyptian Antiquities Service mere institutional ornaments, paid to promote the enlightenment of the *pasha* but unable to fulfill any of their own professed ideals? This would seem to be an overly harsh assessment. Though perennially understaffed and underfunded, Mariette did make real progress on several fronts, usually with the blessing of the *pasha*. For the first time, anyone who wanted to excavate in Egypt had to agree to a standardized set of regulations overseen by Mariette, with the expectation that a representative sample of any finds would be retained for Cairo. Eventually, what was once a gentleman's agreement would evolve into the legal stipulation of *partage*, which decreed an equal 50/50 division of spoils between the Egyptian government and the archaeologist, with any unique finds going to Cairo. Mariette was also free to reprimand Said—and his successor, Ismail— each time they felt the urge to give away another obelisk as a form of diplomatic capital. In this way, the archaeological "black eunuque" of Cairo insisted on being much more than

Figure 4.3. Auguste Mariette, Director of the Egyptian Antiquities Service, 1858–1881.

a pretty adornment to the *pasha*'s court. In addition, Mariette also trained the first generation of Egyptian archaeologists, ensuring the perpetuation of Egyptology in indigenous guise.

By far the most visible fruit of Mariette's efforts, however, was the establishment of the Bulaq Museum. Opened to the public in 1863, the Bulaq Museum, named after the Cairo neighborhood in which it was located, was the first of its kind in Egypt. At long last, Mariette had a permanent scholarly institution into which he could place the archaeological proceeds of government efforts in the field. Inside the museum, Mariette made no attempt to construct any sort of grand historical narrative about the history of Egypt. Instead, working on the assumption that Egyptian visitors to the museum would be too unsophisticated to grasp any higher purpose in the displays, Mariette and his curators hearkened back to the aesthetics of a *wunderkammer*: a hodgepodge arrangement of visually striking artifacts that aimed to please the eye more than the mind. Nevertheless, the very existence of a government-funded museum in the nation's capital was testament enough to a very real truth. That is, in spite of their inevitable shortcomings, the Bulaq Museum, along with its companion Antiquities Service, were representative of a permanent institutional commitment by the Egyptian government to the same field of scholarly inquiry once claimed exclusively by Westerners. Among literate Egyptian elites who participated in the government, Moses vs. Pharaoh had finally been laid to rest.

In Constantinople, similar developments were underway. As early as 1846, Sultan Abdulmejid I decreed the establishment of a new museum inside the Hagia Irene, a Greek Orthodox Church. In 1869 it was renamed the Imperial Ottoman Museum. Inside one could stroll among ancient weapons of the Ottoman armies as well as specimens of Greek art. The goal was to impress European visitors, not the sultan's mostly Muslim subjects, who would have to wait another two decades before any Islamic artifacts were deemed worthy of inclusion. Perhaps the most striking display in this museum was a collection of mannequins built to resemble the Janissaries, an elite military corps only recently abolished by the sultan's father, Mahmud II. The idea for the mannequins likely came from a visit to London in 1837 by an Ottoman official who saw some of Madame Tussaud's figures on display. The mannequins in Constantinople, however, were intended to deliver a carefully tailored message to European visitors: we, too, are a dynamic and progressive people. The Janissary mannequins were intended to prove that the Turks were capable of evolving beyond their own outdated institutions of rule, while simultaneously preserving a carbon copy of these abolished relics in an educational display. By such means, the Ottomans hoped to counter the European charge that all Orientals were mired in stagnation and incapable of change.

And indeed, at least one European visitor to the Imperial Ottoman Museum left with his horizons broadened. "It is only twenty-seven years since the massacre of the Janissaries took place," he said, "yet it seems as though it were a hundred, so radical is the change that has been worked. The old national forms have been destroyed, and almost contemporary costumes have become historical antiquities." This was precisely the message Ottoman officials hoped to project. "Until now," wrote one of these officials, "Europeans have used various means to take the antiquities of our country away, and they did this because they did not see an inclination toward this in us. For a long time this desire has been awakened among Ottomans and recently even a law was passed concerning antiquities. Since the foundation of the Imperial Museum is the greatest example of this, we can now hope that the Europeans will change their opinions about us."

But did they? In the more than three decades since Muhammad Ali's famous 1835 decree, Ottoman elites had come a long way in their attempt to mimic the Western mode of engagement with the pre-Islamic antiquities of their land. In the process, they had paid little attention to the ideological disposition of their own Muslim subjects, most of who rightly viewed the holdings of both the Bulaq Museum and the Imperial Ottoman Museum as utterly irrelevant to their lives. But was this kowtowing to Western cultural standards enough? Would the Europeans begin to adhere to the logic of their own discourse and cede the archaeological proceeds of Ottoman lands to Ottoman museums? After all, the mass

Reorienting the Orient, 1846-1877

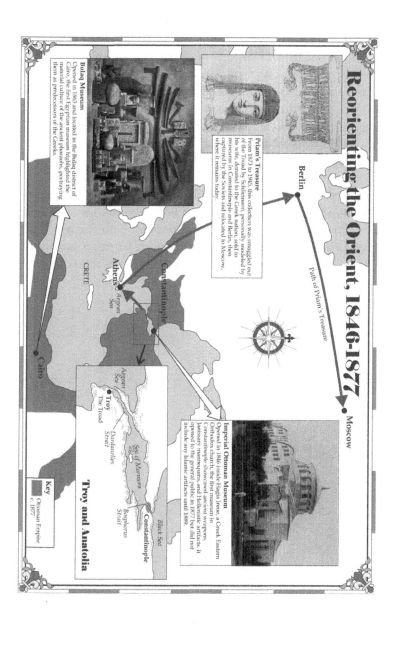

Priam's Treasure
From 1873 to 1945, this collection was smuggled out of the Troad by Schliemann, personally modeled by his wife, donated to the Greek nation, sold to museums in Constantinople and Berlin, then captured by the Soviets and relocated to Moscow, where it remains today.

Bulaq Museum
Opened in 1863 and located in the Bulaq district of Cairo, the first Egyptian museum highlighted the material culture of the ancient pharaohs, portraying them as predecessors of the Greeks.

Berlin

Path of Priam's Treasure

Moscow

Athens
Aegean Sea

CRETE

Constantinople

Cairo

Imperial Ottoman Museum
Opened in 1846 inside Hagia Irene, a Greek, Eastern Orthodox church, the first museum in Constantinople showcased ancient weapons, Janissary mannequins, and Hellenistic artifacts. It opened to the general public in 1877 but did not include any Islamic artifacts until 1889.

Troy and Anatolia

Aegean Sea

Troy
The Troad

Dardanelles Strait

Sea of Marmara

Bosphorus Strait

Black Sea

Constantinople

Key
Ottoman Empire
c. 1877

exodus of Near Eastern antiquities to European lands had previously been predicated on the near total absence of any visible care or concern for such things among the Ottomans, both highborn and low. Now, with the establishment of Western-style museums and Western-style antiquities services in Constantinople and Cairo—all run by Western or Western-educated Ottoman scholars—accusations of neglect and indifference among Ottoman elites began to ring hollow. For Ottoman elites, both in word and deed, were now Western-*ized* elites—and Westerners found it increasingly hard to pretend otherwise.

And yet pretend they still did. In order to understand just how blind most Westerners could be to the changes wrought by reformist Ottoman circles, we need look no further than Heinrich Schliemann. Born into a poor German family in 1822, Schliemann left home at a young age and learned the

Figure 4.5. Heinrich Schliemann, the promoter of Troy.

trade of a merchant. Eventually, he made his way to San Francisco, where he made a small fortune selling shovels and picks to prospectors during the California Gold Rush. His wealth then further multiplied as a military contractor for the Russian government during the Crimean War. By middle age, Schliemann was fabulously rich. But one thing he continued to lack: respect. For his was "new money," utterly bereft of name, legacy, and tradition. So Schliemann decided to do what overnight tycoons have done since time immemorial: launder crudely acquired money into social respectability by investing in cultural pursuits. Of those available to him, Schliemann chose the most reliable avenue: the ancient Greeks.

In the decades following the literary excoriation of Lord Elgin and his marbles, public sympathy for the plight of modern Greece had reached a fever pitch throughout Europe and America. As we have seen, few of these sympathizers identified in any way with the actual Greece of the present; when they talked of Greece, what they really meant was ancient Greece. The ugly warts and mongrel demographics of modern Greece were explained away by reference to the Turks, whose "oriental despotism" had resulted in the dilution and stagnation of the once noble Greek spirit. Now it fell to the West, the reincarnation of that spirit in modern guise, to revive and rescue the Greeks from the Ottoman menace. This Euro-American fantasy was embodied in a sculpture known as *The Greek Slave*. First carved by the American sculptor Hiram Powers in 1844, *The Greek Slave* showcased a nude woman, chained at the wrists, said to be captured by the Turks during the Greek war of independence and sold at a slave market in Constantinople. A cross and locket hung from her hand, one representing Christian piety and the other fidelity to her Greek homeland.

Exhibited at fairs and galleries across Europe and America and sold in replica form to consumers both rich and poor, *The Greek Slave* was the single most popular and well-known statue in the nineteenth century. In its romanticized view of Greece, its demonization of the Turks, and foregrounding of a Christian identity in Ottoman lands, *The Greek Slave* echoed both popular and scholarly narratives about the history of Western civilization then in vogue throughout Europe and

North America. Only those who contributed to the preferred narrative of Western civilization were to be celebrated, and only Westerners were qualified to identify the most worthy contributors to that civilization. "Probably," wrote Jacob Flanders, the elusive protagonist in Virginia Woolf's modernist novel *Jacob's Room*, "we are the only people in the world who know what the Greeks meant." By "we," of course, Woolf was referring to someone like Jacob, a privileged British boy educated at Cambridge and reared to regard the world as his oyster.

Figure 4.6. Hiram Powers' The Greek Slave.

In order to earn the respect of his newfound peers, Schliemann needed more than just money. He needed culture. And the ancient Greeks could provide that culture in spades. In 1859, Schliemann wrote in his diary that he "yearned to travel and visit Greece." Not just any Greece, however. The Greece of Schliemann's imagination, later mythologized via a childhood memory of a drunken miller reciting the *Iliad* and the *Odyssey* in Greek, was accessible only "with Homer and Thucydides in hand." In 1864, at the ripe age of forty-two, Schliemann retired from active business life and embarked on a world tour. During one of his stints in the eastern Mediterranean, he decided to visit the straits of western Anatolia, just across the Aegean Sea from Greece. On European maps, the westernmost part of Anatolia was known as the Troad—after the fabled city of Troy—and the adjacent peninsula just to the north, framing the maritime approach to Constantinople, as the Dardanelles. It was here that he met Frank Calvert.

Calvert was a British expatriate whose family had long provided consular services for the Dardanelles region of the Ottoman Empire on behalf of several different countries. (Prior to the twentieth century, this was a common arrangement in many parts of the world.) More importantly, he also fancied himself an amateur archaeologist, and delighted in giving guided tours of the surrounding countryside to European and American visitors en route to Constantinople. By the time he met Schliemann, Calvert had already amassed a respectable collection of antiquities unearthed during the course of his own modest excavations. Not surprisingly, they were nearly all collected with an eye toward highlighting the ancient Greek presence in Anatolia. For, much like Schliemann and most other educated Western elites of his day, Calvert had the remarkable ability to cast his gaze over Ottoman lands and see nothing but Greeks, Romans, and Christians. And among them, one site loomed larger than any other: Troy.

Troy was the setting for the legendary Trojan War, of Homeric fame. The bravery, cowardice, and strategies of its assorted heroes and villains—Achilles, Agamemnon, Helen, Paris, Hector, Priam, and Odysseus—had been immortalized in poetic verse for more than two thousand years. Every European and American schoolboy was familiar with the broad outlines of the tale, and most educated Western elites could recite lengthy passages by heart. But was there any truth to the story? Had Troy actually existed? Both then and today, most scholars have cast doubt on the historical fidelity of Homer's epic poem, preferring to view it as a legendary embellishment of what was likely a confusing mix of real and unreal events, peoples, and places. Calvert and Schliemann, however, unencumbered by any professional training in history or archaeology, chose to believe in the Trojan War as an actual historical event, its participants as actual flesh-and-blood humans, and Troy as an actual place. For them, Achilles and Agamemnon were real people, and the Trojan Horse had actually been used to penetrate the walls of the city during the siege.

Up until 1868, the year he met Schliemann, Calvert had financed all of his own excavations in the Troad. But Calvert was running out of money, and his family fortunes had recently taken a sharp turn for the worse. Schliemann saw in Calvert a vulnerable target, someone who had gotten close to Troy but could not get any closer. The wealthy German—now an American citizen by virtue of marriage—offered to continue Calvert's excavations at his own expense. For some years,

Figure 4.7. Excavating Troy.

Calvert had been digging into an earthen mound at a site in Hisarlik, on land he had purchased from its previous Turkish owners for precisely this purpose. Now Schliemann took over, hiring a team of local laborers to excavate down to the bedrock. The discovery of some Bronze Age pottery, jewelry, and building foundations encouraged Schliemann to expand the scope of his dig into a neighboring mound that lay on the property of a local Turkish landlord. When the landlord rebuffed Schliemann's offer to purchase it, he decided to dig anyway, despite his lack of either a *firman* to dig or title to the land.

With every layer of sediment his men removed, Schliemann instantly declared the recovery of something that he claimed bore a direct connection to the events narrated in the *Iliad*. In 1873, he produced his most spectacular find yet: a collection of gold, utensils, goblets, weaponry, and jewelry that he touted as "Priam's Treasure," named after the legendary king of Troy. With the gift of a salesman, Schliemann announced this find in dramatic fashion by publishing a picture of his wife adorned in "the jewels of Helen." Needless to say, this was not in line with standard archaeological practices of the day. Far more serious was the response of the Ottoman government, which learned of the existence of Priam's Treasure for the first time upon publication in a foreign newspaper of the infamous photograph of a bejeweled Mrs. Schliemann. Naturally, Constantinople had some pointed questions for Schliemann. For instance, where was his *firman*? Did he have a title to the land he was digging up? And how had Priam's Treasure managed to pass through Ottoman customs?

The answers to the questions would be very distressing indeed. For Schliemann had neither *firman* nor deed, and his method for removing his finds from Ottoman lands was dishonest in the extreme: by smuggling them out via bribes to choice members of the customs house. This was an intolerable affront to the dignity of Westernized Ottoman elites. After all, Schliemann knew that Constantinople was home to the Imperial Ottoman Museum, and that this museum—in accordance with the wishes of its Western and Westernized curators—privileged the display of Greek antiquities precisely such as those found by Schliemann. He also knew that the

Ottomans had their own antiquities service, also run by Western and Westernized scholars. And finally, he knew all too well that the Ottomans now had laws on the books prohibiting the export of antiquities abroad. What, then, inspired him to disregard the ubiquitous signs of Ottoman reform in the fields of archaeology and museum management?

As it turns out, deeply ingrained attitudes of Western superiority and Oriental incompetence died hard. Simply put, Schliemann looked upon Westernized Ottoman institutions with scarcely concealed scorn. He was backed in this belief by one of the American consuls in the region, who, in the midst of all the uproar, gave Schliemann emboldening advice. "It would be worse than throwing away the articles which you have discovered," he wrote, "to permit any part of them to go into the absurd collection of rubbish which the Turks call their 'Museum.'" Rather than hand his finds over to "ignorant barbarians," Schliemann was advised to remain faithful to the dictates of a "man of science." That meant one of two things: either smuggle the artifacts abroad to a Western museum or rebury them on site. Because the Turks were still deemed incapable of understanding Western science, only Schliemann was fit to determine the fate of his discoveries at Hisarlik.

The Turks thought otherwise. Before long, the Ottoman government cracked down on Schliemann's dig and tossed the corrupt customs officials into jail. Schliemann, hoping to stave off Ottoman hostility, now duly applied for his belated *firman*. Not surprisingly, the application was rejected. In addition, a local Turkish *pasha* was induced to purchase all the land upon which Schliemann was digging—later donating it to the state—thus ensuring that all legal niceties were on Constantinople's side. Schliemann, backed into a corner, responded by "donating" Priam's Treasure to the "Greek nation" and attempting to elicit sympathy for his actions in the international court of public sympathy. The Ottomans, preferring to use the actual courts of international diplomacy, moved to file a formal lawsuit in Athens for the recovery of Priam's Treasure. Much to Schliemann's surprise, the Greek state, far more interested in maintaining positive relations with its Ottoman neighbor than in waxing nostalgic over an indeterminate pile of jewels, honored the Ottoman lawsuit and ordered the confiscation of the golden diadems. But Schliemann was one step ahead of them, having skipped town with the treasure just as the Greek state moved to freeze all his assets in the country.

Faced with the stark disconnect between the *realpolitik* concerns of the modern Greek state of today versus the imagined virtues of the ancient Greek nation, Schliemann decided to seek a rapprochement with Constantinople. Of course, he had no intention of relinquishing Priam's Treasure. After all, that was his ticket to social and intellectual respectability among the old moneyed elites. On the contrary, he continued to display the treasure throughout the globe for various social occasions and public lectures, before finally donating it to the Royal Museum of Berlin, where the Soviets found it in 1945 (it now resides in the Pushkin Museum of Fine Arts in Moscow). Where Schliemann was willing to cede ground was in his financial ledgers. This took the form of monetary compensation for the missing treasures and artifacts, along with a negotiation of new terms for the operations at Hisarlik. In the end, the Ottomans accepted a one-time payment of £2,000 in exchange for dropping any and all claims to Priam's Treasure. Schliemann also agreed to a barter sharing arrangement for any future proceeds to emerge from the site, all of which would continue to be funded by Schliemann rather than by Constantinople.

We might call this "the Schliemann precedent." What it meant was simple: money still talked. Even after the Ottomans had aped Western institutions, discourse, and personnel to perfection, the global imbalance of wealth and power still dictated the terms of all geopolitical interactions between states. Certainly in a legal sense, and almost just as certainly in a moral sense, Schliemann was in the wrong on nearly every possible score of the Troy affair. The Ottomans were in the right. And yet none of that mattered. All that mattered was that Schliemann had the money and means necessary to do as he wished. Because the Ottomans were still militarily weak and economically backward, customs officials could still be bribed and the sultan could still be induced to accept a cash settlement for the archaeological proceeds of his realm. After all, this was the only form of compensation he could hope to obtain. The Greeks had respected the Ottoman lawsuit, but would the Germans do so, too? And if the Germans did, what about the United States or France? Sooner or later, a wealthy European man who parroted the familiar yet outdated discourses of Western science and Oriental stagnation would manage to find safe haven somewhere from the growing reach of the Ottomans.

For their part, the Ottomans took away a valuable lesson from this latter-day Trojan War. Museums, antiquities services, and laws on paper were all fine and well, but they meant little when push came to shove. In the end, Europeans and Americans, despite their righteous words about science, preservation, and education, had no intention of leveling the playing field on their own. The Ottomans could practice their own science, preserve their own artifacts, and educate their own subjects, and still the Westerners would find a way to circumvent these new roadblocks and continue to take art and artifacts back to their own countries. In the face of a resourceful and determined Western foe, the Ottomans, enlightened or otherwise, would lose every time. To redress merely the cultural imbalance between the two sides—museums, personnel, and export laws—was not enough. The excavations at Troy had demonstrated that all too clearly. Somehow, the Ottomans would need to find a way to raise the stakes of non-compliance for Western archaeologists and the consular officials who enabled them. Unfortunately for the Ottomans and so many other peoples throughout the world, an opportunity to do so would not come about until the advent of World War I. That is the subject of chapter 6, when the Age of Discontent gives way to the Age of Confrontation.

In the meantime, however, "Schliemann's precedent" would continue to set the tone for nearly all interactions between Western explorers and Middle Eastern governments for another forty years. And yet the kerfuffle at Troy did initiate one important change in the way things were done. Perhaps the Ottomans couldn't last the full twelve rounds in a bout with the West. But their willingness to step into the ring was no longer in doubt. Moreover, they had managed to land some impressive blows, none more so than the successful lawsuit against Schliemann in Greece, heretofore a cherished refuge for the German-American tycoon. In the end, Schliemann got what he wanted, but it was an ugly victory, bereft of both honor and dignity. Neither side clamored for a rematch. But how was one to be avoided? The answer lies in the rather swift embrace by both parties of the face-saving arrangement of *partage*. The idea of *partage*—a French word meaning "division," "partition," or "sharing"—was that each vested party in an excavation would receive an equal share of the material proceeds. Usually this meant 50/50: half for the host government and its museums and half for the foreign archaeologist and his sponsoring institutions back home. (If the excavated land was owned by a third party, then the ratio would be 33/33/33.) In theory, the host government was supposed to decide which artifacts went into which pile, reserving the most precious and unique items for itself. In reality, the same forces that led to the Schliemann precedent continued to ensure that foreigners nearly always took home the best pile.

Regardless of the continued perpetuation of such slights, both real and perceived, most Ottoman elites continued to hold Western archaeologists and their consular allies in relatively high regard. After all, they remained united by social, cultural, political, and financial ties that were just as strong, if not stronger, than those they held with their own, mostly Muslim subjects. Both Western elites and Westernized Ottoman elites were committed to the preservation and veneration of artifacts from the pre-Islamic past throughout the Near and Middle East. This commitment was designed to validate and celebrate their collective identity as "modern" and "scientific," in direct opposition to the "backward" and "unenlightened" masses over whom they ruled. Much as in Europe, the educated elites of Cairo and Constantinople did not look upon their lower-class brethren with detached indifference. More often than not, they looked upon them with a missionary zeal, hoping to transform them—kicking and screaming, if need be—into ideological mirror images of themselves.

In order to accomplish this, the *pasha* and the sultan needed the help of Western elites. And on this front, they got it. The Ottoman and Egyptian antiquities services stood as the most prominent symbols of this social and cultural alliance. Both services bore deep imprints of the Western scholarly agenda. The one in Constantinople was run at first by a German archaeologist, before a pioneering French-educated Ottoman scholar by the name of Osman Hamdi Bey succeeded him in 1881. The Egyptian service, however, was headed by an unbroken succession of Frenchmen for nearly a century, from Auguste Mariette in 1858 to Étienne Drioton in 1952. (A revolution that year ended both the Albanian dynastic line of Muhammad Ali and the French monopoly of the director-ship of the Antiquities Service.) Be they Turkish, Egyptian, German, or French, however, all these directors peddled essen-tially the same ideological line regarding the antiquities of the Near East: the only antiquities worth preserving were those claimed for the narrative of Western civilization.

As heirs to this intellectual tradition, most of us are famil-iar with its general contours today, via repeated exposure to textbooks, mass media, and museum exhibits. By contrast, however, most of the illiterate and poverty stricken Muslim commoners of Egypt and Turkey were not even vaguely aware of the Western historical narrative that had been imposed upon their lands. (The lone exceptions, of course, being those who worked in the tourist industry as guides, interpreters, or escorts for foreigners). As a result, in the decades after the Schliemann affair, the Westernized elites of Egypt made a concerted effort to foist upon their own subjects the Western version of Egyptian history to which they themselves sub-scribed. With the Antiquities Service playing a leading role, the age of the pharaohs soon assumed a visible prominence in the public sphere. As part of this initiative, the Westernized elites of Cairo went to great lengths to adorn new government buildings in the artistic motifs of ancient Egypt and to dissem-inate the iconography of pyramids and obelisks throughout public spaces, most notably in postal stamps and street names. We call this phenomenon *secular pharaonism*. One of the most prominent examples can be seen in the Cairo train station, through which the majority of Egyptians will pass at one time or another. Not only does the very name of the station itself—Ramses Station—pay tribute to an ancient pharaoh, but the halls inside are bedecked in a painstakingly reconstructed pharaonic décor, one that would make Ramses himself blush.

From the 1920s onward, secular pharaonism was official government policy, infused throughout publicly funded institutions and spaces. Before long, it gave rise to another movement, this time outside government auspices, known as *literary pharaonism*. Inspired by the Western vision for a modern identity intertwined with the pharaonic past, Egyptian writers and directors proceeded to weave mummies, pharaohs, and pyramids into their novels and films. For the first time, they produced Arabic literature and screenplays featuring plot lines and dramatic themes drawn from the Egyptomania pulp fiction craze of the Victorian era. In order to appeal to a radically different domestic audience, however, these themes were reworked to reflect the concerns of an educated Egyptian elite. For instance, when mummies come back to life in Western stories, they do so in order to take revenge on all of mankind, without regard to race or creed (though they may make an exception for gender). In twentieth-century Egyptian versions, however, the mummies chase only foreigners, leaving their "descendants"—modern Egyptians—free to run the country on their own.

Patriotic mummies made for good theater. So, too, did the lives of the pharaohs themselves. Naguib Mahfouz, the most famous proponent of literary pharaonism whose work would earn him the Nobel Prize late in life, attempted to turn the history of ancient Egypt into an allegory for the plight of modern Egypt. Mahfouz lamented the "hollow Pharaonic anthems" of government-led secular pharaonism, "which provoke in us only a superficial zeal because they do not emanate from a genuine connection between ancient Egypt and us." Mahfouz took it upon himself to forge just such a genuine connection. He called for ancient Egyptian texts to be translated into modern Arabic, and for "images of ancient Egyptian life, in all of their shades, to be drawn in the Arabic language, that a strong bond be forged between ancient Egyptian monuments and youths at every stage of their development." More specifically, he demanded that the "lives of Ahmose, Tutmose, Ramses, Nefertiti and others like them be within the grasp of every school child and advanced student and for ancient Egyptian myths to come alive in nurseries." One of his more famous novels, *Kifah Tiba* (*The Struggle for Thebes*), published in 1944, made every effort to fulfill this promise. The plot narrates in fictional guise the overthrow of "foreign" Hyksos rule in Egypt by a "native" pharaoh in the fifteenth century B.C. The expelled Hyksos, a light-skinned nomadic race from the Middle East, were thinly veiled representations of either the Turks (Ottomans) or the Europeans, whose imperialist rule is resisted and defeated by the "rightful" rulers of Egypt: the pharaohs.

Despite his best efforts, Mahfouz failed to plant the seeds of a pharaonic craze among the masses of Egypt. His reception of the Nobel Prize in 1988 was premised mostly on his later work, not that of literary pharaonism, which was plagued by poor sales and lukewarm receptions. Nor could the promoters of secular pharaonism, despite a huge investment of government resources, claim much success in the hearts and minds of the Egyptian people. Why? After all, the notion that Egypt should base its modern identity on its ancient past took fertile root among Western minds well over two hundred years ago, and has been further embraced ever since. What, then, can account for the starkly different reception this idea encountered among Egyptian audiences? Part of the answer can be found in the degree of political and economic prosperity associated with the ruling elite of modern Egypt. Generally speaking, politicians who preside over an era of economic and political progress will find it much easier to disseminate their associated ideological programs among their subjects. This is because most people, wont to confuse correlation with causation, will view the arrival of "good times" as the direct product of human agency; that is, the ideas and beliefs of their rulers. By contrast, those who preside over "bad times"—i.e., political humiliation and economic stagnation—will find it difficult to combat the perception among the masses that the ruling ideology of the governing elite is to blame.

In other words, when the king or president of Egypt drapes himself in the rhetorical and aesthetic regalia of Ramses II, he had better succeed in reclaiming at least a slice of the imagined glory of that age for the benefit of his people. Otherwise, the luster of both current and ancient rulers will suffer. The author of an opinion piece published in an Arabic-language newspaper in 1932 captured this logic quite well when he observed how "the Pharaoh rising from the tomb would be shocked by the lowly state of his countrymen under foreign domination." A similar analogy could have been made for nearly every Middle Eastern state of the nineteenth and twentieth centuries, from Egypt to Iran. As a result, Western ideas about the roles of history and culture in the Middle East failed to resonate among the Muslim commoners, because they did not present a credible plan for the improvement of their economic livelihood. In their place, a far more familiar and accessible idea continued to hold its ground: Moses vs. Pharaoh. If Ramses II could not save Egypt, then perhaps the Prophet and his Companions could. Among the Muslim masses, the Quran continued to evince an appeal unmatched by that peddled by the more secular and Westernized elites. After all, one did not have to be wealthy or educated in order to access Quranic teachings. Thus, while the rulers of Egypt attempted to confirm their worth by sending their sons to Oxford and vacationing in Mediterranean villas, their subjects needed only to walk into the nearest mosque for confirmation of their purpose in life. Here, through the promise of eternal salvation to all, they could obtain the social equality and economic liberation denied them in life.

It was an attractive premise, made all the more attractive for the fact that it could not be disproven by any worldly setbacks—for all true accounting took place in the afterlife. In 1928, a man named Hasan al-Banna took this message and used it to recruit followers into a new grassroots organization: the Muslim Brotherhood. According to al-Banna, the Brotherhood promised to reverse the political and economic humiliation visited upon his Egyptian brethren over the past century. Al-Banna gave talks at factories and labor camps, where he saw the suffering of Egyptians first hand. "We are weary of this life of humiliation and restriction," they told him. "We see that the Arabs and the Muslims have no status and no dignity. They are mere hirelings belonging to the foreigners." According to al-Banna, more than sixty percent of the Egyptian populace lived below the subsistence level, a moral stain that he placed squarely on the shoulders of the secular Westernized elite. By 1932, al-Banna moved his recruiting efforts from the British-dominated Suez Canal zone into Cairo itself. It was there that he discovered a rallying cry that transcended the boundaries of Egypt and appealed to Muslims throughout the Middle East: Palestine. Membership in the Brotherhood ballooned, drawing the attention and ire of the political status quo. As a result, throughout the 1930s and 40s, the Brotherhood faced intermittent bans on its participation in national politics.

Al-Banna's views on history and culture were a direct refutation of those promoted by the Westernized rulers of Egypt. Though he claimed to be "interested" in the age of the pharaohs and "welcomed" study of their scientific accomplishments, he vowed to "resist with all our strength the program that seeks to re-create ancient Egypt after God gave Egypt the teachings of Islam and provided her with honor and glory beyond the

Figure 4.8. Hasan al-Banna, founder of the Muslim Brotherhood.

ancient past." More specifically, it was the honor and glory of the Islamic caliphates that he sought to re-create in the present, for they had risen to power after God rescued his followers from "the filth of paganism, the rubbish of polytheism, and the habits of the pagan age." Al-Banna's vision for Egypt's relationship with its past was one that hearkened back to the medieval Quranic discourse encountered earlier in this chapter: a few wondrous curiosities overshadowed by the moral lessons of Moses vs. Pharaoh. In the end, the pharaohs were pagans, forever disqualified as role models for a Muslim nation.

In working toward his goals, Hasan al-Banna did not advocate the use of violence, and he deplored the tactics of the terrorist. Not everyone agreed with him, however, and in 1949, al-Banna himself was shot and killed as he left a youth group gathering. More radical leaders then took over his movement, including a man by the name of Sayyid Qutb. Qutb, once an avid consumer of secular and literary pharaonism, later came to reject these projects after a disillusioning course of study at Stanford. Upon his return to Egypt, Qutb warned his followers that the age of *jahiliyya*—pre-Islamic heathen ignorance—had once again taken over the world, and that the materialistic West and its "running dogs" in the Middle East were to blame. Though a failed assassination plot led to Qutb's execution in 1966, his strident influence has lived on: one of his brother's followers later became a key mentor to Osama bin Laden and was instrumental in the rise of the terrorist organization al-Qaeda.

More generally, it is remarkable to see how the ideas and concepts that once animated the activities of the historical Indiana Jones continue to emerge in the present-day politics of the Middle East. After all, it was Western archaeologists and scholars who played a leading role in the rehabilitation and celebration of the once long-forgotten pharaohs. Not everyone in Egypt was appreciative of their efforts, however. The clearest demonstration of this came in 1981, with the assassination of the Egyptian president Anwar Sadat. The gunmen were Islamic fundamentalists serving in his military, inspired in part by Sadat's conclusion of a treaty with Israel. Any such treaty, of course, would come at the expense of Palestine, whose welfare had long served as the most reliable rallying cry for the Muslim Brotherhood and its sympathizers. Most revealing, however, were the words shouted at the scene of the attack by one of the assailants: "I have killed Pharaoh!" It is difficult to imagine a more direct—and chilling—refutation of the secular Western agenda once peddled by the historical Indiana Jones throughout the Middle East. Indiana Jones may be long gone, but "Pharaoh" is still used as a pejorative label for any Muslim who follows in his ideological footsteps.

Most recently, during the Egyptian elections of 2012, the Muslim Brotherhood succeeded in capturing the majority of the popular vote. Less than a year after its candidate for president took office, however, a military coup returned a more secular politician to power, one with many years of experience in British and American institutions. The battle of Moses vs. Pharaoh continues, with casualties on both sides. The West tends to back Pharaoh in all his Middle Eastern incarnations, while the Muslim masses tend to back his more fundamentalist rivals. And yet neither has proven capable of replicating the "honor and glory" of their promised golden ages. The secular Westernized clique has repeatedly failed to re-create the imagined prosperity of the ancient Egyptian pharaohs, much as the fundamentalists have repeatedly failed to re-create the imagined prosperity of the ancient Islamic caliphs.

Indiana Jones is gone. The Age of Discontent, however, lives on.

Continue the journey at indianajonesinhistory.com:

- EPISODE VII: The Sultan and the Pasha
- EPISODE VIII: The Trojan War
- EPISODE XI: Moses vs. Pharaoh

CHAPTER FIVE

The Treasures of China

"A man of Song who sold ceremonial hats made a trip to Yue, but the Yue people cut their hair short and tattoo their bodies and had no use for such things." Thus spoke the ancient Daoist philosopher Zhuangzi sometime in the fourth century B.C., in what is today northern China. Though most people are familiar with Zhuangzi's memorable butterfly conundrum—had he dreamt of being a butterfly or had a butterfly dreamt of being him—his tale of a hatter from Song is a more apt analogy for the topic at hand. This brief passage speaks to the Daoist theory of relativity, more than two thousand years before Einstein. The lesson is simple: when the customs of one place differ from those of another, practices that are familiar in the first will be regarded as unfamiliar in the second. With just a slight tweak here and there, we can reword this anecdote into a crude but serviceable description of the initial encounter between Western archaeologists and their native hosts throughout much of the Middle East: "A man from Europe who collected Pharaonic, Greek, Roman, and Judeo-Christian antiquities made a trip to the Ottoman Empire, but the Ottoman people believed in Islam and had no use for such things."

China would be different. For the first time, Westerners would come face to face with a cultured elite whose degree of education and obsession with antiquity far exceeded their own. In China, the highly educated Confucian elite had been studying, collecting, appreciating, and preserving their own art and antiquities for thousands of years, long before the first Western scholar ever set foot in their land. Furthermore, unlike the Europeans, they didn't have to rediscover their classical heritage during a Chinese "renaissance." For in China, the

Confucian elite subscribed to an ideal of unbroken cultural continuity with its ancestors as far back as the historical record took them. What constituted the "historical record"? Simply put, anything written in Chinese characters. It didn't matter if the author of those characters was Han, Mongol, Manchu, Tibetan, Turkic, Khitan, Jurchen, Tabgatch, Sarbi, Korean, Japanese, Vietnamese, Xiongnu, Uighur, Arab, Persian, or even a Jesuit. If they wrote in Chinese, then they were viewed as having played some role in the history of Chinese civilization.

We have a phrase for this: the perception of cultural continuity. As in previous chapters, emphasis must be laid on the word *perception*. Contrary to popular belief, there is just as much actual cultural discontinuity in Chinese history as anywhere else in the world. Consider, for instance, the customs and beliefs of the Shang dynasty (c. 1400?–1050 B.C.), the earliest state in East Asia for which written records survive. The Shang kings practiced gruesome human sacrifice, entrusted crucial affairs of state to shamans, held most of their subjects in onerous bondage, relocated their capital up to thirteen times, and had never heard of Confucius, Buddha, or Laozi. In what sense, then, were they "Chinese"? The answer, of course, is that they were no more "Chinese" than Roman pagans were Italian Christians or the pharaohs were Muslim Arabs. What enables the myth of "three thousand years of Chinese civilization" to thrive is the unique role of the Chinese script. Though the Chinese script has undergone several major transformations over the past three thousand years, it is still fundamentally and recognizably the same script, one that represents the sounds and meanings of closely related Sinitic forms of speech.

No other script anywhere else in the world has managed to remain continuously in use for three thousand years, unless the form of that script has evolved so dramatically that it became, in effect, two or more distinct scripts. The ancient Egyptian hieroglyphs are a case in point: technically, they never went extinct. They simply evolved into a diverse group of scriptural offspring, such as demotic, hieratic, and Phoenician. This last gave rise to the Greek alphabet, which in turn provided the basis for the Latin and Cyrillic scripts. Despite an unbroken lineage of scripts, however, someone who reads Greek or Latin cannot make head nor tail of the common ancestor—Egyptian hieroglyphs—from which his own script is ultimately derived. Of course, someone who learned to read and write the Chinese script as it appeared in the year 1000 A.D. would also find it difficult to read a sample of the Chinese script as it appeared in its original form some two thousand years earlier. But his learning curve was nothing compared to that faced by anyone proficient in Greek, Latin, or Arabic who hoped to read the Egyptian hieroglyphs.

The consequences of all this were enormous. The Europeans did not start to collect Greek, Roman, and Pharaonic antiquities until they began to rediscover the cultural virtues of these ancient civilizations in the sixteenth century, and in some cases much later. But the educated elites of China, by way of continuous engagement with their own antiquity—made possible by the unique nature of the Chinese script—didn't have to rediscover anything at all. As a result, despite the historical fact of recurrent cultural, political, social, and economic discontinuity on the ground, an ideal of unbroken civilizational continuity continued to persist in the minds of anyone educated in the Chinese script. This durable perception, as strong today as ever before, meant that the Chinese both identified with and cherished the material remains of any past dynasty whose elites—Han or otherwise—were proficient in writing classical Chinese. Those who lived in 500 B.C. eagerly collected the wares of their perceived cultural ancestors from 1000 B.C., those who lived in 1000 A.D. moved heaven and earth to preserve the wares of their perceived cultural ancestors from 100 A.D., and those who lived in 1900 A.D. competed with each other to own and display the wares of their perceived cultural ancestors from 1200 A.D.

This was the world of Chinese art and antiquities into which stepped the historical Indiana Jones. Of course, long before they arrived in China, Europeans were already familiar with one particular form of Chinese art: porcelain. As early as the eighteenth century, with the arrival of Dutch and British merchant vessels in East Asia, the Chinese had begun to produce porcelain designed specifically for the European market, giving rise to an entire fashion craze known as *chinoiserie*. But *chinoiserie* motifs reflected European tastes, not Chinese. As a result, neither side yet coveted what the other possessed. That began to change in 1860, when the Second Opium War witnessed the arrival of British and French armies into Beijing for the first time. The details of the conflict need not detain us here; what is important from our perspective is that this conflict led to the first demonstration of Western military superiority before the eyes of the emperor himself (the first Opium War in 1839 had been fought in the south, far from the Forbidden City).

In more ways than one, the Anglo-French assault on Beijing in 1860 was similar to that of the Anglo-French conflict in Egypt some six decades prior. In both instances, despite being enemies in one (Egypt) and allies in the other (China), the French and British gave notice to the long-standing powers of the Orient that a new hegemon was in town. At the same time, both invasions also facilitated a more intimate European engagement with the art and antiquities of civilizations unfamiliar to Western eyes. In the case of China in 1860, the British and French finally managed to grab hold of the same sort of aesthetic wares the Chinese themselves valued, as opposed to the exported motifs of *chinoiserie*. The precipitating event was a decision by French officers to allow their soldiers to loot and ransack the Old Summer Palace in Beijing. This was followed two weeks later with an order from Lord Elgin—yes, the son of *that* Lord Elgin—to destroy all remaining structures on the premises as retaliation for the torture and execution of a group of French and British envoys. Much of the loot was subsequently auctioned off in Beijing and soon found its way into the international art market.

Moral quandaries aside, this was the first time that Western collectors found it possible to acquire—with relative ease and in larger quantities than before—the same sort of art cherished by the Chinese (in this case, the emperor himself). Though they continued to favor porcelain, it was porcelain now decorated in the same motifs treasured by the Chinese. It took a little longer for Europeans and Americans to warm up to the type of artifacts most esteemed by the Chinese—bronzes, steles, and calligraphy—but these, too, gradually revealed their charms. In 1901, another invasion of Beijing, this time by a coalition of eight nations in what became known as the Boxer War, precipitated yet another exodus of pilfered antiquities. By this point, China's secret was out. Nearly half a century had now passed since the first appearance of Chinese antiquities on the Western market, more than enough time for the exotic to become familiar. In addition, repeated exposure to the arts of Japan—far more accessible than those of China—bred in many Westerners the same sort of respect and appreciation of Chinese art that many Japanese themselves had. As a result, by the turn of the twentieth century, most Western museums were eager to acquire Chinese art in all its forms.

But how to go about it? For the director of a respectable museum, military pillage was bad form, legally suspect, and

Figure 5.1. The U.S. Ninth Infantry in the courtyard of the Forbidden City.
In 1901, following the occupation of Beijing by an eight-nation military alliance during the Boxer War, foreign soldiers proceeded to loot the palace precincts.

morally odious. True, the sacking of the Old Summer Palace in 1860 and raid on the Forbidden City in 1901 had broadened the horizons of anyone still convinced that the Chinese were capable only of producing fine porcelain rather than fine arts. But such methods of acquisition were neither sustainable nor morally defensible, a point taken up by an increasing number of critics back home. Unlike in Egypt and most of the Ottoman Empire, however, the bulk of antiquities in China were not just languishing under the sun untended, waiting patiently for a foreign "savior" to give them a new home. They were lovingly tended by their Chinese owners, locked away in storage until a suitable pretext arose to place them on temporary display for a privileged guest. For with the exception of porcelain, lacquers, silks, folding screens, spiritual idols, and architecturally fused sculptures—say, a bronze lion's head attached to a railing or door—art and antiquities were rarely flaunted by their Chinese owners. The typical guest to a great house or

Figure 5.2. Chinese bronzes.
In addition to bronzes, the highly educated Confucian elite of China had been collecting, preserving, studying and cherishing steles, jades, calligraphy, paintings, sculptures, books, scrolls, seals, and rubbings continuously for more than three thousand years prior to the arrival of the first Western collectors.

palace in China would not see any of its most prized possessions—bronzes, steles, jades, calligraphy, paintings, seals, or
rubbings—unless he was deemed worthy enough to have them
removed from storage and put on display.

Were Western collectors worthy enough? In a word, no. At
least not initially. Much like his European counterpart, the
Chinese man of means had been raised to regard himself as
a gentleman. And whenever, asked the Confucian philosopher
Mencius in the fourth century B.C., "has there been a gentleman for sale?" Of course, this was the ideal, not the reality.
Lots of Chinese gentlemen posted their aesthetic wares for sale.
But when they sold their most prized possessions—the material embodiment of their moral and cultural credentials—they
tried very hard to pretend that it was not a sale. This meant that
a potential Western buyer, in order to gain access to the cream
of the Chinese crop, first had to convince its owner that he not
only appreciated, but also understood his collection in the same
way that a Chinese gentleman would. Otherwise, the transaction would be exposed for what it really was: a commercial
exchange between merchants. And if that occurred, the reputation of the gentleman, who professed to despise merchants,
would suffer. The Japanese collector Okakura Tenshin has
described the delicate dynamics of such performances. "A small
number of pieces will be shown in the course of an afternoon
mostly spent in dining and exchanging courteous sentiments,"
he wrote in 1912. "To 'do' a large collection requires a series of
appointments and an infinity of patience."

This was a dance that few Westerners could join. John
Dewey, an American philosopher whose students included the
famous Chinese intellectual Hu Shi, knew just how difficult it
could be to impress a Chinese gentleman on his own terms. The
educated classes of China, he once observed, talk about their
ancient script "with all the art jargon. 'Notice the strength of
this down stroke, and the spirituality of the cross stroke and
elegant rhythm of the composition.'" Failure to master the
jargon meant failure to prove oneself worthy of having the
best calligraphic specimens unfurled before one's eyes, much
less offered for "sale." In other words, in trying to gain access
to elite Chinese circles and the treasures they hoarded, the

cultural bar was high. This is why a good number of the earliest Western acquisitions of Chinese art—those not pilfered by Western armies—came about not through direct purchase, but rather as gifts tendered to foreign institutions by Chinese dignitaries eager to curry political favor. For example, when the high-ranking Qing official Duanfang visited Chicago in 1906, he also made a bequest of an inscribed 8th-century B.C. Daoist stele for the Field Museum. In practice, these sorts of transactions were scarcely any different from the gifting of pharaonic obelisks to Western governments by the *pashas* of Egypt. Both turned ancient artifacts into modern diplomatic capital.

So far, none of this constitutes an exodus of art. With the exception of two instances of wartime looting noted above, the Chinese had by the dawn of the twentieth century managed to retain possession of the vast majority of their art and antiquities. Though Western governments and museums might obtain a worthy sampling of steles, paintings, and bronzes from the hands of Chinese diplomats or perhaps the emperor himself, the domestic art market was still *terra incognita* to most Western collectors. The transfer of art and antiquities in China mostly took place in the homes of the rich and famous, and here Westerners—if they could get their foot in the door at all—were often outmaneuvered by other Chinese or Japanese collectors. For unlike the Westerners, the others knew exactly what they wanted, where to get it, how much it was worth, how to determine a fake, and—most importantly—how to convince their similarly educated Confucian counterpart that the hopeful buyer was worthy of its sale.

Until the status quo underwent a profound change, the historical Indiana Jones found it difficult to carve out his own private niche in the Chinese art market. The usual channels of acquisition were dominated by Confucian and Japanese connoisseurs, both of who perceived the entirety of China's three thousand years of recorded history to be within the purview of their collecting agenda. It soon became clear that if Western collectors wanted to fill their museums with Chinese art, they would have to tap into a new supply of antiquities, one that lay outside the Sino-Japanese cartel. Prior to the 1911 revolution, there was only one way for a Western collector to get the better of his East Asian rivals: dig for it himself. Well, not exactly *himself*: in practice, it would always be the peasants of China who dug on his behalf. But the essential point remains: it was only through the yields of freshly excavated sites that the Westerner could hope to compete with his Chinese counterparts. We can place these freshly excavated sites into three types of categories: tombs, oracle bones, and the desiccated treasures of the Silk Road.

Much as in Egypt, in China the lavish graves of the rich and powerful had been dug into by peasants since time immemorial. There they found exquisitely manufactured bronzes, jades, jewelry, steles, scrolls, and occasionally even murals. Sometimes the peasants stumbled upon these sites by accident in the course of plowing their fields; at other times they set off in deliberate search under the cover of nightfall. Such activities always carried an inherent risk: depending on the disposition of the local magistrate, the peasants could very well be punished for having disturbed the bones of someone's ancestor. But such scruples were not adhered to across the board, and it was just as likely that the local magistrate would accept the newly discovered antiquities as a gift from his subjects in recognition of his or the emperor's virtue (in exchange for a financial reward, of course). This was even more likely if the peasants could successfully hide the fact that they had obtained these goods by digging into a grave. Even some landlords were known to scour their fields for signs of underground vaults. Either way, the raiding of tombs was an established practice in China, mostly because the Confucian elites, inspired by the perception of cultural continuity, infused value into almost anything that was inscribed with Chinese characters. As a result, in stark contrast to the situation in Egypt, even if Chinese tombs yielded nothing of intrinsic value—precious metals, jade, and jewelry—they still offered the promise of indirect financial compensation in the form of gifts or sales to the educated elite.

What changed in the early twentieth century was the appearance of a new customer in China, one with deep pockets and nowhere to spend it. Sure, Western collectors had managed to procure a handful of serviceable specimens from private collections, but now their demand far outstripped supply. Into this tightly restricted market stepped the enterprising proprietors of antique and curio shops. Attuned to the potential of a neglected market, they began to send their purchasing agents directly to the countryside and thus bypass the previous channels of exchange through the hands of local gentry, officials, and governors. Before long, antique shops in all major Chinese cities began to display a wide array of authentic wares dug fresh from ancient tombs. The most famous of these was the Liulichang market in Beijing. Of course, in Liulichang as elsewhere, the Chinese and Japanese were free to bid on such items as well, and they gobbled up their fair share. Nevertheless, Western dollars (mostly American, as we shall see) had finally managed to stimulate the rise of a new domestic chain of supply, one that stripped the market of its social and intellectual baggage and made the purchase of genuine Chinese art by Western collectors a more feasible—if still dicey—task.

Having duly invigorated the tomb raiding business, Western collectors also found themselves well positioned to exploit another cache of newly available artifacts: oracle bones. Much as with grave goods, Westerners played no part in the initial discovery, leaving all the heavy lifting to the Chinese. The story of the oracle bones begins in 1899, in a little village near Anyang on the banks of the Huan River, a tributary of the much larger Yellow River. The village had long been known as a good source for what the locals referred to as "dragon bones." These bones, mostly turtle shells and ox scapula, were highly sought after by Chinese pharmacists and apothecaries, who crushed them into a powder and inserted the auspicious particles into various medicinal concoctions. In 1899, the Huan River flooded its banks again, revealing a generous bounty of dragon bones in the eroded soil. Fan Weiqing, an antiquities dealer from Shandong passing through Anyang in search of bronzes, came across the bones and noted traces of what appeared to be some form of writing on the surface. So he decided to buy several batches of them and took them north to Tianjin to see if any Chinese scholars would buy them. Several did, and the oracle bone business was born. (The oft-told tale of a Chinese scholar sick with malaria stumbling upon the bones at his local apothecary appears to be entirely apocryphal.)

In the beginning, no one called them oracle bones, for no one yet knew of their original function as divination tools. In 1903, after several years of intense study, a scholar named Liu E published the first account of what would eventually be confirmed as the earliest record of the Chinese script, having survived on "oracle bones" used by the kings and shamans of the Shang dynasty as early as 1250 B.C. In trying to track down the ultimate source of these bones, Chinese scholars spent many years pursuing false leads and dead ends. They were also repeatedly frustrated by the antiquities dealer Fan Weiqing, who did his best to conceal the location of the villages near Anyang and hoard all the profits for himself. In the meantime, Fan and his associates sought out customers all along the eastern seaboard. Not only that, but landlords in the villages near Anyang, increasingly aware of the rising value of their local "dragon bones," also began to organize their own aggressive excavations. In some cases, they even competed directly with Fan, taking their stashes of bones straight to known collectors in major cities. As with freshly uncovered tomb loot, oracle bones were made available to any collector with deep pockets, absent any social, cultural, or political restrictions. The first Westerners to take advantage of this situation were Samuel Couling and Frank Chalfant, American and British missionaries living in Shandong Province. Together, they managed to collect several thousand pieces. Eventually, many tens of thousands of oracle bone fragments would end up in the collections of foreign scholars, diplomats, and missionaries, most of who later donated or resold their bones to Western museums and universities.

In sum, tomb raiders and oracle bones dealers had enabled Western collectors to claim a seat at the table of Chinese antiquities for the first time. But it was still just one seat among many, and the elbows of rival Chinese and Japanese collectors ensured the limits of their reach. Apparently, if China was to yield its treasures as the Ottoman Empire had once done, it would only do so under similarly compromising conditions: political instability and a perception of cultural discontinuity with the ancient past. So far, neither of these criteria applied anywhere in the Han heartland. But at least one of them did exist in the non-Han borderlands: the perception of cultural discontinuity. Far out along the northern and western frontiers of the empire, Confucian officials exercised a loose and often indirect authority over the lands of Tibet, Mongolia, and Xinjiang. Tibet, with its vast frozen plateaus and enormous stretches of uninhabited land, offered little of interest for the hunter of antiquities. Mongolia, with its rich history of powerful nomadic confederations and recurrent interactions with the fertile agricultural lands of the south, was of slightly more interest, but still lacked dense concentrations of the sort of classically designed art and antiquities coveted most by collectors.

The same could not be said of Xinjiang. Often referred to by Westerners as "Chinese Turkestan" or "Eastern Turkestan," Xinjiang had long been subject to intermittent conquest at the hands of expansive polities based in the Han heartland to the east. Just as often, however, it had been subject to the rule of Tibetans from the south, Mongols from the north, and various Muslim and other Central Asian peoples from the west. This has earned Xinjiang the epithet of being the "crossroads of Eurasia," better known to the layman as the chief geographical backdrop for the oft romanticized Silk Road. Less well known were the many ancient Buddhist kingdoms and Chinese military outposts buried beneath the sands of the Taklamakan Desert, untouched by human hands for more than a thousand years, and in some cases far longer. As was the case with the oracle bones, the exodus of Silk Road treasures from China began at the hands of enterprising peasants, continued under the financial encouragement of modestly educated elites, and concluded in the glass cabinets of distant scholars. In this case, however, the peasants were Turkic-speaking Muslims rather than Han; the modestly educated elites were Russian and British consuls instead of a Chinese antiquities dealer from Shandong; and the distant scholars were from Europe, not Beijing.

The origins of these expeditions date to the mid-nineteenth century, when the Russian and British empires began to bump up against one another in Central Asia: the former eastward across the Kazakh steppe and down into the khanates of

Kokand and Bukhara, the latter northward from India into the Punjab and Kashmir. This heated imperial rivalry was forced to call a truce at Afghanistan, which both powers warily conceded as a buffer state. The towering mountain ranges that stretched all along the eastern and northern frontiers of Afghanistan, however, were fair game. In the name of king, queen, and czar, geographers from both empires raced to scale the peaks of the Pamirs, Himalayas, Karakoram, and Kunlun ranges. Once there, they had an unparalleled view of the deserts of Xinjiang. It was thus only a matter of time before Russian and British diplomats each managed to secure permission from the emperor in Beijing for the establishment of dueling consulates in the sprawling oasis of Kashgar. By the last decade of the nineteenth century, two men jealously guarded their respective interests: Nikolai Petrovsky for the Russians and George Macartney for the British.

Petrovksy and Macartney played the same role for European explorers in Xinjiang as Henry Salt had once played for Giovanni Belzoni in Egypt (and as the antiquities dealer Fan Weiqing had played in Anyang). In short, they were all modestly educated enablers who put distant scholars into direct contact with the incidental fruits of local peasant enterprise. In southern Xinjiang, both the peasants and their local headmen (*begs*) were Turkic-speaking Muslims (known today as "Uighurs," but referred to at the time by their Chinese rulers as "Turban Heads"). Together, they represented some seventy to eighty percent of the population of Xinjiang, along with a smattering of Kazaks, Mongols, Kyrgyz, Hui (Chinese Muslims), and Han merchants. Above them all stood a small handful of Chinese officials, who in most cases ruled over a populace that was almost entirely alien in culture, language, and ethnicity. All of these factors combined to re-create the same favorable conditions for Europeans in Xinjiang that they had faced in Egypt a century prior. Even the climate was similar: the deserts of northwestern China were so barren and the air so dry that almost anything placed beneath the sands or inside a cave—corpses, paper, wood, paintings, sculptures—would retain much of its original appearance for thousands of years.

The oasis dwellers of Xinjiang, having long tilled their fields along the fringes of the Taklamakan Desert with the aid of melted alpine snow, had likely been stumbling upon the remains of ancient Buddhist kingdoms for hundreds, perhaps even a thousand years. But it was only with the arrival of Consuls Macartney and Petrovsky in Kashgar that they began to realize such things could yield a material profit. Previously, only the chance discovery of a rare deposit of jade, gold, silver, or gems motivated anyone to venture out beyond the pale of cultivation. If what they found instead were merely the financially worthless remains of ancient stupas, walls, and wooden tablets, these would be promptly quarried for fertilizer. If they happened upon a birch-leaf document or clay figurine, it would be handed over as a plaything to children or perhaps regarded as a charm and placed into safekeeping. Sometimes, fearing the powers of a malevolent *jinn*, they would be left in place or destroyed. Whatever they did with them, none of the diverse peoples of Xinjiang had yet to see in these objects what Petrovsky and Macartney managed to see: themselves.

Much like Lord Elgin in Athens and Heinrich Schliemann in Troy, the European consuls of Kashgar had a penchant for detecting the greatness of Western civilization in even the remotest corners of the world. But it was one thing to see evidence of the Greeks in Athens and Troy. It was quite another to see Greeks in the sands of Central Asia. So what were they seeing? We need only invoke the name of one person: Alexander the Great. In the fourth century B.C., this young Macedonian king embarked on more than a decade of unprecedented military conquest throughout the lands of Anatolia, Persia, and what are today the lands of Afghanistan and Pakistan. Everywhere Alexander's armies marched, they left their mark by mixing their language, culture, and customs with those of their newly acquired subjects. Though the empire itself was short lived, the hybrid cultures left in its wake were not.

Now fast forward to the nineteenth century, when all that was known of Alexander's exploits among European scholars was limited to what they could read in books. For them, the British incorporation of much of the Indian subcontinent had opened up new scholarly vistas undreamt by previous generations. Far out on the northwestern borders of the Raj, Europeans could travel through the same lands once settled by Alexander's armies. There they found traces of what they called "Gandharan" art: a fusion of Asian and Hellenic (Greek) motifs, styles, and craftsmanship, often expressed through a Buddhist medium. Of course, only the Greek elements of such creations were singled out for praise. In the 1920s, while attempting to describe a sculpture "reminiscent of types in the Gandharan art," the German archaeologist Albert von Le Coq gave voice to this prejudice when he observed how the "drapery falls in noble lines, not yet degraded by Eastern Asiatic misunderstanding of classic forms." But only tantalizing fragments of Gandharan art survived within the borders of the Raj, much of it having been destroyed or repurposed at the hands of Hindu and Muslim successors. Afghanistan, reputed to hold the one of the richest stores of surviving Gandharan wares, was also off-limits, largely due to its status as an acknowledged buffer zone between the Russian and British empires.

Figure 5.3. A Gandharan fresco in Xinjiang.
Western archaeologists were lured to Xinjiang by images such as these, which suggested the ancient presence of partially Hellenized migrants from South Asia.

That left Xinjiang. Though no one knew it at the time, ancient migrants and refugees from the hybrid communities of northwestern India had taken their culture, religion, languages, and scripts over the forbidding mountain ranges of Central Asia and into the oases of the Taklamakan Desert. For about a thousand years, they left their footprint upon fortuitously irrigated sands, until those same sands decided to take back what they had ceded. With once flourishing oases now buried beneath the desert winds, their residents became migrants once more, relocating to new settlements that soon fell under the sway of Tibetan, Muslim, Mongol, or Chinese influence. The Gandharan impact upon the peoples of the Taklamakan Desert thus passed into legend; that is, until Petrovsky and Macartney showed up. Petrovsky was one of the first to spot what looked like traces of Buddhist and Gandharan art on the shelves of local curio shops and in the homes of known treasure-seekers. He also noticed strange forms of writing preserved on wooden tablets and birch leaf manuscripts, some of which later proved to record various Indo-European languages and scripts. These he bought and shipped to scholars in Europe. That in turn initiated a predictable chain reaction: the scholars, already inclined to see themselves in anything bearing traces of Greek art, were now eager to recover any object that might shed light on the triumphal march of Western civilization into Asia.

Of course, the local Muslims of Xinjiang were more than happy to supply the Europeans with all the Gandharan art their hearts desired. The art, antiquities, and manuscripts found in the desert meant little to them, and in some cases they had even intentionally defaced Buddhist murals preserved in caves. Before long, however, the Europeans began to suspect that the locals were profiting off their enthusiasm by filling the bazaars with forgeries and other objects of dubious provenance. It was becoming increasingly clear that if Gandharan art was to be recovered in its entirety, someone would have to go into the desert himself, bypassing all local intermediaries. The first person to do so was Sven Hedin, a daring Swedish explorer who in the 1890s twice proved the feasibility (and potential folly) of venturing into the Taklamakan Desert for weeks at a time.

This was a necessary benchmark for any prolonged excavation of a buried oasis. In 1900, the Hungarian turned British scholar Marc Aurel Stein—named for the Roman emperor Marcus Aurelius—followed in Hedin's footsteps. Unlike Hedin, however, Stein came ready to dig. Over the course of three separate expeditions spanning the next fifteen years, Stein would fill the museums of London and New Delhi to the brim with Gandharan art and antiquities. He also brought back tens of thousands of ancient manuscripts written in numerous scripts and languages, some long dead and forgotten.

Figure 5.4. Aurel Stein in Xinjiang.
Pictured here in the Taklamakan Desert with his Chinese, Uighur, and Indian assistants, along with a beloved pet dog, Dash. The pecking order in Stein's party was clear: Stein, the classically educated Chinese assistant, and Dash. After the dog came the uneducated or merely technically educated Uighur and Indian assistants. "The petty ways of my Indian Assistants & their indifference to any higher aims put my Chinese helpmate's value into double relief," Stein confessed in a letter to a friend in 1907. "He and eager little Dash are always pleasant companions. With the rest one is again & again reminded that one is dealing with mercenaries."

Other explorers followed. Today, the art, antiquities, and manuscripts of northwestern China can be found all over the world, from St. Petersburg to New Delhi to Tokyo. The Silk Road expeditions constituted the first mass exodus of art and antiquities from China to occur outside of a military looting operation. This was a direct result of the fact that most of the earliest explorers went to Xinjiang in search of Indian Buddhist artifacts buried on the fringes of Muslim communities. In other words, the stuff that left the country was, much as in Egypt, perceived as culturally discontinuous by the contemporary inhabitants of the land, who were generally content to earn a commission on its removal. Yet despite the fact that most of the Silk Road explorers were interested only in recovering traces of Gandharan art and Indo-European scripts—hence their primary training as Indologists—it did not take long for them to stumble upon ancient Chinese antiquities and scripts as well. This presented an unusual scenario, for, as we have seen, educated Chinese elites tended to regard anything written in the Chinese script—even if it was written by a Manichaean Persian—as part of their own cultural tradition.

The handful of Chinese officials who governed Xinjiang on behalf of Beijing were all familiar with the Confucian classics and Chinese historical annals, both of which made reference to the ancient lands of the distant northwest. The histories, in particular, often discussed the Chinese presence in Xinjiang during the Han (206 B.C.–220 A.D.) and Tang (618–907) dynasties, back when it was known as the "Western Regions." Not only that, but the Chinese officials stationed in Xinjiang were also sympathetic to Buddhism, it being one of the major religions of the Han heartland from whence they came. This raises an important question: Why did Chinese officials in Xinjiang, who appreciated, preserved, and identified with many of the exact same sorts of antiquities and manuscripts unearthed from the desert sands by Western explorers, allow so many of them to leave the country for good? We can concede that they might not have cared all that much about the Sanskrit materials, but what of those bearing the Chinese script or images of the Buddha? We cannot explain the Silk Road exodus of antiquities from China purely by reference to the gross power imbalance that

The Treasures of China

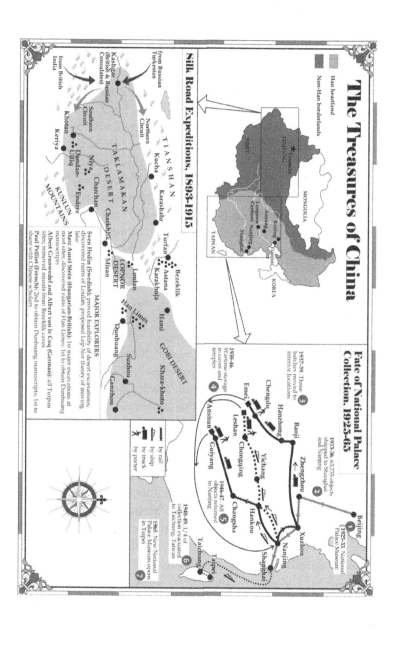

Han heartland
Non-Han borderlands

Silk Road Expeditions, 1893-1915

from Russian Turkestan

from British India

Kashgar (British & Russian Consulates)

Northern Circuit

Southern Circuit

Khotan

Keriya

TIANSHAN

Kucha

Karashahr

Turfan

Astana

Karakhoja

Bezeklik

TAKLAMAKAN DESERT

Niya

Domoko

Uluq

Charchan

Endere

Charkhlik

Miran

Loulan

LOPNOR DESERT

KUNLUN MOUNTAINS

Hami

Khara-khoto

Han Limes

Dunhuang

Suzhou

Ganzhou

GOBI DESERT

MAJOR EXPLORERS

Sven Hedin (Swedish): proved feasibility of desert excavations; discovered ruins of Loulan; proposed Lop Nor theory of moving lake

Marc Aurel Stein (Hungarian-British): 1st major excavations at most sites; discovered ruins of Han Limes; 1st to obtain Dunhuang manuscripts

Albert Grunwedel and Albert von le Coq (German): all Turfan sites; removed murals from Bezeklik caves

Paul Pelliot (French): 2nd to obtain Dunhuang manuscripts; 1st to share with Chinese scholars

Fate of National Palace Collection, 1925-65

1925-31, National Palace Museum ①

1933-36, 63,735 objects shipped to Shanghai and Nanjing ②

1937-39, Three batches moved to interior locations ③

1938-46, Wartime storage in caves and temples ④

1946-47, All objects returned to Nanjing ⑤

1948-49, 1/4 of collection evacuated to Taichung, Taiwan ⑥

1965, New National Palace Museum opens in Taipei ⑦

Beijing

Zhengzhou

Xuzhou

Baoji

Hanzhong

Chengdu

Emei

Leshan

Anshun

Guiyang

Chongqing

Yichang

Hankou

Changsha

Nanjing

Shanghai

Taichung

Taipei

by rail
by ship
by truck
by porter

existed between China and the Western powers of the day. This is doubly so in light of the fact that there appears to have been little coercion involved: at least in these early years, it is clear that the Chinese did not attempt to obstruct the removal of a single bodhisattva's ear from their land.

So how to explain all this? In short, there are three things we need to understand about what happened in Xinjiang. First, despite striking similarities in climate and a similar perception of cultural discontinuity among the masses, Xinjiang still was not Egypt. In Egypt, the archaeologist could disembark from his comfortable barge on the Nile and find himself surrounded by ancient stone monuments and temples in mere minutes. (The Valley of the Kings is only five miles by foot from the Nile and the comforts of Luxor.) In Xinjiang, however, the archaeologist had to suffer severe physical hardship before he came anywhere near the sand-buried treasures of the Taklamakan. Nearly all of the ruins required a multi-day trek straight into the forbidding desert. Furthermore, due to the punishing summertime heat, the journey could only be made during the subzero winter, when frozen blocks of ice could be brought along and melted for drinking water. Even then, the frigid winds could be brutal, resulting in severely chapped hands and faces. For the foolishly unprepared, death was in the offing: in 1895, two of Hedin's local Muslim guides died of thirst after the party mismanaged its water supplies. But even responsibly outfitted expeditions faced daily hardships. In 1907, during his second expedition, Stein described the scene near a marshy spring in the Gobi, where the air was "thick of mosquitos and the ground swarming with equally bloodthirsty creatures wherever we camped." The next year Stein lost a toe to frostbite; in 1914, he nearly died when his horse reared back and fell on top of him, leaving him with a badly crushed leg.

Were the Chinese officials willing to endure such misery themselves? Not in a million years. In fact, we know exactly what they thought of Stein's treks through the desert. In 1902, Wan Rong, a Chinese official stationed in the provincial capital of Urumchi, compared the admiration of his colleagues for Western science and technology with their reticence for the fieldwork upon which such advances were made. "They all marvel at the natural sciences and are in awe of Western weapons and technology," Wan wrote. "Yet when it comes to seeing Mr. Stein crossing mountains and rivers, or traveling through the desert, they laugh at his folly." Some officials had a different reaction. In 1908, Zhu Ruichi, the prefect of Guma, wrote a letter to Stein in which he recounted the harsh conditions the latter had faced. "While on the road," Zhu wrote, "you encountered snowcapped mountain peaks and a bitter cold air that pierced through to the bone and rendered all clothing immaterial." When he heard that Stein had lost a toe to frostbite, Zhu's sympathy turned to admiration. "What I mourn is the thought of the hardships you must endure while scaling mountains and fording bodies of water, and of the difficult straits in which you continually place yourself. What I admire, however, is your stern fortitude and valiant resolve."

Some Chinese officials laughed at Stein. Some praised him. Not one, however, was prepared to follow him into the desert. We can attribute some of their reluctance simply to cultural baggage: the ideal of the Confucian gentleman did not yet include a valorization of manual labor or physical hardship. On the contrary, the leisured classes of China had long taken pride in untrimmed fingernails and pale skin as the mark of a cultured man, someone who labored indoors with his mind rather than outdoors with his hands. But there was more to it than that. Perhaps of greater importance than any supposed cultural bias against dirty work was the fact that most of the Chinese who lived in Xinjiang were, first and foremost, *officials*. Though many had scholarly interests, they were not paid to be scholars. They had a job to do, and it was a demanding one. From the governor on down to the prefect, each official was responsible for fulfilling a host of demanding tasks, from taxes, legal disputes, and irrigation works to agricultural reclamation, infrastructure, and the maintenance of public order. Seen in this light, the question is not why they failed to undertake their own expeditions into the desert, but rather how they managed to find time to express any genuine interest in them at all.

And genuine interest they certainly had. This brings us to our second realization: wherever feasible, the Chinese officials of Xinjiang did in fact undertake their own excavations.

Expeditions they could not do, but excavations were within the realm of the possible, so long as they could direct the work from the confines of their government office. In this capacity the Chinese officials of Xinjiang most closely resembled Lord Elgin, who, it might be recalled, orchestrated the removal of the Parthenon marbles entirely from the comfort of his embassy in Constantinople. In Xinjiang, such an arrangement was replicated most closely in the vicinity of the oasis of Turfan. There, as Stein observed, "the ruins are practically all within village areas & within reach of pleasant quarters." This meant that systematic digs spanning many weeks could be funded, managed, and exploited from the convenience of urban abodes. Though most Western explorers liked to give the impression that the Chinese were largely indifferent to their excavations, it is clear that they, too, were determined to get their share. As Stein noted in his field diary on several separate occasions, the Astana graves at Turfan had been "worked" by a man named Muhammad Jiza "for supplying Chinese at Turfan and Urumchi." Eager to portray his own excavations in a more positive light than those done on behalf of the Chinese, Stein went on to characterize the latter as "unchecked destruction in which the local people and the kwans [officials] employing them have been allowed to indulge."

Underneath Stein's rhetorical gloss we can see that in those few places in Xinjiang where excavations could be organized without the preamble of an expedition, Chinese officials seem to have done as the foreigners did. The result was more or less analogous to what had happened with the oracle bones at Anyang, but with the ratio of distribution reversed. In Anyang, centrally located in the Han heartland and excavated at the same time as the Silk Road treasures, everybody got his share, but the Chinese clearly got the most. Conversely, out in Xinjiang, everybody also got his share, but this time it was the foreigners who left the Chinese in the dust. It is easy to see why. The only permanent residents of Xinjiang who perceived a legacy of cultural continuity with its Silk Road treasures were the Chinese officials, who numbered less than one percent of the population. These men were limited to what Stein derisively referred to as "suburban" excavations at places like Turfan. Even there, however, they faced stiff competition from the Europeans: from 1902 to 1914, the German archaeologist Albert von Le Coq treated Turfan as his own personal stomping grounds, setting up extended shop on four separate occasions. With regard to transportation, it was also much easier for Westerners to get in and out of Xinjiang: the Trans-Siberian Railroad could whisk them to Xinjiang's doorstep in a mere week or two, while Chinese officials were obliged to spend three grueling months on the overland trek to Beijing. Furthermore, the foreign archaeologist was not constrained by official duties or, for the most part, finances. By and large, he could dig to his heart's delight without the distractions of domestic politics, empty treasuries, or administrative burdens.

Common both to the dispersal of the oracle bones at Anyang and the Silk Road treasures in Xinjiang is our third realization: the widespread embrace on both sides of two fundamental principles regarding the disposition of archaeological proceeds in China. The first was the moral validity of "finders keepers." The second, which grew out of the first, was the legal sanctity of personal property. Simply put, we cannot fully comprehend why so many archaeological treasures were removed from China unless we first understand how the people involved in their removal viewed such arrangements at the time. The European thinking on this point was very clear. In 1907, when Stein gained access to a hoard of ancient manuscripts locked away in a secret cave "library" at Dunhuang, he conceded ownership of the hoard to the local *daoshi* (Daoist priest) who had first happened upon the cave. "Tao-shi undisputed owner of collection by right of discovery," he wrote in his journal. He then proceeded to negotiate the purchase of the manuscripts from their first rightful owner (the Daoist priest) to their second rightful owner (Stein).

Did the Chinese agree? It certainly appears so. When word of the Dunhuang cave library reached Beijing, one Chinese scholar, Luo Zhenyu, urged the government to send out an order to the local officials of Dunhuang to secure the remainder of the manuscripts for the Imperial Library. The government obliged, setting aside what it believed to be suitable monetary compensation to the priest for the removal of his manuscripts.

Figure 5.6. The secret cave "library" at Dunhuang. The French sinologist Paul Pelliot in 1908, trying to decide which of the tens of thousands of ancient manuscripts he should take with him back to Paris. He eventually removed about ten thousand, considered by the Chinese to be the cream of the crop.

That the promised funds never reached the *daoshi*, having been appropriated by local officials en route, is less important than the fact that such funds had been earmarked in the first place. In other words, the Chinese government itself tacitly acknowledged the legitimacy of "finders keepers": because the *daoshi* had discovered the hoard, he could not be divested of his property without compensation from the government.

The Chinese expressed their agreement on this point in other ways as well. One of the most telling was in their repeated use of a particular phrase, deployed in discussions of both the discovery of the oracle bones and the Silk Road treasures: "the earth does not love its treasures" (*di bu ai bao*). This phrase, used to suggest the unfathomable bounty of buried antiquities just waiting to be claimed, was in one case preceded by an explicit commentary on foreign acquisitions. In 1910, the scholarly official Wang Shunan, in a survey of recent archaeological endeavors in Xinjiang intended for a Chinese readership, wrote the following:

During the Six Dynasties, Buddhism was transmitted to the Western Regions and flourished. As a result, many of those manuscripts are of the highest quality. Unfortunately, most of them were taken by Westerners. But the earth does not love its treasures. Henceforth, who knows how many more in all will come out of the ground?"

Here we see the attitude of Chinese elites of the day on full display. Without a doubt, it was "unfortunate" or "regrettable" (*xi*) that the Westerners had taken away so many manuscripts. But their right to remove these manuscripts in the first place was not in question. The only thing that was in question was the curious lack of Chinese enterprise in securing their fair share. Fortunately for Wang Shunan, the earth did not love its treasures: there was still hope for more, and to each the spoils of his endeavors. Also worth noting is the type of language deployed in commentaries like these. Until the 1920s, the Chinese never once described Western archaeologists as having "stolen," "plundered," "pilfered," "looted," "robbed," or "raided" their country's treasures. Instead, their actions were consistently mediated through such neutral verbs as "taken," "removed," "transported," "excavated," "shipped," "delivered," or "acquired," all words lacking the element of moral judgment.

It was this conviction in the sanctity of private property that would soon open the floodgates of Chinese art and antiquities. Recall for a moment the difficulties encountered by Westerners who wished to acquire Chinese art in the Han heartland. Unlike in Xinjiang, where the Chinese were few and the antiquities unspoken for, in the heartland the Chinese were many and the antiquities (oracle bones and freshly unearthed tombs excepted) were already spoken for. The 1911 revolution changed all that. With the overthrow of the Qing dynasty, the former empire quickly dissolved into a patchwork quilt of competing warlord domains. Until the reunification of the country in 1949, warfare and material deprivation were constant features of daily life throughout the land, from Shanghai to Xinjiang.

Such chaos reverberated throughout the world of art and antiquities. Within months of the revolution, thousands of former Qing officials found themselves unemployed and their finances in tatters. Some, like the Manchu connoisseur

Duanfang, who had once gifted an ancient Daoist stele to the Field Museum in Chicago, lost their heads at the hands of revolutionaries. Dead or alive, all their families now found themselves in desperate straits. In the face of such hardship, even the most treasured works of art were put up for sale. John Ferguson, a Canadian missionary turned foreign advisor to the new government, was one of the best positioned to exploit the sudden glut. In 1914, Duanfang's family, eager to find a sympathetic buyer for their patriarch's collection, contacted Ferguson to discuss a sale. "The family," Ferguson wrote, "has been left with not much else than the art specimens which the father collected during his life." That same year, Ferguson declared that "the market here has never been so favorable as at present." The reason, he concluded, was "due to the necessity of selling collections on the part of those who are no longer in office. ... It has nearly driven me to bankruptcy to try to buy as much as I have." Fortunately, his patrons had deep pockets: in 1912, the very year the Qing dynasty fell, the Metropolitan Museum of Art gave Ferguson $25,000 with which to relieve former officials of their most prized possessions and display them in America.

All this was perfectly legal by the standards of the day, for there were as yet no laws in China prohibiting the sale of private collections of art, regardless of the nationality of the buyer or destination of the goods. This is why so many of these objects will never be seen in China again: Beijing has no legal grounds to demand their return. The prospects for return are slightly more promising for art and antiquities exported after 1914, if they can be identified. That was the year that the new Republican government, alarmed at the sudden hemorrhage of its artistic heritage, enacted the first laws prohibiting the export of antiquities from China. As in the Ottoman Empire during the late nineteenth century, however, the same conditions that gave rise to "Schliemann's precedent" similarly undermined any and all attempts to enforce this provision in China. In other words, a politically unstable China whose treasury was in gross arrears had little chance of enforcing any of its dictates upon wealthy and powerful foreigners.

As a result, just like in the Middle East, the export prohibition law was flaunted by both foreigner and Chinese alike.

Public religious art was the next major casualty. Graves, of course, had always been looted, and the oracle bones at Anyang continued to fall into the hands of the highest bidder. Prior to the revolution, however, public installations of Daoist and Buddhist art had generally been kept free of despoliation. With hunger and warfare now endemic throughout the land, however, even sites of active religious worship could be targeted for sale. The tragic results were on prominent display at the Longmen Grottoes near Luoyang. The more than two thousand caves, carved out of the side of a limestone cliff spanning more than half a mile along the Yi River, contained tens of thousands of Buddhist statues, inscriptions, and steles. Most could be dated from the fourth to tenth centuries, reaching their apogee during the Tang dynasty. But now it was a free-for-all, as one Western collector was soon to discover:

> Men from across the river wade armpit deep in the river and chip fragments from the surface at night. These they took down to Zhengzhou, where agents of the Beijing dealers bought them. In Beijing, the fragments were assembled, and with zeal copies were made from photographs and rubbings.

Unlike in Europe, most public religious art in China was not stored safely inside churches and cathedrals. Much of it was out in the open, exposed and vulnerable in times of chaos. Western collectors, though quick to criticize local peasant initiative and the Chinese middlemen who paid them, were nonetheless more than happy to fuel this illicit trade by paying handsomely for any inventory that reached the city. C.T. Loo, one of the more successful Chinese antiquities dealers, made a fortune exporting vandalized sculptures and art from Longmen and countless other sites to Western museums and dealers throughout the world. In 1934, years after Longmen had been stripped of its most exquisite treasures, Edward Forbes, the director of the Fogg Art Museum at Harvard, attempted to justify the acquisition of so much dubious loot by pointing the finger squarely at the Chinese. "I think that it is an outrage that the Chinese government should have allowed these great sculptures to be hacked off the walls of the cave and to leave the country," he said. "But I think as we had nothing to do with hacking them off the walls of the cave and first heard of them when the mutilated pieces were in Beijing being put together, we are justified in buying them for posterity in this way even if to accomplish the object of preserving them we have to divide the sculpture into two halves."

What was to be done about all this? For the time being, nothing. Laws prohibiting this sort of activity were already on the books, and had been for some time. But until political stability returned to China, there was simply no way to enforce these laws throughout the realm. Unfortunately for the Chinese, stability was nowhere in sight: the Japanese, who occupied Manchuria in 1932 and invaded the heartland in 1937, made sure of that. No matter how bad the situation got, however, there was one thing the Chinese were determined to hold on to: the treasures of the Forbidden City. Though once looted in 1901 by foreign armies in the aftermath of the Boxer War, the Forbidden City was still home to the most

Figure 5.7. The Longmen Grottoes.
An outdoor smorgasbord of vulnerable Buddhist
sculpture near Luoyang, just waiting to be removed
by desperate peasants in search of an income.

magnificent specimens of Chinese art ever collected by an emperor. Shelves and pedestals emptied by foreign soldiers were quickly restocked, either from abundant reserves in the palace itself or from the splendid supply of art held in the imperial summer retreats in Manchuria.

After the 1911 revolution, the same fate that befell the private collections of unemployed or deceased Qing officials also plagued the Qing imperial collection in the Forbidden City. After all, what were the treasures of the Qing emperors but the most renowned private collection of art and antiquities in all of China? Remember: there were no public collections in China at that time. The idea of a museum—a public building exhibiting the most outstanding examples of artistic achievement for the edification of the general public—was a profoundly alien concept in China. Not that Chinese elites didn't have their own august tradition of collecting and preserving *objets d'art*. They did. In addition, the objects they preserved were also intended to contribute to a public mission of education. But each and every one of these collections was private, available to view through invitation only. And the educational mission was not intended directly for the commoners, but rather for the educated elites. These elites in turn were then expected to exert their moral transformation—derived from contemplation of a private collection—over the poor benighted masses, who themselves could never hope to see anything other than public religious art. This lofty task of mediation was central to the identity of the Confucian gentleman, and can be seen clearly in the lengthy epithet left by a Chinese official in Xinjiang in a letter addressed to Stein: "Written by Changsha native Dai Chengmo, dispenser of moral guidance to the people and Magistrate of Keriya County, Xinjiang."

The Qing imperial collection was viewed by its owners in exactly the same way. That is to say, the bronzes, jades, steles, paintings, and calligraphy held in the Forbidden City were not regarded by the emperors of the Qing dynasty as the "patrimony" of the Chinese people writ large. Instead, they were regarded as a reflection of the personal virtue of the members of the ruling dynasty alone. That dynasty was led by the Aisin Gioro clan, whose Manchu ancestors were credited with having brought peace and prosperity to the peoples of China. Their accumulation of so much art was proof of their virtue, and their accumulation of so much virtue was proof of their right to rule. "The empire is not an individual's private empire," proclaimed the regent of the first Qing emperor back in the seventeenth century. "Whosoever possesses virtue, holds it." Though the empire itself may not have been the private property of the emperor, the collection of art and antiquities acquired by the emperor mostly certainly was.

This was a familiar concept to the Europeans, whose own museums had grown out of royal collections also imagined to reflect the personal virtue of their owners. They understood this logic so well, in fact, that when Lord Elgin mulled his options for punishing the Xianfeng emperor during the Second Opium War in 1861, he chose to lay waste to the Old Summer Palace rather than the city of Beijing. This, he reasoned, would spare the Chinese people—who had played no role in the emperor's perfidy—of any unnecessary suffering. Elgin's logic, if not his actions, was one fully embraced by the Chinese: they, too, were convinced that the Old Summer Palace belonged to the emperor and the emperor alone. As such, the destruction of its treasures had absolutely nothing to do with the Chinese people. Only the virtue of the Xianfeng emperor himself had suffered, exactly as Lord Elgin intended.

Fifty years later, the last scions of the Aisin Gioro clan continued to regard everything in the Forbidden City as their private property. In the aftermath of the 1911 revolution and overthrow of the dynasty, the boy emperor Puyi and his thousands of attendants found themselves in dire financial straits. The articles of abdication had granted them the right to continue to reside within the Forbidden City, but without sufficient funds to maintain their luxurious lifestyle. In order to make ends meet, the eunuchs began to sell the art and antiquities of the palace to private dealers in Beijing. Later Puyi himself, along with his brother Pujie, did the same.

The rulers of the new republic, alerted to the piecemeal sale of palace goods, decided to halt the depletion of China's largest "private" collection of art by turning it into a national museum. The idea of establishing a public museum in China can be dated as far back as 1829, when the British East India Company founded the first museum of natural history in Macau. Similar efforts followed, including the establishment in 1905 of the Nantong Museum near Shanghai, the first such institution to be founded and managed by a Chinese director.

But none of these were open to the Chinese public, none served an audience beyond their locality, and only one (Nantong) was run by a Chinese. In other words, none were national museums. In order to fulfill all three of these criteria, we must return to Beijing. In 1914, the new republican government held the first public exhibition of the emperor's treasures in two small halls located in the outer court of the Forbidden City. Another exhibition followed in 1916. Both occasions marked the first time ordinary Chinese citizens had ever passed through the gates of the Forbidden City without incurring a hundred blows of the bamboo rod. But one serious

Figure 5.8. Aisin Gioro Puyi, last emperor of China. From his abdication of the throne in 1912 until his sudden eviction from the Forbidden City in 1924, Puyi and his retainers sold countless imperial treasures in order to supplement their dwindling government stipends.

problem still remained: Puyi and his attendants all still lived within the palace itself, as permitted by the "Articles of Favorable Treatment" signed in the aftermath of the 1911 revolution. As a result, so long as Puyi and his family continued to reside within close physical proximity to the art and antiquities of the palace, the theoretical distinction between "articles of clothing and daily use" (now deemed the property of the Aisin Gioro clan) and "treasures and historical relics" (now deemed the property of the state) proved meaningless in practice. The imperial clan continued to treat *all* palace goods as privately held economic capital capable of staving off the decline in family fortunes. Until the boy emperor and his attendants were physically removed from the palace precincts, it seemed, there was no way to turn a living household into a national museum.

This ideological quagmire was finally resolved in 1924, when the Christian warlord Feng Yuxiang marched his armies into Beijing. Hoping to make good on a host of bold populist promises, Feng unceremoniously ordered Puyi and his household to vacate the Forbidden City. Puyi did as he was told, retreating to a mansion in the Japanese concession of Tianjin. (Even after he left the Forbidden City, however, Puyi still managed to peddle "family heirlooms" he had smuggled out of the palace for another twenty years.) In 1925, with the Aisin Gioro clan gone at last, the National Palace Museum was able to open its doors to the public for the very first time. Its triumph was short lived. Just eight years after its inauguration, the National Palace Museum fell within the radius of advancing Japanese armies in the northeast. The new Nationalist government of Chiang Kaishek, based in the Yangzi Delta in the distant south, decided to pack up 63,735 objects in crates and ship them to secure storage sites in the foreign concessions of Shanghai. There they would await construction of a new home in the Nationalist capital of Nanjing. In May 1937, all 2,631 crates were relocated as promised and a national exhibition of imperial art opened to the public. Two months later, the Japanese invaded Beijing, followed by the occupation of Shanghai.

Thus ensued what is perhaps the single most remarkable odyssey of art and antiquities the world has ever seen. Here illustrated for the first time in detail (see map), the circuitous route of the National Palace collection would eventually span more than ten thousand miles from beginning to end. The one-time treasures of the Manchu ruling house, now reimagined as the abstract patrimony of the Chinese nation, were deemed so important to the political legitimacy of the Nationalist government that they would be protected more carefully than the lives of the Chinese people themselves. In 1938, as three separate collections of crates were carefully moved inland via rail, boat, truck, and porter to the safety of caves in the interior, the Nationalists attempted to obstruct the Japanese advance by deliberately destroying the dykes of the Yellow River near Zhengzhou. The resulting floods killed somewhere between 500,000 to a million Chinese peasants; the imperial treasures emerged unharmed.

After the war, all the crates were returned to Nanjing. The resumption of hostilities between Communist and Nationalist forces, however, ensured that the journey was not yet complete. By 1948, it was apparent that Chiang Kai-shek's Nationalist government would lose the civil war. This prompted the incredible decision to take as many crates as possible—about one-fourth of the original collection in Beijing, more or less the cream of the crop—with the retreating armies to Taiwan. Once there, the crates were stored in two warehouses of the Taichung Sugar Company (Taichung being regarded as the least humid city in Taiwan), before again being placed inside mountain caves. Finally, in 1965, work on a new National Palace Museum, built to rival the imperial architecture and grandeur of the Forbidden City in Beijing, was at last completed. The treasures were thus moved one last time, to the northern suburbs of Taipei, where they remain to this day. For its part, the Communist government in Beijing, smarting at the loss of so many fine works of art, moved quickly to restock the Forbidden City yet again. Through a vigorous purchasing campaign both at home and abroad, coerced and voluntary donations, new excavations, and the consolidation of other museum holdings, the Forbidden City managed to regain much of its former splendor. Most gratifying to the Communist elite, a good number of the objects sold by Puyi, Pujie, and their eunuchs were successfully identified and reclaimed for the museum.

Today, there are two different National Palace museums in two different Chinese republics. This remarkable fact stands as testament to the stubborn tenacity of Chinese perceptions of cultural continuity with their distant past. Neither museum, however, can claim much success in facilitating the unity of the modern Chinese state. On the contrary, they are both stark reminders of the politicized role often ascribed to art and antiquities throughout the modern world. Nevertheless, despite the persistence of internal schisms in the world of Chinese art and politics, the dueling national museums of Beijing and Taipei have accomplished one very important objective. They have both proven beyond a doubt the Chinese commitment to the Western ideal of the modern museum, as embodied through the veneration of science, preservation, and—for the first time in China—public education accessible to the masses. From this point onward, a Communist from Beijing still might argue, obstruct, and compete with a Nationalist from Taiwan over the disposition of their common cultural heritage. Likewise, the poor peasants of China would continue to struggle against urban scholars and officials in their quest to turn a profit from newly discovered graves and other portable religious artifacts. But all such disputes would now be kept "within the family," so to speak, without the participation of foreign archaeologists or scholars.

Despite its troubled past, divisive present, and uncertain future, the founding of the National Palace Museum represented the death knell of legitimate foreign enterprise in the collection of art and antiquities in China. It should come as no surprise, then, to learn that the first attempts to confront Indiana Jones in China occurred precisely as the general public walked into the National Palace Museum for the first time.

Continue the journey at indianajonesinhistory.com:

- EPISODE XII: The Treasures of China
- EPISODE XIII: The Forbidden City
- EPISODE XIV: The Silk Road
- EPISODE XV: The Guardians of Dunhuang

CHAPTER SIX

Confronting
Indiana Jones

On November 20, 1937, readers of the *Saturday Evening Post* were treated to a short story about hard-hitting cops and the bad guys they busted. Four pages into the action, "The Last Wayne" wraps its text around a one-panel cartoon by David Huffine. The setting depicts a dock somewhere on the Hudson River in New York City, with the Statue of Liberty in the background. On the dock stand three men: a casually attired African-American janitor, a white porter in suit and tie, and a scantily clad black man with an oar in his hand. Beneath them, still floating on the water, are three more men sitting in a canoe, each drawn to resemble the third man on the dock. They, too, have black skin, few clothes, and tribal adornments, all of which suggest a journey from the jungles of Africa. Below them is the punch line, delivered by the African-American janitor to the smartly dressed white porter: "He say dey is a expedition, come heah to get stuff fo' dey museum." In Cambridge, Massachusetts, Langdon Warner, a Harvard professor and curator of Asian art at the university's Fogg Museum, sees the cartoon and cuts it out of the *Saturday Evening Post*. He then mails it to his good friend Roy Chapman Andrews, now the director of the American Museum of Natural History in New York City.

It is easy to understand why Warner sent the cartoon to Andrews: the intended humor is obvious to anyone who, like them, sat atop the racial and political hierarchy of the day. After all, everyone knew that only white people embarked on expeditions to "get stuff fo' dey museum." The British archaeologist

"He say dey is a expedition, come heah to get stuff fo' dey museum."

Figure 6.1. Role Reversal in the Saturday Evening Post.
Cartoon © SEPS licensed by Curtis Licensing,
Indianapolis, IN. All rights reserved.

Aurel Stein certainly agreed. In 1930, during a brief stopover in Japan en route to his fourth expedition in northwestern China, Stein found himself unable to narrate his stay in Japan in the same way that he had done for all his previous expeditions in Xinjiang. Why? In his own words, Japan was "far too 'civilized' and complex a world for that." In short, expeditions were what civilized people did in uncivilized lands. Therefore, the idea that black men from an uncivilized tribe in Africa would undertake an expedition to civilized New York was not only absurd, it was downright laughable. By 1937, however, the year of the Huffine cartoon, the laughter had become bitter-sweet. Stein, Warner, and Andrews were all decorated veterans of the expedition trail in China, responsible for removing tens of thousands of artifacts from the country for display in their own museums abroad. And yet each one had also left China in disgrace, their last expeditions obstructed by a new political force entirely unknown to previous generations of explorers.

We call this force "nationalism." From 1918 to 1937, the period between the first and second world wars, nationalism would put an end to the collecting activities of nearly every Western explorer and archaeologist in foreign lands. But what was nationalism? Simply put, it refers to the veneration and protection of the "nation" as the basis of all political legitimacy. What, then, was the "nation"? Depending on one's tastes, it could be the customs, language, culture, religion, or race of the people whom one claimed to represent in the political sphere. Such things had not previously anchored the validity of any ruler's right to rule. Throughout recorded history, political elites have invariably justified their hold on power by claiming consent or descent from superhuman forces, with God, Heaven, and dead ancestors among the most preferred. Though emperors and kings invariably pronounced their love for and duty to protect their subjects, these were the love and protection bestowed by a stern father upon his children. These children in turn were expected to direct their loyalty back toward their lone earthly sovereign, not the collective nation. By way of example, recall from chapter 1 how Karl Weber professed to undertake the excavations at Pompeii "solely out of love for Your Majesty," i.e., King Charles of Bourbon. To Weber, a Swiss-born German serving a Spanish-born king of French origin in the Italian kingdom of Naples, it would have made little sense to carry out his work on behalf of any single nation.

Nationalism provided an alternative route to power for anyone wishing to subvert the status quo. Instead of claiming consent and descent from God, Heaven, or grandpa, a nationalist need only claim consent and descent from the people who comprised his own nation, with the promise of some sort of political autonomy for that nation—hence the quixotic ideal of the "nation-state." In order to do this, a nationalist must try to convince the members of his chosen community that the cultural and ethnic ties binding them together (their national identity) are more important than the economic divisions (class identities) driving them apart. This is where art and antiquities come into play, in their ability to serve as a sort of cultural glue for the new nation. Not only does a bronze tripod from 1000 B.C. stand as a powerful testament to the artistic genius of the "Chinese nation," but it also suggests that the "Chinese nation" itself has been around continuously for over three millennia, its core identity unaltered by the passage of time.

The new national myths took root fairly quickly in China, where long-standing perceptions of cultural continuity among the elites needed only to be shared with the rest of the population. Progress on this front was much slower in the Middle East, where Muslims from all walks of life, both elite and commoner alike, failed to see much continuity with the pre-Islamic past. From the perspective of Western archaeologists, however, the only thing that mattered was the extent to which the levers of powers in the host country were held by domestic nationalist elites rather than the old imperial guard. If the former, then it hardly mattered whether or not the masses were on board with the new nationalist myths. So long as those in charge of the Egyptian government earnestly believed that their right to rule the "Egyptian nation" rested in part upon the preservation and display of Pharaonic antiquities for the benefit of that nation, then the days of foreign collecting in Egypt were numbered. The ideology of nationalism required that all ancient art and antiquities be regarded as the collective patrimony of the "Egyptian nation." From this logic it followed that artifacts could not be regarded any longer as the private possession of a single person, free to sell, donate, or display as he pleased. With antiquities now viewed as the embodiment of the collective spirit of the eternal nation—and *not* the private, temporary virtue of individual gentlemen—no form of compensation could now be accepted for their removal without committing political suicide. Nationalism had endowed these antiquities with so much ideological value that they were now literally priceless.

But wait a minute. Hadn't nationalist ideas been around for a very long time already? If so, why hadn't their effect been felt earlier? The answer is simple. Yes, nationalist ideas had been around for a long time already, dating back to the pursuit of "authenticity" and the "sublime" among the Romantic poets of the late eighteenth century. And yes, their effects had been felt earlier—just not in the Middle East or China. Recall from chapter 1 that nationalist ideas were in large part responsible for the construction of both the Luxembourg Gallery and the Louvre. The cost of both institutions was initially justified by reference to the role they were expected to play in the improvement of the "French nation." If successful, the patrons of those institutions—first the Bourbons, later the Jacobins—would find the legitimacy of their rule over the French nation to be strengthened. Once Napoleon expanded the territorial domain of the French nation far beyond the original borders of France, however, the Louvre was called upon to represent the entirety of Napoleon's empire, which meant the cultural patrimony of many different nations. All were then brought together in the Louvre as a celebration of French stewardship (nationalism) of the artistic genius of all the nations who were imagined to have contributed their talents to Western civilization (imperialism).

Once these treasures entered the Louvre, they too became priceless—priceless because they now represented French pride in ruling over a diverse empire rooted in the glorious civilizations of antiquity. Failure to ensure that all the artifacts in the French imperial collection remained in possession of the French empire was tantamount to failure to protect both the French nation and the civilizations of which it imagined itself steward. From such awareness emerged the possibility of exploiting a favorable exchange rate toward the acquisition of Ottoman antiquities. Objects regarded as worthless by the Ottomans would be regarded as priceless once removed to a European museum. In this sense, the Europeans were playing a duplicitous game—and they knew it. In 1907, when Aurel Stein managed to convince the "ignorant" Daoist priest of Dunhuang to sell him nearly ten thousand ancient manuscripts from his secret cave "library," Stein privately admitted to having manipulated his foreknowledge of the value of such manuscripts in a distant European marketplace, one inaccessible to the local priest. As Stein himself put it in a letter to his friend, he had secured the priceless hoard "for a sum which will make our friends at the British Museum chuckle." Much like his French rivals, Stein viewed his acquisitions as a reflection of British leadership (nationalism) over a diverse empire (imperialism) rooted in the glorious civilizations of yesteryear.

So what changed? The answer: World War I. The outbreak of the First World War marked a dramatic turning point for the two empires most often targeted by Western archaeologists: the Ottoman and Chinese. Prior to the war, the ruling classes of both empires had viewed themselves much as did their counterparts in European empires: as cosmopolitan gentlemen, nominally tethered to a national identity (Ottoman Turkish or Confucian Han-Manchu-Mongol), and exercising benevolent rule over a diverse array of subordinated nations—none of whose consent, by the way, was required to claim the mantle of leading nation. World War I was responsible, either directly or indirectly, for the actual or feared dismemberment of the former multi-ethnic empire into its distinct national components. With defeat, the Ottomans lost everything. In its place, the empire was replaced by a host of new states that were national in form—Turkey, Egypt, Syria, Iraq—but stubbornly diverse in composition.

In China, the effects of World War I were less direct but equally traumatic. They included the loss of central government control over Outer Mongolia, Tibet, and Xinjiang, along with the intrusion of a significant Japanese presence throughout the northeast and the interior, one that effectively turned parts of China into an informal colony of Tokyo. As a result, by the end of World War I, political elites in the lands of both former empires had been thoroughly conditioned to think in terms of the fate of "their" nation, to the exclusion of all others. To these new leaders, consent and descent from God, Heaven, or dynastic ancestors was no longer necessary or desirable. The validity of their rule was now premised entirely on consent and descent from their earthly nation. In order to demonstrate the support of that nation, the new nationalist leaders were compelled to make a great show of safeguarding the nation's cultural heritage from the covetous advances of anyone deemed outside their nation. Whether this "show" was sincere or not is beside the point. For Western archaeologists, the result was the same: obstruction.

Of course, obstruction itself was not necessarily new. As early as the 1870s, Heinrich Schliemann had faced repeated Ottoman attempts to obstruct his work at Troy. As we saw in chapter 4, the Ottomans had by that time already begun to mimic the Western treatment of antiquities and were desirous of removing such artifacts to their own museum in Constantinople. Schliemann, however, had managed to use his wealth and political connections to overcome principled Ottoman resistance. We referred to this phenomenon—the steamrolling of principled non-Western resistance by unprincipled Western force and money—as "the Schliemann precedent." One of the more significant effects of World War I, beyond its enshrinement of the national ideal, was to destroy the conditions that made possible the Schliemann precedent. How did this come about? First, the war diverted nearly all resources and personnel away from Western interests abroad and back into Europe. This initial withdrawal, followed by their mutual destruction on the battlefields of Europe, meant that the French and British (but not the United States) had to re-establish their empires abroad after the war with far fewer resources than were available to them before the war. Some, such as the Germans, never returned at all. Others, such as the Russians, were sidelined from the imperialist game for many years—and when they did return, in the guise of Bolsheviks, they preached an invigorating anti-imperialist message all their own.

Second, the unrelenting demands of the war had prompted all the European empires to draw upon the economic and political resources of their colonies (or, in the case of informal colonies such as China, subordinated ally). In exchange, they often granted vague promises of greater political autonomy or geopolitical rewards once the war was over. Many of these promises were broken. But the fact that they had been made in the first place was a sign of declining Western strength. The subsequent breaking of these promises was thus the perfect invitation to test that strength. The cumulative effect of all this was the emergence of nationalist Chinese, Egyptian, and Turkish political parties, each of which attempted to mobilize the masses to march in the streets, organize rallies, and cast their vote for nationalist causes. An essential ingredient in the unity of such groups was an insistence from their leaders on the justness of their cause, as legitimized by the consent and descent of all members of the newly besieged nations—nations now said to be rooted in the art and antiquities then being taken out of the country by foreign archaeologists.

The age of nationalist obstruction began with the "Sardis affair." From 1910 to 1914, during the twilight of the Ottoman Empire, Princeton archaeologist Howard Butler excavated the Greek, Lydian, Persian, and Roman ruins of Sardis, a site on the Anatolian peninsula some two hundred miles southeast of Troy. The dig was a product of its time and place. Permission to excavate came from the Ottomans, but all the money came from Americans such as J.P. Morgan, who had close ties to the Metropolitan Museum of Art. As with Schliemann forty years earlier, the Ottomans had enshrined into law their right to claim ownership of any and all finds. But in practice, "Schliemann's precedent" still held sway, and the American financiers of Butler's work—the "Sardis Committee"—expected to get a cut of the proceeds for their museums. Valentine Macy, a trustee of the Metropolitan, went so far as to urge Butler to "follow the policy of having everyone who leaves Sardis, whether they are visitors or not, take some 'fragments' with them."

Butler, who preferred not to antagonize the director of the Ottoman Imperial Museum and wanted to keep the collection intact, demurred. Then the war broke out, and all American personnel withdrew from Sardis. The collection of artifacts was placed in storage in Sardis, to await the outcome of the war. But the conclusion of the war, which resulted in Ottoman defeat and dismemberment, brought only more confusion and chaos. In 1919, the Greeks, acting on Allied promises of territorial gains in Turkey in exchange for wartime support, invaded the port of Izmir. Over the next two years, the Greeks continued to advance inland, coming to within fifty miles of the new Turkish capital at Ankara. Other Allied armies also occupied parts of Turkey. Then, in 1921, a Turkish counterattack on the Sakarya River began to push the Greeks back toward the sea. By 1922, the retreating Greek armies were making a beeline straight for Sardis, and Allied occupying forces were preparing to leave the country. Fearing for the safety of the artifacts still in storage, the American financiers of Butler's excavations made the unilateral decision to remove fifty-eight crates from Turkey and send them to New York for "safekeeping."

In the old days, "Schliemann's precedent" would have come into play and resolved the situation in favor of the Americans. But the Ottoman Empire was no longer—and the Republic of Turkey now called the shots. In no uncertain terms, the Sardis Committee was informed that no American archaeologist would be welcomed back into Turkey until the Sardis collection was returned in full. The committee responded with an offer that would have made Schliemann proud: the Americans would pay for all remaining artifacts at Sardis to be shipped to the museum in Istanbul, in exchange for allowing the Americans to keep the contents of the fifty-eight crates already in New York. They even tried to placate the Turks by promising to label these artifacts "Gift of the Turkish Government." The Turks refused to budge, keeping several American archaeologists and their financial backers in limbo regarding their proposed excavations in Turkey. Eventually, the Sardis Committee realized that nationalist Turkey could not be bullied about like its Ottoman predecessor. In 1924, all fifty-eight crates were shipped back to Istanbul from New York, and the Turks themselves decided which objects the Americans could accept as a "gift from the Turkish Government." (An eleventh-hour proposal to cut the Americans out of the deal entirely was shelved at the last minute.)

The balance of power had finally shifted. But was Turkey the first to shift it? Just barely. Mere months after the Turks resolved to dig their heels in against the Americans, the Egyptians took on the British. In Egypt, however, the prize was the stuff of legends: the tomb of Tutankhamun. Like the Sardis collection, the search for the treasures of King Tut had begun long before World War I. At the center of the search was the British archaeologist Howard Carter. Carter first arrived in Egypt in the 1890s to work as an apprentice alongside more established excavators such as Flinders Petrie and Percy Newberry. Carter, the son of a painter, was employed primarily as a draughtsman, producing color reproductions by hand of ancient Pharaonic temple art and hieroglyphs—an essential task in the era before color photography. In 1899, Carter was tapped by Gaston Maspero, the French director of the Egyptian Antiquities Service, to assume the duties of the chief inspector of Upper Egypt, based at Luxor. For the next five years, Carter was tasked with overseeing the management of important sites. His somewhat pedestrian duties included the installation of gates and electricity, construction of donkey parks, pursuit and persecution of tomb raiders, and paying local farmers not to use nearby ruins as fertilizer for their fields.

In 1904, Carter was promoted to chief inspector of Lower Egypt. Just one year later, a scandal at the pyramid of Saqqara led to his resignation from the government. Carter had made the grave mistake of ordering his Arab staff to defend themselves after they were assaulted by drunken French tourists who had refused to pay admission fees to the site. In a sharp rebuke, Maspero informed Carter that the setting of "natives against Europeans was not a proper thing to do." Carter, however, refused to issue an apology to the French, preferring instead to take his skills and knowledge to the open market. For the next three years, he made ends meet as an antiquities dealer for Europeans and Americans who wished to obtain their own Pharaonic antiquities from afar. Had it not been for the fortuitous arrival of a hopeless gentleman archaeologist, Carter might have continued in that capacity for many more decades.

The hopeless gentleman was the Earl of Carnarvon. Typical of his leisured class, the earl had long sojourned in Egypt, amassing a respectable collection of Pharanoic antiquities for display at his country house back home: the now famous Highclere Castle (a.k.a Downton Abbey). For no particular reason, Carnarvon one day judged himself fit to organize his own excavations in Egypt. Maspero, after issuing the earl a permit and seeing the predictably lax and messy results of his handiwork, urged him to hire a bona-fide scholar who could properly manage his digs. Carter was available and accepted the job, soon drawing an annual salary from the earl. At first, Maspero would only issue digging permits for peripheral areas, keeping them out of the most promising sites. In 1914, however, a permit for the Valley of the Kings suddenly became available. Pierre Lacau, Maspero's successor in the Antiquities Service, agreed to transfer the concession to Carnarvon.

Figure 6.2. The Earl of Carnarvon.

For six years, Carter organized annual excavations through-out the Valley of the Kings on behalf of Carnarvon. At the same time, the British took advantage of the war to abolish what little remained of Egyptian sovereignty, turning the country into a protectorate. As with many such arrangements during the war, however, subordination to the Allies was tendered with a host of promises regarding increased political autonomy after the war was over. In 1919, representatives of the Wafd, a new Egyptian political party, traveled to the Paris Peace Conference and demanded Egypt's independence. Two years of protests, demonstrations, and negotiations followed. In February 1922, the British bowed to the inevitable and declared Egypt independent. That same summer, Carnarvon called Carter to Highclere Castle and informed him of his decision to abandon the Valley of the Kings. To his great disappointment, all the time and money spent there had not resulted in a spectacular find.

Carter, as if acting out a Hollywood script, begged the earl for one last season. He was certain, he said, that the intact tomb of Tutankhamun, the boy pharaoh of the thirteenth century B.C., was still out there. Carnarvon, impressed by

Carter's tenacity, agreed to one final season. On November 1, 1922, Carter arrived back at the Valley of the Kings. Just five days later, he sent his celebrated telegram to the earl: "At last have made wonderful discovery in the Valley. A magnificent tomb with seals intact. Recovered same for your arrival. Congratulations. Carter." Carnarvon and his daughter immediately boarded a steamer and made their way to the valley. From the outset, both men assumed that the old ways of dealing with the Egyptians still constituted acceptable practice. Carnarvon informed both the Metropolitan and the British Museum that he planned on giving them the lion's share of the tomb's contents. Carter was even more blunt, telling a friend that he had found "enough stuff to fill the whole upstairs Egyptian section of the British Museum." Before long, Carter erected an iron door barring entry to the keep. For his part, Carnarvon went ahead and took the liberty of granting the London *Times* a monopoly on all press access to the tomb, a move that infuriated everyone who didn't work for the *Times*.

The sultans of old may have tolerated such shenanigans, perhaps as a means of obtaining precious diplomatic capital.

Figure 6.3. Howard Carter inspects King Tut.

But an independent Egypt, run by nationalist politicians who viewed the pharaohs as their own ancestors, would not. Within weeks of the tomb's discovery, Carter was already at loggerheads with Egyptian officials in Cairo. That communications between the two sides were often mediated through Pierre Lacau and the French-run Antiquities Service mattered not in the least bit. Lacau worked for the Egyptians, and he would do as they told him. First, Carter was ordered to turn over lists of his guests and staff for vetting by Cairo. Then he was told to host a revolving door of domestic and international dignitaries whom the Egyptians wanted to impress. Carter was already irritated at having to play the role of host for Carnarvon's endless acquaintances. Now the demands from Cairo made him bristle even more. In February 1924, not long after the "indignity" of having one of his guest lists approved by the Egyptians, Carter unilaterally closed the tomb. The response from the chief inspector of Lower Egypt—Carter's old job—was telling. He fervently hoped, he said, that he did "not get an order to blow up the disgustingly strong door by means of which you have locked up the treasures of Egypt's ancestors."

A few weeks later, that order came. The Antiquities Service revoked Carnarvon's permit, which had passed into the hands of his daughter following the earl's untimely death from malaria, the result of an untreated mosquito bite. At the same time, Egyptian soldiers traveled in person to the Valley of the Kings and cut the locks to the tomb. Pierre Lacau took the opportunity to remind Carter of his dwindling options. "The Government no longer discusses, but conveys to you its decision." Carter, channeling his innermost Schliemann, responded with a lawsuit and letters of protest to newspapers around the world. It was all to no avail. In the end, neither Carter nor the heirs of Carnarvon got a single artifact from the tomb. For the first time ever in the non-Western world, one hundred percent of the proceeds from an archaeological dig went straight into the museum of the host country. For Carter, the timing of his discovery had sealed its fate: had he discovered Tut's tomb in any of his previous six seasons of digging—before Egypt gained its independence from Britain—most of the artifacts would have ended up in London and New York. Though Carter would eventually make amends with the Antiquities Service and return to the tomb for many more years of work, he would only do so under the terms and supervision of the Egyptian authorities themselves.

"Schliemann's precedent" was over. The "mummy's curse" had arrived. Not the bogus curse conjured up by journalists looking to explain Carnarvon's untimely demise, of course, but rather the very real curse visited upon the heads of every foreign archaeologist hoping to pick up where Carter left off. We might call this "the King Tut effect." James Breasted, a professor of Egyptology at the University of Chicago and director of its Oriental Institute, was to be its first, second, third, and fourth victim. The day after the government's seizure of Tut's tomb, Breasted's son, Charles, described the affair as "only another evidence of Near Eastern bravado, of the decline of occidental prestige, and of the intoxicating effect of sudden freedom and independence upon an ignorant, decadent, mongrel people, totally unfit for self-rule." John D. Rockefeller, Jr., who had funded Breasted's previous digs in Egypt and was eager to fund more, thought little of the Arabs and Turks with whom they were obliged to work. "The men of both races," he said, "seem to have great facility in standing, sitting or lying in the sun and doing nothing."

It should thus come as little surprise to learn that neither Breasted nor Rockefeller was much deterred over the Egyptian treatment of Carter and Carnarvon. After all, the sun may have begun its descent over the British Empire, but it was only beginning to rise over that of the Americans. Surely the Egyptians would not treat the United States, bereft of colonial interests in the region, the same as they had the British? Wedded to a belief in American exceptionalism, Breasted and Rockefeller quickly got to work. In January 1926, just two years after the Tut debacle, Breasted presented a plan for a new national museum in Cairo to replace the current overcrowded one. In support of the initiative, Rockefeller approved a gift of ten million dollars. The catch? The Americans would have de facto administrative control over the museum for thirty-three years—long enough to ensure one more generation of Western initiative in Egypt— and would control the endowment indefinitely.

Incredibly, the Egyptians were not once consulted about the proposal until it was ready for the king's review. But why should that matter? "With this ammunition," Breasted proclaimed, he expected "to intoxicate the king," and boasted that "if that doesn't get a vain and self-conscious Oriental, nothing else will." Much to Breasted's surprise, the king was not in the least bit intoxicated. Instead, he erupted in anger and complained about

Figure 6.4. James Henry Breasted, American Egyptologist.

American "interference." Breasted, ever the optimist, remained unfazed by the king's outburst. He later wrote to Rockefeller's wife to assure her that such setbacks were merely the price one paid "to save these people from themselves." As was his habit, Breasted blamed French perfidy for his failures. The natives, he was convinced, were not capable of standing up to Westerners on their own. The downfall of Carter in Egypt, he believed, had been due to the machinations of Pierre Lacau in the Antiquities Service, not the initiative of Egyptians themselves. Surely the French were manipulating the king from the behind the scenes here, too, in order to make the British and Americans look bad.

The museum project was dead on arrival. But Breasted had his fingers in many pots, and was not so easily deterred. In 1927, in Turkey, he obtained the services of a German archaeologist, Hans Henning Von der Osten, to excavate on behalf of the Oriental Institute back in Chicago. The Turks, of course, had made it abundantly clear during the Sardis affair that, henceforth, anything taken out of the ground would have to remain in Turkey. Breasted ignored this precedent, however, and successfully enlisted the support of U.S. diplomats in

Ankara to press for a new and "reasonable" Turkish antiquities law. Confident that he could succeed in Turkey where he had failed in Egypt, Breasted wrote to Von der Osten to remind him to be on the lookout for "monumental returns for our collections." But the writing was on the wall, had Breasted only cared to read it. The Turks repeatedly rebuffed any and all requests to share the finds of his American-funded expeditions. Breasted's desperate claim that such generosity would "serve as a very desirable type of propaganda, reminding the Western world of the ancient background of civilization in Anatolia," was to no avail. In 1932, Breasted withdrew his team from Turkey. For their part, the Turks began to replace foreign initiative with their own domestic excavation teams. Instead of Greco-Roman ruins, the Turks chose to focus on sites such as Boğazköy and Alacahöyük, where evidence of the Hittites and their predecessors suggested an alternative civilization neglected by Westerners.

Turkey and Egypt were the first Middle Eastern states to obstruct foreign archaeological enterprise. They were also the most successful, neither yielding an inch. Iran and Iraq, two other countries in the region with a rich monumental past, had to settle for less stirring victories. But still the King Tut effect resonated. In Iran, the French, from their base in Susa, had enjoyed a monopoly on excavations throughout the country since the turn of the century. With the overthrow of the old Turkmen Qajar dynasty in 1925, however, the new nationalist-minded leaders of Iran were eager to link their political legitimacy to the country's ancient past. School textbooks were quickly infused with the message that the Iranians belonged to the "white race," which was widely believed to be "smarter and more civilized than the other races"—namely, the Arabs. In order to ground this narrative in the ancient past, the Iranians asked the French to provide a reasonable share of their finds for a new national museum in Tehran. The French, long accustomed to sending all their finds to the Louvre, offered duplicates and plaster casts in return. This snub led to the abolition of the French monopoly in all regions of the country except for Susa. By 1928, a division of 50/50 had become common practice for all foreign digs in Iran.

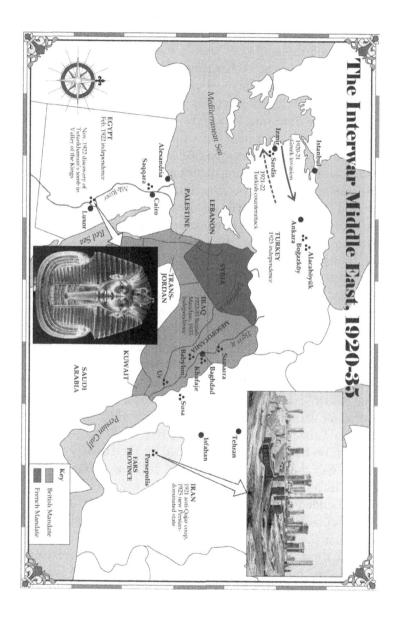

The Interwar Middle East, 1920-35

EGYPT
Feb. 1922 independence
Nov. 1922 discovery of
Tutankhamun's tomb in
Valley of the Kings

Alexandria
Saqqara
Cairo
Luxor

Nile River

Red Sea

Mediterranean Sea

Istanbul

Izmir
Sardis
1920-21
Greek invasion
1921-22
Turkish counterattack

TURKEY
1923 independence

Alacahöyük
Ankara
Boğazköy

PALESTINE

LEBANON

SYRIA

TRANS-
JORDAN

Euphrates R.

IRAQ
1922-33 British
Mandate, 1933
independence

Tigris R.

Samarra
Baghdad
Khafaje
Babylon
Susa
Ur

SAUDI
ARABIA

KUWAIT

Persian Gulf

Tehran

Isfahan

Persepolis

FARS
PROVINCE

IRAN
1921 anti-Qajar coup,
1925 new Persian-
dominated state

Key

British Mandate

French Mandate

In 1930, Ernst Herzfeld, another German scholar employed on behalf of Breasted's Oriental Institute, won the concession for Persepolis. Persepolis, the ceremonial center of the Achaemenid rulers (547–330 B.C.) founded by Darius I, was the most important archaeological site in Iran. Centrally located in Fars Province, now viewed as the Iranian "homeland" by nationalist intellectuals, Persepolis was an attractive target for the new state. Though the Iranians were still obliged to rely on foreign scientific expertise and capital, they increasingly came to view the 50/50 *partage* arrangement as unbecoming for a site as important as Persepolis. In 1934, following several years of work by Herzfeld and Breasted, Tehran decided to take a more principled stand. This took the form of an "exception clause" in the existing *partage* arrangement, one that stipulated a new Tut-like distribution of finds: 100% for the Iranians. Breasted, convinced the Iranians were bluffing, called on American diplomatic support. "The Oriental," he informed his son, "has to be told very decidedly where he gets off." The impasse was resolved with an equitable division for that season, but all future seasons of work at Persepolis would proceed according to the new exception clause. The very next year, Herzfeld halted all work at the site and left the country. Breasted reacted with his typical racist invective. "To put it very mildly," he wrote to one of his friends, "if there are any loathsome vermin anywhere on the surface of the earth worse than the Persians, I do not know where it might be!"

It was on Iraq that Breasted pinned his final hope. A formal mandate of the British since the end of the war, Iraq did not obtain its independence until 1933, one year after the British recommended its entry into the League of Nations. The next year, Sati' al-Husri, the former director-general of education, took over the management of antiquities. Al-Husri assessed the situation in his country and found it most depressing. Records and holdings for the national museum were grossly incomplete, and most of the items on display were from the pre-Islamic period, a reflection of the Western ideological bias. When a foreign visitor to the Iraqi museum in Baghdad told al-Husri how "astonished" he had been upon "not finding Arab or Islamic antiquities in the museum of a city that was once the Abbasid capital," al-Husri resolved to correct the imbalance. He began by drafting new, stricter export laws, and vowed to enforce existing stipulations that had long since been neglected. Just as with Schliemann during the Ottoman empire a half century earlier, the laws themselves were already on the books: they just needed someone willing to enforce them.

Sati' al-Husri proved more than up to the challenge. First, he informed all foreign expeditions that their excavations would have to be supervised by Iraqi officials, in accordance with the law. Second, and more important, he announced that the practice of *partage*, long manipulated by foreign excavators to their own benefit, would now be subject to Iraqi oversight. In early 1935, al-Husri decided to make an example of a site at Khafaje under the direction of one of Breasted's colleagues. After the available antiquities were laid in two equal rows along a long table, al-Husri asked Julius Jordan, his German director of antiquities, which objects were unique and unrepresented in the Baghdad museum. Jordan, unaware of what al-Husri intended to do, duly pointed them out. Al-Husri's next move stunned everyone present: he moved seventeen artifacts identified by Jordan to the side, and informed those assembled that these would not be part of the division. The message was clear: the foreigners would no longer determine which share of the spoils went to Iraq, and which share went abroad. The Iraqis would now take the best of everything—or the foreigners would get nothing.

Breasted was furious. Now, he said, he would have to take it upon himself to deal with "these ignorant and fanatical Iraqis." Apparently, Breasted had not learned anything from his past experiences in Egypt, Turkey, and Iran. Taking a page from the playbook of Howard Carter, who had accused Lacau of hindering the goals of science, Breasted made the same appeal to al-Husri, suggesting that Iraqi "obstruction" of his excavations was tantamount to the obstruction of scientific progress itself. In other words, if the young Iraqi state wanted to prove its credentials as a modern, enlightened nation, it could only do so by bending to the will of the more progressive Americans. Al-Husri would not be intimidated. The Oriental Institute had received so many antiquities from Iraq, he said, that Chicago now had a better collection than did Baghdad. As for science, its interests could be served just as well in Iraq as anywhere else. Nor was the specter of instability in his country persuasive to al-Husri: World War I, he said, had deprived Westerners of all moral high ground on that front. Finally, in an ironic inversion of the Sardis affair, when the trustees of the Metropolitan Museum of Art offered to attach to the artifacts in its possession a label reading "Gift of the Turkish Government," al-Husri promised to do the same for any artifacts found by foreigners and placed in the Baghdad museum.

By the end of 1935, James Breasted was dead. His passing marked the end of an era. Before long, the outbreak of the Second World War led to yet another withdrawal of foreign personnel and money from archaeological sites throughout Iraq and the rest of the Middle East. In the meantime, Sati' al-Husri sponsored the first Iraqi-led dig at Samarra, a short-lived Abbasid capital north of Baghdad. There, his team focused on recovering antiquities related to Islamic and Arabic history. Much like the Egyptians, Turks, and Iranians before them, the Iraqis, too, would now determine which of their country's many pasts were most suitable for present-day nationalist agendas. By the time World War II was over, the training of native archaeologists in all four states was complete. The mummy's curse, destined to be celebrated in the novels of literary Pharaonism, had finally driven the foreigners from their country.

The situation in China revealed strange parallels with what had occurred in the Middle East. As in Egypt, the Paris Peace Conference served as a backdrop for the assertion of nationalist indignation among intellectuals back home. Led to believe that participation in World War I on the side of the Allies would lead to the return of German colonial holdings in Shandong, the Chinese were shocked to learn of a secret agreement promising the transfer of these territories to Japan instead. The "betrayal at Versailles" prompted demonstrations in the streets of Beijing and eventually compelled the Chinese representative in Paris to withdraw his signature from the peace treaty. Similarly, as in Turkey, the postwar Chinese state was beset by military confrontations throughout the land. Though these were distinct from the Greco-Turkish wars in mostly pitting Chinese against Chinese, they produced a similar result: few expeditions or excavations could proceed while the land was at war. During this chaotic interlude, nationalist political parties seized upon China's various humiliations to organize the masses and agitate for a new central government capable of restoring Chinese sovereignty throughout the land. From 1919 to 1923, much like the emergence of the Wafd Party in Egypt, Sun Yat-sen reassembled his long-suffering Nationalist Party and established a new base in Guangzhou. At the same time, in 1921, the Chinese Communist Party was founded in Shanghai.

But here the parallels with the Middle East end. Unlike in Egypt, Turkey, Iraq, or Iran, the wartime exodus of Westerners in China did not lead to a reprieve of any sort for the Chinese. For into the space vacated by the Europeans and Americans immediately stepped the Japanese. This meant that China, though still formally independent, was subject to continuous and unrelenting political and military pressure throughout the age of Western expeditions. Amid such a hostile environment, no Chinese central government would be able to exercise effective control over the entirety of the country until after the Japanese were defeated in 1945. Even then, the outbreak of civil war would push back the restoration of full sovereignty for another four years, to the rise of the Communist government in 1949. What were the implications of all this for foreign archaeology in China? Above all, it meant that the first, second, third, and fourth priorities of every politician in China were the restoration of domestic political sovereignty. In other words, Chinese politicians were consumed with the confrontation of other Chinese warlords or the Japanese. They had precious little time or resources to confront Indiana Jones.

As a result, nearly all the frustrations experienced by foreign archaeologists in China during the 1920s and 30s would ultimately trace their origins to nationalist-minded individuals or organizations operating outside the auspices of the government. The central government, first in Beijing and later in Nanjing and Chongqing, was too preoccupied with self-preservation and nonstop warfare to take the initiative. Of course, once galvanized, both warlords and the

Nationalist Party would make belated room in their political agendas for the concerns of nationalist scholars—but only if those scholars raised a sufficiently loud ruckus first. Unlike in the Middle East, politicians in China did not take the lead in matters of cultural sovereignty. Instead, this role would fall to Confucian gentlemen in nationalist guise. True adherents of the old Confucian order, men such as Luo Zhenyu, who led the first major breakthrough on the oracle bone script, were not nationalists. Even after the 1911 revolution, these men had remained loyal to the old cosmopolitan imperial order, respecting the principles of "finders keepers" and the private ownership of art. They were also willing to collaborate with anyone—Japanese scholars, European sinologists—who were interested in the Chinese past, regardless of present-day political sympathies or past removals of Chinese art. This was a *culturalist* orientation, not a nationalist one. So long as Chinese art and antiquities were preserved, cherished, and studied, it did not matter who did the preserving, cherishing, and studying—or where they did it—provided they shared the fruits of their labor among one another.

The new breed of nationalist scholars was represented by men like William Hung. Born in 1893 to a Qing official and educated in the Confucian classics, Hung later enrolled in foreign missionary schools and obtained fluency in English and German. His childhood familiarity with Western education, evident in his adoption of a foreign first name (his Chinese name was Hong Ye), culminated in two degrees from American universities, including a master's from Columbia. In 1922, upon his return to China, Hung joined the faculty of Yenching University, a leading Christian university in Beijing founded by foreign missionaries with ties to Harvard. The very next year, Langdon Warner, whose preservation of the *Saturday Evening Post* cartoon kicked off this chapter, arrived in Beijing. With him was Horace Jayne, curator of Oriental Art at the Pennsylvania Museum in Philadelphia. Their goal was Dunhuang, where they hoped to acquire photographs and artifacts that would assist in the development of the "Oriental collections" of the fledgling Fogg Museum and encourage "advanced studies in Far Eastern art and archaeology" at Harvard University.

The first expedition (1923–24) was considered a modest success. Upon reaching Dunhuang, Warner and Jayne saw for the first time the destruction visited upon some of the cave murals by White Russian soldiers who had been interned at Dunhuang by Chinese authorities two years earlier—a grim reminder of the priorities of Chinese officials, for whom the preservation of law and order loomed larger than the preservation of desert art. Seeing the damage, Warner resolved to remove twelve of the hundreds of cave murals to "safekeeping" in America. The unsightly holes left by Warner are still visible today. Confident that his actions had not aroused any suspicions—the local Chinese officials knew what he had done and seemed to be okay with it—Warner left China and prepared for a second expedition to Dunhuang. This time, intending to remove even more murals and artifacts for the Fogg, Warner brought along a team of five additional specialists to aid in their removal. In 1925, they secured their visas from the warlord government in Beijing and set off for Dunhuang.

Unbeknownst to Warner, prior to his team's departure from Beijing, the Chinese interpreter from his first expedition, Wang Jinren, had paid a secret visit to William Hung, now the dean of Yenching University. In that meeting, Wang told Hung about what Warner had done at Dunhuang the previous year. Hung mulled his options. Neither he nor Wang could do anything about the larger political situation in China, where a revolving door of warlords in Beijing routinely issued permits and visas to any foreigner able to make it worth their while. As a result, it was clear that nothing could prevent Warner from reaching Dunhuang. Once there, however, it just might be possible to restrict his freedom of movement. Hung decided to meet with Qin Fen, the minister of education, and asked him to send a secret telegram to all the local officials along Warner's route. In it, they were ordered to "provide these friends with ample protection and courteous treatment, but on no account allow them to touch any historical relics."

Their plan worked. Everywhere Warner's team went, they were politely informed by the local Chinese magistrate that they could not allow the removal of any antiquities, though they were permitted to take photographs and make

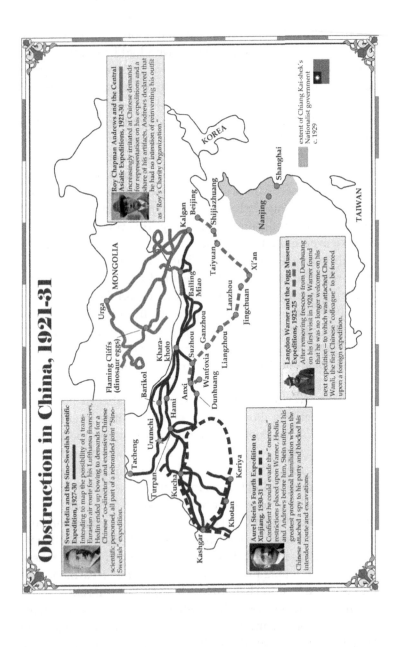

Obstruction in China, 1921-31

Sven Hedin and the Sino-Swedish Scientific Expedition, 1927-30 ▬▬▬
Intending to map the possibility of a trans-Eurasian air route for his Lufthansa financiers, Hedin ended up bowing to demands for a Chinese "co-director" and extensive Chinese scientific personnel, all part of a rebranded joint "Sino-Swedish" expedition.

Roy Chapman Andrews and the Central Asiatic Expeditions, 1921-30 ▬▬▬
increasingly irritated at Chinese demands for representation on his expeditions and a share of his artifacts, Andrews declared that he had no intention of reinventing his outfit as "Roy's Charity Organization."

Langdon Warner and the Fogg Museum Expeditions, 1923-25 ▪▪▪▪
After removing frescoes from Dunhuang on his first visit in 1924, Warner found that he was no longer welcome on his next expedition – to which was attached Chen Wanli, the first Chinese "colleague" to be forced upon a foreign expedition.

Aurel Stein's Fourth Expedition to Xinjiang, 1930-31 ▪▪▪▪
Confident he could evade the "onerous" restrictions placed upon Warner, Hedin, and Andrews before him, Stein suffered his greatest professional humiliation when the Chinese attached a spy to his party and blocked his intended route and excavations.

extent of Chiang Kai-shek's Nationalist government c. 1929

KOREA

MONGOLIA

TAIWAN

Urga
Flaming Cliffs (dinosaur eggs)
Kalgan
Beijing
Shijiazhuang
Taiyuan
Xi'an
Shanghai
Nanjing
Bailing Miao
Kharakhoto
Suzhou
Ganzhou
Lanzhou
Liangzhou
Jingchuan
Barkol
Anxi
Wanfoxia
Dunhuang
Hami
Tacheng
Urumchi
Turpan
Kucha
Keriya
Kashgar
Khotan

transcriptions. When they reached Dunhuang, the restrictions tightened even further. Unlike in Xinjiang, where the Muslim masses expressed indifference toward the Buddhist antiquities in their midst, the peasants of Dunhuang were Chinese—and they were Buddhists. This meant that the cave murals of Dunhuang were still objects of active worship by the local population. To be sure, Stein, Pelliot, and others had managed to take tens of thousands of ancient manuscripts from the Dunhuang caves. But these things were not cherished by the illiterate masses. The murals and Buddhist statuary removed by Warner, however, most definitely were. The local magistrate, Yang Yiwen, explained the situation to the Americans. Suffering from a failed harvest and the prospect of starvation, the locals seemed to have put two and two together and associated Warner's removal of the murals with the wrath of the gods. As a result, once the removal of the murals became known, "the local people went *en masse* to the magistrate to question him about this matter." They then declared that they would not "release" the magistrate until he "returned those wall paintings peeled away by Warner."

Faced with both the threat of physical violence from his own subjects in Dunhuang and a heartfelt nationalist plea from the minister of education in Beijing, Magistrate Yang decided to prioritize his own career over that of Warner's. Nationalism, with a little bit of help from starving, superstitious peasants, had raised the value of the Dunhuang murals beyond what any politician was willing to pay. For the first time in modern Chinese history, a foreign expedition was forced to leave China empty-handed. It would not be the last. In 1926, just one year after Warner's retreat from Dunhuang, the Swedish explorer Sven Hedin returned to China with the intent of mapping a trans-Eurasian air route through Inner Mongolia and Xinjiang for his Lufthansa financiers. To the Chinese, he framed his expedition primarily in terms of its archaeological and geological research agenda. In support of these ostensibly scientific aims, Hedin also proposed an "investigation into whether or not airplanes could be used to survey the land."

Thirty years had passed since Hedin's last expedition to Xinjiang. Back then he had been a nameless upstart eager to prove his mettle, with two dead Uighur porters to show for it. Now he was a world-famous explorer who wrote best-sellers, consorted with royalty, and flaunted his many honors and titles. By contrast, Langdon Warner was a modest college professor who shied away from the public limelight. Hedin, however, was an international celebrity who craved the stage. Stopping Hedin would require far more manpower than that marshaled by William Hung to obstruct Warner. Throughout the second Fogg Expedition, Hung had opted to maintain a low profile, work from behind the scenes, and maintain face for all parties involved. Such methods would not work against Hedin, who would be quick to turn any Chinese resistance into an international media debacle. To take down the wily old Swede, the Chinese would not only have to unite—they would have to make a public show of their nationalist unity.

No help, of course, could be expected from the warlord government then in possession of Beijing. Zhang Zuolin, the "tiger of Manchuria," duly affixed his seal to Hedin's passport and ordered the local officials en route to provide all necessary protection and assistance. In response, Chinese scholars at several universities and research institutes in Beijing managed to organize a united front. It took the form of a hastily convened Association of Chinese Scholarly Organizations, which proceeded to issue public pronouncements in the press expressing concern for the ultimate fate of any antiquities collected in the course of the expedition. In addition, they noted the glaring absence of any Chinese personnel among Hedin's ranks. In this day and age, they noted, the only acceptable solution was to reorganize the Swedish-German expedition as a joint Sino-Swedish expedition. Furthermore, the very use of the word "expedition"—*yuanzhengdui* in Chinese, literally "long-distance marching team"—was now deemed derogatory. In a telling preview of the *Saturday Evening Post* cartoon published ten years later, these Chinese scholars apparently also believed that "expeditions" were what civilized people did in uncivilized lands. Therefore, to allow Hedin to undertake an "expedition" in China was to concede that China was indeed uncivilized.

The end result, hammered out over six months of grueling negotiations, was the formation of a joint Sino-Swedish

Northwest Scientific Survey. Instead of only Swedish and German personnel, the "survey" now contained five Chinese scholars and five additional Chinese students. Not only that, but one of the Chinese scholars, Xu Bingxu, dean and professor of philosophy and history at Beijing University, was appointed co-director of the survey alongside Hedin. The symbolic importance of such a power-sharing arrangement was unprecedented, both in China and the Middle East. (This was not the first time the faculty of Beijing University had attempted to insert their colleagues into a foreign expedition, however. In 1925, they prevailed upon Langdon Warner to take into his party Chen Wanli, a professor in the School of Medicine. Though Chen was a legitimate member of Warner's team, he did not share any decision-making authority with Warner himself.) Now, having attained a status equal to that of the foreigners, one of the Chinese archaeologists included in Hedin's survey, Huang Wenbi, made it clear that henceforth, the Chinese would be in charge. "Our task was twofold," Huang wrote in his diary. "On the one hand, we were to supervise the foreigners, and on the other hand we were to carry out scientific investigations." The order in which these priorities was expressed was not a coincidence.

Figure 6.7. Sino-Swedish Expedition Commemorative Stamp. The decision by Hedin in 1927 to bow to demands from Chinese scholars in Beijing for a joint expedition was deemed so momentous by the Chinese government that a special stamp was commissioned to commemorate the event.

With the appointment of Xu Bingxu as co-director of the expedition and the support of numerous Chinese scholars on Hedin's dime, the Chinese intellectual community of Beijing had accomplished what their warlord leaders either would not or could not. In the end, nationalist scholars employed outside of government auspices had effectively shamed their own politicians into compliance with the new nationalist appraisal of the value of Chinese antiquities. Roy Chapman Andrews, Hedin's friend and fellow explorer, seconded this conclusion when he observed that the Association of Chinese Scholarly Organizations, "an entirely unofficial organization," had managed to arouse "such popular indignation that the government authorities dared not ignore its activities." Much like the King Tut effect, "the Hedin effect" resonated through-out archaeological circles in China. Aurel Stein, writing several years later in 1930 on the eve of his own expedition, noted the appraisal of a British diplomat, who foresaw in Stein's proposed expedition "difficulties ... on account of the unsatis-factory conditions which have been imposed upon & accepted by Chapman Andrews & Sven Hedin."

Hedin was the first foreign explorer to succumb to the demands of Chinese scholars in Beijing. Roy Chapman Andrews was the second. Since 1919, Andrews had been leading successive paleontological expeditions to Inner and Outer Mongolia on behalf of his home institution in New York, the American Museum of Natural History. Supported by Henry Osborne, the museum's president, Andrews set out to find fossil evidence of the "missing link" between man and ape. If found, it would provide fodder for a highly racist yet fashionable theory peddled by Osborne: that *homo sapiens* were descended from the more palatable "Mongoloid" stock of Central Asia rather than the undesirable "Negroid" stock of black Africa. In more than a decade of exploration, Andrews found nothing of the sort. But he did find some dinosaur eggs, which he used to drum up popular and philanthropic support for his expeditions in influential New York circles.

By 1928, Andrews was ready for yet another expedition to Chinese-held Inner Mongolia. He knew full well the fate of Hedin's expedition of the previous year, and resolved to avoid its fate. Working in tight secrecy, Andrews managed to secure his passport through the auspices of (who else?) Zhang Zuolin, the warlord of Beijing. Shirking all public fanfare and press, Andrews' team slipped out of Beijing without being detected by the Association of Chinese Scholarly Organizations. But the association could not be deceived for long. Upon his return to Beijing, the Chinese scholars again worked to shame their own politicians into action and force Andrews to share his finds with them. Andrews, a proud and arrogant man, could not imagine doing as Hedin had done. Dismissing the Chinese scholars as "returned students who absorbed a superficial level of Western culture" and suffer from an "inferiority complex," Andrews decided to cancel his next expedition and instead listened to Japanese proposals for a new expedition in their colonial domains in the northeast. Walter Granger, a colleague of Andrews and a frequent participant in his expeditions, said that submission to Chinese demands would reduce the Central Asiatic Expeditions to little more than "Roy's Charity Organization."

By this time, the loose conglomeration of Chinese scholarly organizations had coalesced around a much more tightly knit body: the Commission for the Preservation of Chinese Antiquities. Founded in 1928 in Beijing in the wake of the Sino-Swedish expedition, the commission faced the same intractable problems confronted by both William Hung and the Association of Chinese Scholarly Organizations before it: their own leaders. It wasn't that Chinese politicians were entirely unprincipled. Most of them had principles. But in the trying domestic conditions of the 1920s and 30s, they had to prioritize these principles. For them, national and political survival always came first. If they thought about art and antiquities at all, the first thing that came to mind was probably the fate of the collection of the National Palace Museum, which lay right before their eyes. Foreign expeditions to the distant borderlands, however, were out of sight and out of mind. Furthermore, the backing of powerful foreign governments meant it was often possible to squeeze precious diplomatic capital or other favors from these governments in exchange for a passport. And last but not least, against the backdrop of a divided China torn by rival warlord jurisdictions, it was also an opportunity for the central government—be it in the hands of warlords or an organized political party—to impose its authority upon domestic rivals by forcing them to accept the marching orders of a distant government. In other words, this was infiltration by foreign scientific proxy, a modern-day version of the Trojan horse.

This was clearly the thinking behind the approval of Aurel Stein's fourth and final expedition to Xinjiang in 1930. But this time, instead of warlords, the seal on Stein's passport was none other than that of the Minister of Foreign Affairs in Chiang Kai-shek's Nationalist government, which had recently moved the national capital to Nanjing. The Nationalists, as their name suggests, were a highly organized Leninist par-ty-state devoted to the restoration of nationalist Chinese sovereignty throughout the former Qing Empire. To this day, from their island of exile on Taiwan, the Nationalist government continues to produce maps that portray "Outer Mongolia"—the independent state of Mongolia—as part of the Republic of China. In 1930, however, this same Nationalist Party was willing to grant Stein a passport for another expe-dition to Xinjiang without throwing a single obstacle in his way. After obtaining his passport in Nanjing, Stein revealed his own amazement at how easy it had been. In his meeting with Wang Zhengting, the foreign minister, Stein later noted how "no reference had been made to that 'National Council' at Peking [Beijing] and the conditions it might wish to impose." According to Stein, Eric Teichman, one of the British diplo-mats in charge of his passport negotiations, was "pleasantly surprised of easily secured result."

Why were the Nationalists so eager to grant Stein a pass-port? By this time, a clear precedent had been established by the nationalist Chinese scholars in Beijing, who had already sabotaged or otherwise impeded the expeditions of Langdon Warner, Sven Hedin, and Roy Chapman Andrews. Stein knew all about these precedents, as did his American patrons who still hoped to fill the cabinets of the Fogg Museum at Harvard. In fact, the only reason the Americans even approached Stein in the first place was because they believed that he—and he

Figure 6.8. Marc Aurel Stein.

alone—had the prestige, experience, and close relationships with Chinese officials in Xinjiang capable of overcoming the principled opposition of the scholars in Beijing. Again and again, Stein assured his patrons that "Old China," which respected the principles of "finders keepers" and a gentleman's right to dispose of art and antiquities as he saw fit, could still prevail over the forces of "Young China," which viewed all art and antiquities as the non-negotiable patrimony of the "Chinese people."

So why, to answer our question, did the Nationalists, the political embodiment of "Young China," continue to treat Stein as the mandarins of "Old China" once did? The answer is a familiar one: politics. The Nationalists, despite having obtained global and domestic recognition of their authority over all of China, did not actually exercise that authority anywhere on the ground outside of the Yangzi River delta. The rest of the country was still run by the same old warlords of yesteryear, each of which had simply exchanged his previous titles and flags for Nationalist titles and flags. Therefore, to send Stein into Xinjiang with Nationalist papers was one more way for Nanjing to force the warlord governor of that province, Jin Shuren, to recognize and respect the authority of the new government at Nanjing. The Sino-Swedish expedition had also benefitted from this strategy. In 1929, just one year before Stein obtained his passport, Hedin and his colleagues were expelled from Xinjiang by Governor Jin, who rightly feared political infiltration of his province under the unobjectionable guise of science. When Hedin arrived in Nanjing to protest this treatment, the Nationalists were quick to lock horns with the governor on his behalf. After providing Hedin with a new passport, the Nationalists urged him to return to Xinjiang without delay, for "an order from the Central Government required no answer since in practice it must be obeyed." When Jin continued to resist Hedin's re-entry, Liu Fu, a professor of literature at Beijing University, warned Nanjing of the consequences should the governor's will prevail. "It seems that orders from the central government must be approved by Governor Jin first," Liu wrote from Beijing. "For a Chinese citizen equipped with a passport issued from his own central government to be unable to travel within the borders of our country—this is a frightening prospect."

Unfortunately for Stein, neither Liu Fu nor any other member of the Beijing intelligentsia was willing to go to bat for him as they had once done for Hedin. Hedin, after all, had submitted to their demands, most notably by sharing leadership duties with a Chinese co-director, paying the expenses of Chinese scholars appointed to his expedition, and leaving all archaeological proceeds in China. Stein had not even met with the commission, to say nothing of offering any concessions to nationalist sentiment. This left both Stein and, ironically, his patrons in the *Nationalist* government vulnerable to a nationalist counterattack from the Antiquities Commission in Beijing. In the summer of 1930, as Stein prepared to cross over into Xinjiang via an old Himalayan route, the commission issued a devastating press release. In it, nineteen of the most eminent scholars in China accused him of having engaged in "commercial vandalism" on his first three expeditions. Stein's acquisition of ten thousand manuscripts from the cave library at Dunhuang in 1907 was described as a "dishonourable act," one that Stein "gleefully" recounted in his books "without the least shame." With that, the first nationalist salvo was launched. Other Chinese scholars soon entered the fray, calling Stein the greatest "thief" ever to "plunder" China's national heritage.

As with the expeditions of previous explorers, nationalist scholars employed outside of government had managed to shame their own leaders into compliance with new nationalist principles. Now that all of the antiquities sought by Stein had been infused by Chinese nationalists with a new value—i.e., priceless—the political benefits of impinging on the domain of a rival warlord in Xinjiang were subsequently devalued for the Nationalist government. Anyone responsible for the removal of antiquities from Chinese territory would now be branded a traitor to the "Chinese people" themselves. Stein's reputation as a scholar *outside* of China could—and did—withstand such an assault. But Nationalist aspirations of claiming a reputation as the defender of Chinese sovereignty *inside* China could not. In a desperate attempt to stave off political suicide, the Nationalists cancelled Stein's passport and ordered him out of the country. "The duplicity and craftiness on display here is truly despicable," wrote Chiang Kai-shek himself. "Send a stern telegram to the provincial government in Xinjiang that they are to observe and implement the many orders we have issued, and expel him from the province."

For Stein, the sense of betrayal was acute. As he left China for the last time, this time in disgrace, the old Hungarian deplored "the obstacles which unjustified agitation has raised against the continued work of a confrere who had done as much as any one to throw light on the great and beneficial part played by ancient China in the history of Central Asia." In Stein's eyes, he was a "confrere" of China—a colleague. The cosmopolitan Confucian elite of "Old China" would have fully concurred with that sentiment. But the nationalist Chinese intellectuals of "Young China" did not. To them, he was a criminal. Such was the dramatic transformation wrought by the power of nationalist ideas, all in the course of a single generation.

Six years after Stein's disgrace, Langdon Warner and Roy Chapman Andrews took solace in the pages of the *Saturday Evening Post*, where the notion of anyone but a white man undertaking an archaeological expedition was roundly mocked: "He say dey is a expedition, come heah to get stuff fo' dey museum."

But the Chinese, now masters of their domain, had already begun to imagine a world in which the role reversals suggested by the Huffine cartoon came true. "When will our countrymen measure up to the Stein and Pelliot spirit," asked one Chinese pundit in 1936, "venture out into the world, unearth and gather up exquisite cultural treasures, and bring them back to our country, all for the greater glory of our nation?"

For any Westerner long accustomed to getting his way in foreign lands, the laughter was bittersweet, indeed.

Continue the journey at indianajonesinhistory.com:

- EPISODE IX: Tutankhamun
- EPISODE X: The Mummy's Curse
- EPISODE XVI: Foreign Devils Begone

CHAPTER SEVEN

Scholars at War

On July 2, 1937, the famed American aviator Amelia Earhart vanished somewhere over the southwestern Pacific Ocean. Over the next eight decades, many theories would be put forth to explain her disappearance, some of them outlandish. One of the more provocative is the suggestion that the Japanese had something to do with it. After all, the nearby waters and atolls of Micronesia, seized by Japan from Germany during World War I, were home to numerous military fortifications built in violation of the League of Nations "mandate" granted to Tokyo after the war. Perhaps the Japanese had shot down Earhart's plane after she "inadvertently" flew over one of their illegal bases? Or maybe, after an innocent crash landing, the Japanese navy found her first, concluded she was a spy, and threw her in jail? If any evidence ever emerged to support the theory, it would go some way toward explaining why some Pacific Islanders later claimed to have seen Earhart in a remote part of the Marshall Islands after her supposed capture by Japanese authorities.

A likely story? No. A plausible one? Absolutely. The idea that the Japanese suspected Earhart of being an American spy—and treated her unlikely passage through Micronesia accordingly—was merely the projection of a long established Euro-American precedent onto a geopolitical rival. That is to say, the outlandish rumor of Japanese perfidy was able to gain so much traction precisely because Western explorers and archaeologists themselves nearly *always* doubled as intelligence agents for their home governments. It stood to reason, then, that the Japanese probably did the same, and would naturally suspect explorers from rival states of also engaging in such time-honored practices. In the final analysis, Amelia

Earhart was probably not an American spy, and accusations of Japanese treachery are almost certainly off the mark. But if new evidence ever emerges to suggest that she was a spy, it should not surprise us in the least.

Why? The answer is simple: for nearly two hundred years, explorers and archaeologists possessed a rare yet easily transferable skill set, one whose ultimate application depended upon the wishes of their patron. More often than not, that patron was the government—if not always in terms of money, then certainly in terms of diplomatic support. As a result, no explorer or archaeologist desirous of gaining entry into distant lands could expect to avoid the inevitable request, often tendered with a subtle dose of patriotic encouragement, to help collect sensitive information about the internal conditions of a rival state. As for their rare skill set? It usually consisted of several (and sometimes all) of the following talents: cartography, navigation, engineering, prospecting, wilderness survival, fluency in foreign languages, proficiency in firearms, knowledge of foreign cultures and customs, and proven leadership abilities. Nearly all of these skills were acquired either in universities or the military. It is thus little wonder that the majority of Western explorers and archaeologists were veterans of both institutions. (Recall from chapter 1 that both Alcubierre and Weber, the first men to oversee the Pompeii excavations, were military engineers by training.)

All four expeditions of Aurel Stein into Xinjiang even went so far as to include Indian assistants on loan from the armed services of the British Raj, responsible for producing maps, elevations, and other geological data. The French sinologist Paul Pelliot, who took the cream of the Dunhuang cave library crop just one year after Stein, had even distinguished himself on the actual field of battle, earning recognition as a chevalier of the Legion of Honor for his valor and bravery during the Boxer War of 1901. That men like Stein and Pelliot in turn expected strict martial compliance from anyone serving on their expeditions is evident in the language Stein once used to describe an attempt to test his decision-making authority by one of his Indian assistants. "Had to hurry on Ram Singh who was taking his meal at 8 AM declaring he could not get up earlier," Stein wrote in his diary entry for December 14, 1906. "Insolent attitude & outburst on account of my remonstrating. Attempts to leave by asking camelmen to unload. Stopped this barefaced insubordination." *Insolent. Insubordination.* These are the words of an officer who has been challenged by an enlisted man. Even more galling to Stein was the fact that his Indian subordinate had further "presume[d] to state his opinion about me personally." The next day, after Ram Singh had "come to better sense" and apologized, Stein nonetheless insisted on a "written reply to my Memo calling for explanations." This was military discipline, and Ram Singh was lucky to get off so lightly: Hasan Akhun, the camel factotum, was once sentenced by Stein to a public whipping for his part in a brawl. The resulting welts, Stein informs us, "had a very salutary effect upon the young offender."

All this is to say that most archaeologists felt quite at ease in the presence of soldiers and guns, and did not distinguish as clearly between military and civilian spheres as we might do so today. This meant that topographical and geological data, easily collected in the course of hunting down antiquities, would invariably be shared with the relevant government organs back home. Stein, who made a point of avoiding routes already mapped by others, turned all of his survey data over to the Trigonometrical Survey of the Raj as a matter of course. But he was not alone in making detailed field notes of foreign topography. The journal of Gustav Mannerheim, a Finnish member of Paul Pelliot's 1907 French expedition to Xinjiang, also reveals an acute interest in local defense capabilities and strategic infrastructure. "The improvements necessary to make the road suitable for heavy vehicles are insignificant," he noted in the oasis town of Yangi-hissar. On another occasion, he described "one more valley that crept up to within about 300 paces of the fortress and might some day afford welcome protection to an advancing enemy." He then crossed over what he described as "an easily destructible bridge over the moat, about 35 feet wide."

Not surprisingly, the Ottomans and Chinese were none too keen to permit such observations. In fact, prior to World War I, the only consistent objections raised by Ottoman, Egyptian, or Chinese officials tasked with hosting foreign expeditions related not to their removal of antiquities, but to their attempts to gain access to sites of potential strategic significance. On his first expedition in 1901, Stein noted the contrasting reception afforded him by the local civilian and military authorities. "On the 19th I went to call on Pan-Darin," Stein wrote in his diary, referring to the local civilian magistrate, "with whom I had a long and cheering interview." Later that same day, however, after a clearing in the weather revealed the outline of a nearby mountain range, Stein found that "permission to use the ramparts of the Yangi Shahr for theodolite observations was refused by the Military Commandant, evidently to Pan-Darin's regret." Surely the British could sympathize with the commandant's fears: from 1902 to 1914, when Count Otani Kozui organized three Japanese expeditions to Xinjiang in search of Buddhist manuscripts and antiquities, the British consul in Kashgar was absolutely convinced they were a thinly veiled pretext for espionage. The British made their suspicions of Japanese motives so well known, in fact, that in 1910 Count Otani took the remarkable step of hiring a sixteen-year-old boy named Orlando Hobbs from England to accompany the final expedition, with the sole intent of allaying British suspicions. (Tragically, Hobbs contracted smallpox and died just a few months after his arrival.)

These examples reveal a disturbing trend: science as a cover for espionage. The reason the British suspected the Japanese of using an archaeological expedition as a clever pretext for spying was because they did the same thing themselves. Science was the perfect cover, for anyone who questioned its pursuit risked branding himself an obstacle to progress. And from there it was a short step to the enduring stigma of labels such as "backward," "reactionary," and the dreaded "uncivilized." As a result, most archaeologists found it possible to operate in a sort of grey zone, where tactfully disguised scientific pretexts often enabled the collection of sensitive strategic data. Nor should we suppose that such practices posed any moral quandaries to the men who undertook them. Art and politics had always been intertwined, with the production or acquisition of the former invariably leading to the glory of the latter. Espionage was no different. Much as with art and antiquities, nearly any means that contributed to the progress of one's nation, empire, or civilization could be justified on the grounds that the betterment of one's own homeland was in fact equivalent to the betterment of humankind at large. After all, "our" ideals are the most noble, so what is good for us is naturally good for everyone else.

This is what psychologists refer to as "cognitive dissonance": the ability of the human brain to hold two contradictory ideas simultaneously. Science, the supposedly neutral pursuit of empirically verifiable transcendent laws of nature, is all too often subordinated to the selfishly mundane goals of politically or financially motivated patrons. In times of peace, such cognitive dissonance lay deep within the subconscious and likely occasioned little mental stress. In times of war, however, the gaping disconnect between ideal and reality became harder and harder to ignore. In the end, some scholars found the stress too difficult to bear and decided to pull back the curtain on what they regarded as the unholy marriage of science and politics. Their exposé would produce a very public divorce. As we shall see, however, it would not preclude the taking of many different scientific mistresses behind the scenes.

The outbreak of World War I marked the first systematic co-optation of archaeologists for the cause of the battlefield. For American scholars, enlistment began in 1917 upon U.S. entry into the war. In the Far East, Roy Chapman Andrews of the American Museum of Natural History served as intelligence officer #241 for the Office of Naval Intelligence. Under the scientific cover of "comparative zoological studies of Chinese mammals," Andrews filed reports dealing with political conditions in China, communication and rail facilities, troop movements, industrial output, armaments, shipping and ports, and evidence of foreign intervention in China and Manchuria. In 1917, when the Russian civil war broke out, Andrews traveled to Siberia to collect information on the prospects of White loyalists, the preferred victor of the Allies. In Siberia, Andrews brushed shoulders with Harvard art historian Langdon Warner (of later Dunhuang infamy) and David Barrows, an anthropologist at the University of California in Berkeley. Warner worked for the Department of

State and operated under the cover of "acting vice consul" at Harbin. Not all agents were Americans, however. Paul Pelliot served as military attaché for French forces in the Far East. At one point, he, Warner, and Barrows all traveled together to track down the whereabouts of Grigory Semenov, the leader of White Russian armies in the Transbaikal.

Back on the home front, the U.S. Office of Naval Intelligence (ONI) began to enlist American archaeologists to help police its own backyard. In February 1917, the British intercepted the so-called Zimmerman Telegram, which revealed an offer by the German ambassador to Mexico of "generous financial support" toward any effort to retake Texas, Arizona, and New Mexico from the United States. Though never seriously considered by Mexico, the telegram was enough to prompt widespread paranoia among Washington policymakers. After all, the Germans commanded the single most destructive weapon of the war: "undersea boats" (U-boats, or submarines), which sunk on average 300,000 tons of shipping per month throughout the Atlantic. The Americans were well aware of the dangers of German U-boats, having lost 128 of their own citizens in the sinking of the *Lusitania* in 1915. But that attack had occurred off the coast of Ireland, far away from the borders of North America. Now that the United States had joined the war against Germany, however, it was reasonable to expect that German U-boats would begin to set their sights closer to the American mainland. The Panama Canal, for instance, provided endless targets for German torpedoes. Then there was the potentially crippling dependence of the British Royal Navy on Mexican oil fields, which supplied sixty percent of its total fuel needs. And, of course, there was the unthinkable: a U-boat attack on American ships in sovereign U.S. waters.

But how would the U-boats reach these targets? For that, the Germans would need coastal bases and ports somewhere within striking distance of the Americas. Before long, rumors of U-boat sightings and German agents in Mexico and Central America appeared to confirm the suspicions bred by the Zimmerman Telegram. As a result, the ONI decided to conduct its own reconnaissance of coastal waters to the south, either to prove or disprove the presence of secret German bases. But there were two problems with this plan. First, none of the Central American countries had openly sided with Germany in the war. Either they were neutral or they supported the Allies. This meant that there was no legitimate pretext for U.S. agents to search for evidence of German collaboration within their sovereign territories, unless Washington was prepared to acknowledge its insulting lack of confidence in the ability of its southern neighbors to police their own borders. Therefore, any such reconnaissance would have to be covert. Second, the United States had never before deployed intelligence agents overseas. The only men even remotely proficient in the arts of espionage belonged to the FBI and Secret Service—and they had their hands full with domestic concerns.

So where was the Office of Naval Intelligence going to obtain its spooks? The answer was obvious: from those Americans already familiar with the lands, peoples, and languages of regions most likely to elicit German strategic interest. In practice, this meant the recruitment of prominent archaeologists and anthropologists, who came equipped with a plausible alibi. Within a year of the U.S. entering the war, the ONI had deployed thirty intelligence agents to Mexico and Central America. The head of this latter group was Sylvanus Morley, a Mayan archaeologist with a degree from Harvard. When the war broke out, Morley was working as a curator for the Peabody Museum in Cambridge, Massachusetts, and drawing a salary on a research grant from the Carnegie Institute. Not only did Morley volunteer his services for the ONI, but he also provided a list of "available anthropologists" who were willing to be deployed. It seemed like an ideal arrangement for all concerned: the Carnegie was relieved of Morley's salary, the Peabody got an opportunity for free fieldwork, and the ONI got a ready-made spy in need of little training. As Morley and other thinly veiled academics transited through New Orleans en route to Belize, journalists clamored for a parting interview. One of them told a reporter that they were going to Guatemala to study primitive developments of food values still in use among the natives. Wilson Popenoe, an avocado researcher for the Department of Agriculture and ONI agent #219, departed under the cover of "agricultural explorer" for the University of California.

Figure 7.1. Sylvanus Morley's mugshot for the Office of Naval Intelligence.

Perfectly harmless, right? No need to worry about insulting foreign governments: these men were nothing more than unobjectionable scholars carrying out fieldwork within perfectly sensible geographical parameters—it was not Morley's fault if ancient Mayan ruins just happened to be located within sight of suspected German U-boat base sites. But alas, there was far more than avocados and native food preparation techniques on the agenda. Logistical arrangements were carefully planned in advance, with anonymous transfers of money handled by the National City Bank of New York (now Citibank). All communications from agents in the field were mailed to fictive Japanese and German recipients in New York or Boston—Taro Yamamoto or Karl Hoffmeyer, perhaps—on the belief that such names would be less likely to arouse the suspicions of the host governments. And transportation, lodgings, supplies, and telegraph services were provided by the many commercial outposts of the United Fruit Company, which kept the most detailed and accurate maps of local topography and whose managers were more than happy to share them with Morley.

Morley's first job was to report on possible U-boat base sites. It did not take long for him to conclude the extreme unlikelihood of any submarine docking station being built anywhere along the shallow and turbulent waters of the Central American coastline. With regard to the Mosquito Coast, for instance,

Morley reported back to Washington that "all things considered, therefore, it would seem that the physical conditions of this littoral are such as to practically preclude its use by the Germans for submarine bases." Similar assessments followed nearly everywhere Morley reached. "The war in Europe is so remote," Morley wrote on one occasion, "that the people here are as indifferent toward it as they are toward the ancient races I study." With the overt military threat debunked, Morley and his fellow spies needed something else to do. On occasion this meant indulging in actual fieldwork—just as their passports claimed—though always with an eye out for possible German machinations. "Kosbiel once asked me to go out to Saccacal with him and see some ruins that were on the place," Morley recorded in his notes, "and if I hear anything further about this alleged Champoton wireless plant I will take an archaeological *pasear* out that way before we leave."

Mostly, however, Morley and his colleagues filled their many idle hours in pursuit of less morally defensible tasks. In a preview of more aggressive measures that would be undertaken during the Second World War, Morley spent considerable time and effort attempting to sabotage the German economic presence in Central America. This resulted in the creation of a "black list," on which Morley placed the names of German expatriates who worked in local factories and businesses. The most vulnerable were those employed by U.S. firms, who could be fired in accordance with the "Trading with the Enemy Act." In the Mexican state of Campeche, Morley filed a report on two Germans named Adolf Raab and Gustav Walker. "As both are being employed by an American firm their discharge can easily be procured at that end if you deem the matter of sufficient importance to take it up." On another occasion, Morley passed along a list of names "so that you can notify the proper people, if you see fit, and thus scotch this promising little viper's nest in the embryo stage." At times Morley feared that the viper had already left its nest. When he learned of ongoing labor strikes at three banana factories in Honduras, Morley rushed to investigate. "As anxious as the Hun undoubtedly is, to cause just such disturbances as this," Morley conceded, "I think that for this once at least, we may probably exonerate him from all complicity."

Morley and his colleagues were so zealous in their persecution of German expatriates that the British minister in Guatemala City began to complain about the unfair application of "pro-German" or "anti-American" labels upon local firms unable to appeal such ruinous—and often arbitrary—designations. But Morley did not stop at persecuting Germans alone. Even certain U.S. citizens were targeted for reprisals. At a United Fruit factory in Tela, Honduras, Morley heard of the arrival of a young man from Milwaukee, who was said to be pro-German and fond of describing his escape from the draft. "If I find out that he really is a draft-dodger, I will try to have him fired just to show him that there are no hard feelings."

In the eyes of Morley and his colleagues, Latin America was a hotbed of potential agitation against U.S. interests. If there were no U-boat bases, then there must be German wireless stations. If there were no wireless stations, then there must be German strike organizers. If there were no strike organizers, then there must be American draft dodgers. And if there were no draft dodgers, then there were still the local governments themselves, whose vows of neutrality and pro-Allied postures counted for little in Washington. In fact, one of the jobs of the ONI spies in Central America was to assess the prospects for fomenting domestic unrest in the event one of those governments "should force our hand by allying herself with Germany and declaring war on us." The situation on the Yucatan Peninsula seemed most promising to Morley, who believed that "with any sort of encouragement from us the Yucatecans would throw off the Mexican yoke, separate themselves from the rest of the republic and declare themselves an independent state." What form would such U.S. "encouragement" take? "A gunboat at Campeche, another at Progreso to prevent the Mexicans from sending any reinforcements over here," Morley explained, "and the Yucatecans themselves could easily take care of the thousand-odd Mexican soldiers now maintained here."

All in all, Sylvanus Morley covered just under two thousand miles in thirteen months of intelligence work, having traversed both the coastlines and interiors of Nicaragua, Honduras, Guatemala, and Mexico. After the war, he

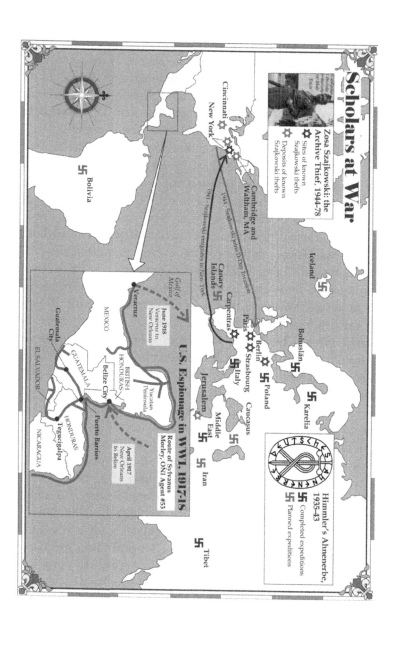

transitioned seamlessly right back into the academic career he had put on hold two years prior. Morley saw no conflict of interest between the two. But others did. In December 1919, *The Nation* published a letter to the editor by Franz Boas, then considered the most famous anthropologist in America and now viewed as the father of the discipline. As it turned out, Boas learned of the ONI's collaboration with archaeologists and anthropologists quite by accident: in the summer of 1917, two anthropologists about to embark on an ONI mission tried to use contacts in the Mexican government that they had obtained through their relationship with Boas. Suspicious, Boas inquired further into the matter and soon learned all about Morley and the others.

In his letter to *The Nation*, Boas claimed that Morley—whom he did not name—and his colleagues had committed the ultimate betrayal. "A person who uses science as a cover for political spying, who demeans himself to pose before a foreign government as an investigator and asks for assistance in his alleged researches in order to carry on, under this cloak, his political machinations," he wrote, "prostitutes science in an unpardonable way and forfeits the right to be classed as a scientist." Boas was a man ahead of his time. Though his critique would eventually win the day, leading to an institutional divorce between the intelligence and academic communities, Boas would not live to see his victory. On the contrary, just ten days later, at the annual meeting of the American Anthropological Association, that organization's governing council voted to censure Boas and remove him from its ranks. Not only that, he was also forced to resign his position on the National Research Council, and openly denounced as a "Hun" in bed with the Germans.

The Western world, it seemed, was not yet ready to confront the moral quandaries raised by the longstanding intimacy between science and politics. It should come as little surprise, then, that sympathy for Boas was in short supply on both sides of the Atlantic. In fact, the decade leading up to World War II would witness some of the most politically charged applications of ideas about art, antiquities, and the ethical duties of scholars that the world had ever seen. At the center of the maelstrom was a group whose name needs no introduction: the Nazis.

What we can add to the oft-painted portrait of the Third Reich is an emphasis on the unique geopolitical context of interwar Germany. It is easy to forget that the Nazis had few original ideas of their own; most were derivative of theories about race and history that existed among intellectuals and politicians living in every other Western state. The Nazis, however, were unique among these states in presiding over the only Western industrial empire to have been stripped of its overseas colonial territories and business holdings—a consequence of defeat in the First World War. In other words, the larger an empire, the more diverse its people will be. And the more diverse its people are, the more likely their leaders will subscribe to an inclusive cosmopolitan vision of the body politic.

Take that diversity and cosmopolitan impulse away, and you remove the single greatest check on ethnic chauvinism run amok. Germany wasn't the first empire in world history to be stripped of its diversity overnight. The Ottomans also lost everything after the war, and the Chinese faced the perennial threat of a similar fate. What was different about Germany was that it was the first Western *industrial* empire to be treated by its rivals as all other non-Western empires before them had been treated. Humiliated on the battlefield, stripped of their colonies, and made financially dependent on the victors, the Germans now knew what it felt like to be an "Oriental" in the age of Western supremacy. Unlike the Ottomans or Chinese, however, the Germans had the technical know-how and industrial foundation required to hit back against their "oppressors." Their riposte on the battlefield led to World War II. But it is their riposte in the realm of culture that is most relevant to the worlds of art, antiquities, and archaeological expeditions.

The Nazis pursued the ideal of the nation-state to its most logical—and grotesque—conclusions. Unrestrained by a cosmopolitan vision of a global empire, the Nazis scapegoated their most visible internal "other"—the Jews—for the failure of the German race and nation to achieve its full potential. In the world of art, this translated into a designation of "degenerate art" for any painting that either depicted Jews or was produced by a Jew. Throughout the 1930s, it became common for such "degenerate" works of art to be seized by Nazi authorities and

Figure 7.3. Nazi art seizures.

placed for sale on the international auction circuit. According to the director of the Nazi-affiliated Combat League for German Culture, such measures were deemed progressive. "There must no remorse and no sentimentality," he announced, "in uprooting and crushing what was destroying our vitals."

Jewish art was not the only category deemed "degenerate," however. Also included was much of what passed for modernist and realist art. Modernist art, with its abstract reflections on contemporary life in non-linear form, was criticized as "nonsense" or the work of crazy men intent on insulting the people and isolating art from the nation. Conversely, realist art, if it portrayed the common man and woman in an unflattering light, was charged with draining the morale of the German people. In 1937, Adolf Ziegler, a German painter tasked by Hitler with purging the nation of degenerate art, gave voice to this sentiment when he declared that "he who paints our youth as wasted idiots, and the German mother like a Neanderthal woman, has shown undeniable proof of his degenerate character." In place of such specimens, most Nazi leaders venerated the same sorts of artistic productions that European elites before them had admired: Greek and Roman sculpture, along with the "Old Master" paintings of the Low Countries. Like Napoleon a century and a half earlier, Hitler and the top Nazi leadership managed to acquire—by conquest, confiscation, coerced sales, and legitimate purchase—thousands of such works of art. Instead of depositing them in the Louvre, however, Hitler made meticulous plans for the cream of the crop to be displayed in a never-completed showcase museum in his hometown of Linz, Austria.

But it was not enough simply to eliminate the enemy within. Once cleansed of the Jewish parasite, the German race must still reconnect with its own forgotten roots. These roots were imagined to be synonymous with what was referred to as the ancient "Aryan" race. Originally a linguistic term coined to invoke similarities between classical languages such as Sanskrit and Latin, "arya" increasingly came to be used by scholars throughout Europe as a convenient shorthand for an "Indo-European" race whose ancestors were credited with the very birth of civilization itself. In short, every accomplishment of humankind was chalked up to an Aryan ancestor of some sort, with less impressive achievements attributed to the "degeneration" brought about by mixing with an inferior race. Thus the rise of civilization in India was attributed to Aryan migration into the subcontinent, with its subsequent "decline" explained by racial mixing with the inferior native races. Even then, however, the Aryan vigor could not be fully extinguished: elite social classes such as the Brahmans, with their "generally lighter skin," "narrower face and nose," "brown hair," and a height of "six to nine centimeters taller than the rest of the population," were said to have most successfully resisted miscegenation with the local savages.

In 1935, Heinrich Himmler, head of the *Schutzstaffel* ("Protection Squad," or SS), founded a scholarly organization dedicated to research into the origins of the Aryan race: the Ahnenerbe ("something inherited from the forefathers"). Within two years, the Ahnenerbe claimed 137 scholars on its payroll, with an additional 82 employees as support staff. Their agenda was clear: to "recover" the lost wisdom and achievements of the Germanic branch of the Aryan race as inspiration for the revitalization of the German nation. Here Himmler differed from Hitler. For Hitler, the Aryans only flourished in Greece and Rome, where the balmy climate unleashed the full potential of the race. The Germanic tribes of early Europe, however, were something of an embarrassment to him. "People make a tremendous fuss about the excavations carried out in districts inhabited by our forebears of the pre-Christian era," Hitler once remarked. "I am afraid I cannot share their enthusiasm, for I cannot help remembering that, while our ancestors were making these vessels of stone and clay, over which our archaeologists rave, the Greeks had already built an Acropolis."

Hitler was referring to the archaeological work of the Ahnenerbe. On Himmler's instructions, Ahnenerbe scholars worked feverishly to produce "scientific" evidence of "Nordic" accomplishments in the distant past. From 1935 to 1939, Himmler bankrolled expeditions to four remote sites outside of Germany in hopes of proving a causal link between the glories of the "Nordic Aryans" and the "Greco-Roman Aryans." In June 1936, the first group of scholars was sent to Bohuslän, a rural farming village in southwestern Sweden which boasted thousands of rock art engravings from the Bronze Age. Just one month later, another expedition was sent to Karelia, a remote site in eastern Finland said to be home to witches and shamans in possession of ancient Scandinavian folklore. In 1937, the Ahnenerbe financed the work of scholars in northern Italy and the Balkans who promised to study prehistoric rock inscriptions that "proved" the founding of ancient Rome by the Nordic Aryans. There were many other activities funded by Himmler's scholarly outfit, including several proposals that were cancelled once the war broke out. Among the aborted missions was an expedition to Iran to study rock inscriptions containing the word "Aryan"; a mission to Bolivia to assess the possibility that Nordic sailors had built South American ruins; a trip to the Canary Islands to investigate reports of white-skinned natives with blond hair; a tour of rural Iceland to collect rural Scandinavian folklore; and an investigation of racial types in the Caucasus region, with special attention paid to the so-called "mountain Jews."

Perhaps the most ambitious undertaking of the Ahnenerbe, however, was the one that elicited admiration from both Hitler and Himmler alike: the 1938–39 expedition to Tibet. Led by Ernst Schäfer, a zoologist and naturalist who had traveled widely throughout China and Inner Asia, the purpose of this mission was to uncover evidence of ancient Aryan migrations

Figure 7.4. The Ahnenerbe Expedition to Tibet, 1938–39.

in the remotest parts of Asia. Inspired by evidence of Aryan symbols he claimed to have found in Tibetan graves in Kham and Sichuan—on the Chinese side of Tibet—Schäfer proposed entry through British India on the pretext of collecting zoological specimens. After an initial refusal from the British, Schäfer managed to gain a conditional entrance to the kingdom of Sikkim. From there he and his men marched brazenly onward toward Lhasa, where they were met with a disappointingly simple reception and a vague Tibetan interest in the Nazi appropriation of the Buddhist swastika. En route, they dangled the prospect of free medical services as an enticement to local populations to submit to anthropometric measurements of their skulls and facial features, on the belief that such data could prove or disprove the presence of Aryan blood. This view was inspired by the work of the German racial scholar Hans Günther, whose immensely popular books posited an Aryan pedigree for East Asian elites. According to Günther, the Chinese and Japanese "aristocracy" evinced "a decidedly long skull and an almost white skin, sometimes combined with handsome European features."

The Nazis were by no means unique in using anthropometry as a means of determining the degree to which certain races were capable—or incapable—of making contributions to civilization. In fact, this is still one of the most discomfiting realities encountered by any historian who conducts research on archaeologists active during the late nineteenth or early twentieth centuries. From Egypt to China, Western scholars of all political persuasions routinely took anthropometric measurements of the local peoples wherever they found them, and often commented on the unexpected presence of striking "European" features among the more "admirable" types. Western archives in possession of the papers of these explorers are filled with tens and sometimes even hundreds of anthropometrical mug shots and accompanying data sheets. In 1906, for instance, Aurel Stein bemoaned the resistance of local hillmen in Xinjiang to his scientific entreaties, "just as if real live heads were to have been taken instead of mere measurements and photographs with perfectly harmless instruments." In 1907, the Finnish explorer Gustav Mannerheim noted in his diary that "people were fetched for my anthropological measurements" from among the Torgut Mongols of Karashahr. On his last expedition in 1930, within a decade of Schäfer's trip to Tibet, Stein commented on the wonderful opportunity in the Himalayan valley of Hunza to collect "anthropometrical materials among an interesting ethnic 'relict'."

Figure 7.5. Nazi anthropometry.

The scholars themselves were mostly harmless, be they German, Finnish, or British. But if political and economic conditions were toxic enough, the ideas they promoted could be invoked by political elites to justify the most horrific slaughter of human beings the world had ever seen. And that is precisely what happened throughout Nazi domains. The scientific method may be an admirable ideal in the abstract. But when it is practiced by humans—as it always and ever will be—it is beholden to the same sort of political agendas that animate the rest of the mundane world. The Holocaust and other ethnic cleansing campaigns were all justified via reference to "scientific proof" of their necessity. But "scientific proof" is a moving target, interpreted differently in various times and places. The Nazis were not the only wartime belligerents to utilize the discourse of science for dubious ends. They were simply the most odious in its application, and the ones least deserving of the historian's redemptive touch.

Other figures deserve a more sympathetic appraisal. Foremost in this category is Zosa Szajkowski, a Jewish refugee and soldier whose turbulent career as an amateur historian spanned both sides of the Atlantic. Szajkowski (pronounced "Shy-KOV-ski") was born in 1911 into a poor Jewish family in east-central Poland. Unable to afford a formal education, Szajkowski instead followed his brothers to Paris when he was sixteen years old. There he found work as a journalist and came under the wing of Elias and Rebecca Tcherikower. In 1925, the Tcherikowers had helped to create the Yiddish Scientific Institute (YIVO), an organization dedicated to the study of Jewish life in eastern and central Europe. That same year, the Hebrew University of Jerusalem officially opened its doors. Both institutions represented the nationalist aspirations of the Jewish diaspora, but for different constituencies: YIVO promoted the interests of Yiddish-speaking Jews of central and eastern Europe, while the university in Jerusalem encapsulated Zionist aspirations for an independent Hebrew state in Palestine.

As a Polish Jew, Szajkowski naturally gravitated toward YIVO, writing articles and gathering research materials for the Tcherikowers. When the war broke out in 1939, Szajkowski put down his pen and volunteered for the French army, in part to prove his loyalty to his adopted state and in part to escape possible anti-Semitic backlash. Just one year into the war, a bullet through the shoulder and lungs led to Szajkowski's discharge from the French army. Hoping to avoid his deportation to an internment camp, the Tcherikowers managed to secure an American visa for Szajkowksi on the pretext that he was a Jewish intellectual worth saving. Incredibly, after his arrival in the United States, Szajkowski again volunteered for military service, receiving training as a paratrooper. On June 5, 1944, just twenty-four hours before D-Day, he jumped out of a plane over German-occupied Normandy and exchanged fire with German troops on the ground. Over the next year, often working as a translator for Allied forces in Europe, he would see first-hand the destruction wrought by the Nazi occupation of France and Germany.

Before we delve into Szajkowski's postwar awakening, it might be appropriate to recall Newton's third law of motion: for every action, there is an equal and opposite reaction. This dictum is equally applicable to the realm of scholarship as it is to the realm of physics. Of course, Szajkowski had long experienced the effects of anti-Semitism in Europe. But what he saw on his postwar patrols through Paris and Berlin would galvanize him in ways that peacetime discrimination had not. He learned, for instance, that the wartime puppet government of Vichy France had facilitated the deportation of 76,000 Jews to Nazi death camps. Untold numbers of Jews had suffered the loss of property and possessions through government-sanctioned confiscations, with little to no compensation after the war. As for the Jews themselves, Szajkowski was distressed to learn that the horrors of the war had done nothing to unite them against a common enemy. In Paris, he deplored the sight of Jews "doing nothing to put damaged Jewish life in Paris back together." On the contrary, they continued to "talk about world problems, about everything in the world except Jewish problems."

The world saw Jews as Jews—and persecuted them as such. But Jews saw themselves as minority members of their individually adopted states, and strove to be accepted as such. Szajkowski was determined to change all this. It was not enough simply to formulate a political plan of action for the Jews, such as that provided by a Zionist platform. What they needed more than anything else, Szajkowski believed, was a cohesive cultural identity that transcended the parochial national identities into which the global diaspora had placed them. The Nazis said that all Jews were the same: one coherent, filthy nation that needed to be exterminated. Szajkowski wanted Jews everywhere to agree with the first part of this statement, while putting a positive spin on the second part: yes, the Jews are one coherent nation, but it is a glorious one worthy of the pride of each of its far-flung members. The Nazi action of mistreating the Jews as a deplorably homogenous race would thus produce an equal and opposite reaction of Szajkowski proudly treating the Jews in similar taxonomic fashion.

How could Szajkowski, a refugee paratrooper who had once worked as a journalist, realize this vision? The answer: by rearranging the organizational building blocks of history itself. This is not as confounding an answer as it may appear on first blush, for Szajkowski was in an excellent position to sift through the voluminous paperwork of the Third Reich. In Berlin, as an armed translator for Allied occupation forces, Szajkowski could gain access to most vacant German government offices without being noticed. On one occasion, he described the delight he took in defacing a Nazi publication. "Is it barbaric to rip apart Nazi books?" he asked in one of his letters to the Tcherikowers. "Yesterday as I sat and tore pages out of a Nazi book, a German girl started crying. Her beastly Nazi soul couldn't bear to see a Jew calmly tearing pages out of a German book. I told her to keep working and stop her games."

Most of the time, however, Szajkowski elected to preserve the documents he found in Nazi offices, not destroy them—especially if they related to the treatment of Jews. But he was no longer willing to allow them to remain in Europe. In Szajkowski's mind, the unconscionable treatment of European Jewry over the past decade meant that the continent had forfeited any right to pose as a defender of the Jewish people. Nothing related to the Jews could ever be safe in Europe anymore. Now, the only safe repository for any sort of Judaica was abroad. With his military superiors turning a willfully

Figure 7.6. Szajkowski's revenge.
Szajkowski sifting through documents in the Nazi
Propaganda Ministry during the Allied occupation of Berlin.
Archives of the YIVO Institute for Jewish Research.

blind eye to his activities, Szajkowski got to work, rummaging through Nazi archives and storage rooms for any materials related to the lives and livelihoods of Jews in Europe. Before long, box after box of such materials were mailed to YIVO offices in New York, courtesy of the U.S. military postal service.

Szajkowski's wartime "looting" of Nazi government offices was technically illegal, but easily forgiven. Once the war ended, however, Szajkowski found it harder and harder to quit old habits. Before long, he found himself in less morally defensible territory. From the end of the war until 1961, Szajkowski would successfully steal tens of thousands of documents from French municipal archives, mostly from Strasbourg and Carpentras—all without permission, tacit or otherwise. Of course, like every daring scientist and adventurous scholar before him, Szajkowski justified his actions by reference to a globally accepted standard of altruistic science. After all, he made prompt use of everything he stole, publishing three books and hundreds of articles on the history of the Jews in Europe. He then sold them, but not just to the highest bidder. Much like the archaeologist who sells his wares to a museum, Szajkowski only peddled his documents to reputable scholarly institutions, ones that embodied the ideal of politically disinterested scholarship. Among these reputable purchasing institutions, none of which cared to inquire too deeply into the provenance of their acquisitions, was Brandeis University (Waltham, Mass.), Harvard University (Cambridge, Mass.), Hebrew Union College (Cincinnati, Ohio), the Jewish Theological Seminary of America (New York), Yeshiva University (New York), YIVO (New York), and the Central Archives for the History of the Jewish People (Jerusalem).

Yet the scholarship Szajkowski produced from these documents before he sold them was anything but disinterested. In his politically motivated narratives, the Jews were a coherent race and nation wherever he found them, shorn of their parochial contexts. Szajkowski's approach to Jewish history is well illustrated by an incident that took place at the Strasbourg archives in 1961. Sifting through the folders of the archive, Szajkowski found that all of the files relating to the history of Jews in France had been classified by the archival staff according to the racially blind priorities of the French state. This meant that there were no files on the Jews *per se*. Instead, files related to Jewish life were dispersed across multiple government departments, alongside files on non-Jewish French citizens. A historian who passively followed such an administrative arrangement in the writing of his historical narrative would likely portray the Jews in France as "French Jews"—not as Jews who just happened to live in France. According to the French state, the Jews were French first and Jewish second. The postwar French state even went so far as to declare all documents produced by the wartime Vichy regime as illegal, since they had classified the Jews on the basis of race rather than their place in French society. But to Szajkowski, the Vichy emphasis on race and nation was entirely appropriate, provided it was given a benevolent gloss: to him, the Jews were Jews first and French, German, Italian, or Polish second.

In order to reflect this new organizational scheme, Szajkowski ripped out the files on French Jews from their many different folders in the archives and rearranged them in his briefcase as a newly formed subject: Jews who just happened to live in France, without the context of the larger French society that dominated their daily lives. When he later sold these files to scholarly institutions abroad, they retained Szajkowski's new Jewish-oriented classification for all future historians who consulted them. But these particular documents from Strasbourg never got that far. Acting on a tip from the local archivist, Strasbourg police followed Szajkowski back to his hotel room and demanded to see the contents of his briefcase. His crime was readily apparent. At first, however, unaware of his many years of theft in the same archive, the French authorities characterized Szajkowski in sympathetic terms: to them, he appeared to be nothing more than an "impassioned scholar" with an "excess of interest in his subject." As such, he was allowed to leave the country following the submission of a written confession. When the stunning extent of his decades-long theft was later discovered, however, French authorities convicted Szajkowski to three years in prison *in absentia* and a 5,000 franc fine.

Now barred from France, Szajkowski turned his sights to the New York Public Library. Seventeen more years of unchecked theft followed. Then, in 1978, he was caught in the act there, too. Aware of the likely consequences of this exposure—loss of employment and access to YIVO, libraries, and archives; likely prison time; and the inevitable strain on his marriage—Szajkowski chose to end it all. On September 26, 1978, he was found dead in a bathtub in a Manhattan hotel.

In the realm of science and scholarship, we might think of Himmler's Ahnenerbe as the action and Szajkowski's archival labors as the reaction. Yet this binary deduction hardly exhausts the list of scholars who were willing to subordinate the ideals of science to the demands of politics. Like Himmler and Szajkowski, they all felt their actions to be justified because they all felt themselves to be on the side of right, not might. Throughout the war, perfectly respectable professors from nearly every major American university—but mostly from the prestigious Ivy League—thought nothing of lending their services to the U.S. government for the infiltration of war-torn lands. Though most of these scholars stayed well behind the battle lines and were often limited to producing a trail of paperwork, they nonetheless provided valuable translations of foreign news reports, interviews with refugees, and first-hand knowledge of distant lands and peoples. Most well known are the so-called Monuments Men: university professors and museum curators who advised Allied commanders on ways to minimize destruction to historical buildings during the invasion of Europe, and then later worked to identify the original owners of Nazi looted art for the purpose of restitution. Less well known—and omitted from the 2014 Hollywood adaptation—is the fact that twenty-five of the Monuments Men felt compelled to sign a letter, now known as the Wiesbaden Manifesto, protesting orders to relocate 202 German-owned paintings to the National Gallery of Art in Washington, D.C. Despite all claims to the contrary, it seems, the United States simply couldn't resist doing unto the Germans what the Germans had done unto Europe.

Such tensions between scholars and government became more common with the passage of time. Lingering in the shadows was the scathing critique of Franz Boas nearly three decades prior: that scholars who went to war could no longer be considered scholars. Be it through Morley, the Ahnenerbe, Szajkowski, or the Monuments Men, the use and abuse of science and scholarship for political agendas was becoming increasingly clear to all. Other trends also favored the separation of science from politics. First, the process of decolonization had given a global voice to non-Western scholars and politicians, who proceeded to criticize what to them was a painfully obvious subordination of science to politics. Second, the unprecedented destruction of two world wars, the specter of nuclear warfare, and revelations of unimaginable human cruelty such as the Holocaust shook like never before the faith of Western intellectuals in the moral superiority of Western civilization. And, finally, government itself had outgrown its longstanding reliance on temporary "contract" scholars to carry out what was becoming an increasingly specialized and complex world of espionage. This last point is best illustrated by the creation in 1941 of the Office of the Coordinator of Information and its institutional successors: the Office of Strategic Services (OSS) and, finally, the Central Intelligence Agency (CIA).

It is no coincidence that the CIA headquarters in Langley, Virginia, has always been referred to by its employees as "the campus." For that was exactly what the creation of the CIA represented: an in-house training campus for government agents who would combine the area studies knowledge of previously employed university scholars with the technical (and sometimes martial) training of a professional spy. The establishment of such a bureau as the permanent home base for politically indoctrinated "scholar-soldiers" effectively freed university and museum personnel from the moral dilemma of having to mix scholarship with politics. Not that this would always be the case in practice. But at least now there were some safeguards on the preservation of the ideal of politically disinterested science. The end result was an institutional divorce between universities and museums, on the one hand, and government agencies on the other, one that remains in force today. (Incidentally, before I decided to pursue a Ph.D. in history, my foreign language skills, travel experience, and area studies expertise proved sufficient to advance me through several stages of interviews for the CIA's Clandestine Service. Had I continued along that route, I could not have become a college professor. Now a professor, I face a host of professional safeguards that effectively prevent me from ever performing clandestine work for the government.)

In the end, Franz Boas won the day.

Divorce, however, does not preclude the taking of a second spouse. But with the union of scholars and government now increasingly frowned upon, any future partner could not be openly embraced. In other words, it would have to be a mistress. The geopolitical context of the Cold War set the stage for the taking of the first scientific mistresses of the postwar world. By this time, the golden age of Western archaeological expeditions was more or less at an end. Henceforth, future excavations of archaeological sites the world over would be carried out on terms dictated by the host government, power imbalance be damned. No matter: the great museums of the Western world were already overflowing with more treasures than they could ever possibly display. Now, instead of science being used to justify expeditions into distant lands for the recovery of cultural artifacts, it would be used to justify entry into the new geographic frontier of the Cold War: space.

Space was exciting. Space was sexy. Space was free of the "ungrateful natives" whose Westernized scholars and politicians shrilly demanded an equal piece of the scientific pie. Space, in other words, was the last virgin frontier. The first nation to colonize space would achieve a measure of international prestige equivalent to that which Napoleon's armies had once brought to France, what Lord Elgin had once brought to Britain, and what Himmler's expedition to Tibet had once brought to Germany. As President Lyndon B. Johnson would later put it, "In the eyes of the world, first in space means first, period; second in space is second in everything." So space was clearly prestigious. But unlike museums, whose acquisitions rarely required seven-figure disbursements, national prestige alone would not be enough to convince the U.S. legislature to open its pocketbook and write check after check for the billions and billions of dollars needed to explore this last frontier.

The only thing capable of justifying such a price tag was the promise of strategic applications. In the context of the Cold War, that meant rockets. By 1949, both the Soviet Union and the United States had successfully tested their own nuclear bomb. But these bombs were only a credible military threat if they could be delivered to the doorstep of their intended target. Strapping a nuclear bomb to an aircraft and dropping it from the sky only worked if the enemy did not possess any means of shooting that aircraft down. That was the case with Japan in 1945: the only reason Hiroshima and Nagasaki could be nuked from above was because Japan's mangled air force and obliterated anti-aircraft capabilities had already ceded complete control of the sky to the Americans. Neither Washington nor Moscow could expect such aerial license from the other. The science of rocketry, however, held out the promise of a nuclear strike from a safe distance. In order to cover such a vast distance, however, the rocket must be capable of breaching Earth's atmosphere. Otherwise, the Earth's gravitational pull would only allow it to travel so far. Not only that, but it would also be vulnerable to interception before it reached its target. Space, however, could solve both problems. By launching a rocket into space beyond Earth's gravitational pull, a nuclear warhead could travel halfway around the world. It would also make the possibility of enemy detection or interception far less likely.

But how was the United States going to get a rocket into space? The answer: by taking a Nazi rocket scientist out to dinner. Throughout the 1930s and 40s, four bodies of military science had been advanced by scholars working for one of the major wartime belligerents: radar by the British; chemical and biological weapons by the Japanese; nuclear bombs by the Americans; and rockets by the Germans. Each technological breakthrough was deemed so valuable by the victors of the war that they nearly tripped over one another in their collective rush to take custody of the scientific personnel of the vanquished. In the case of the Japanese biological and chemical warfare program, the well-known fact that thousands of unwilling Chinese captives—and even some American

Figure 7.7. The V-2 rocket.
The V-2 rocket, originally developed by Nazi scientists, would provide the basic template for the Jupiter-C rocket, which launched the first U.S. satellite into orbit.

POWs—had been used for live experiments posed no moral quandary whatsoever. On the contrary, such knowledge made possession of the resultant data more valuable than ever. "Such information could not be obtained in our own laboratories because of scruples attached to human experimentation," observed Edwin Hill, chief of basic sciences at Camp Detrick in Frederick, Maryland, without a hint of irony. Instead, the Americans granted immunity from prosecution to all the Japanese scientists and paid them handsomely for the repellant results of their handiwork.

The Nazi rocket scientists would be treated even better. Why? Because their brains alone held out the promise of beating the Soviets to space. During the war, while the Americans worked toward a nuclear bomb, the Nazi scientists had labored to perfect the V-2 ballistic missile, capable of delivering a payload more than two hundred miles away. The deadly result was thousands upon thousands of grisly civilian deaths throughout England and the Scandinavian countries. By the time the Germans surrendered, their scientists had already drawn up blueprints for the world's first intercontinental ballistic missile (ICBM): a multi-stage rocket with a range of 3,200 miles. The most prominent of the Nazi rocket scientists, Wernher von Braun, took advantage of the chaos in the war's closing months to seek out U.S. forces on his own initiative and offer his services. As he later characterized his decision, "We despise the French; we are mortally afraid of the Soviets; we do not believe the British can afford us; so that leaves the Americans." In a show of good faith, von Braun led the Americans to the Nazi rocket factories, where the components of a hundred V-2 rockets were disassembled for delivery to New Mexico.

Wernher von Braun had clearly made the right choice. Despite having presided over a system of Jewish slave labor in Nazi missile factories for many years and bearing direct responsibility for the deaths of thousands of Allied civilians, von Braun and his team of Nazi rocket scientists were given immunity from war crimes prosecution and a comfortable new life in America. Even then, however, proper appearances had to be maintained. Soviet propagandists would have a field day if they learned that the American race to space was being

Figure 7.8. Ex-Nazi Wernher von Braun.
Much like the pardon given to Japanese scientists who conducted
live experiments on human subjects during World War II,
Wernher von Braun (in civilian suit), who once oversaw Nazi
rocket factories employing thousands of enslaved Jews, would
be given a second chance in the suburbs of America in exchange
for sharing everything he knew about the science of rocketry.

directed by a former Nazi war criminal. Therefore, Wernher
von Braun had to be kept out of the public spotlight. In the
end, he was put in charge of the Army's ballistic missile development camp in Huntsville, Alabama, and tasked with the
development of the "Redstone" arsenal. Though von Braun's
rockets had proven themselves in test flights as early as 1953,
his team was actively restrained from setting their sights too
high, and Army inspectors were posted to Huntsville to ensure
that none of von Braun's rockets "accidentally" reached orbit.

Why all the fuss? The reason is simple: the United States
wanted effective weapons of mass destruction, but it wanted to
develop them on a suitably benign pretext. As such, it simply
would not do for Hitler's rocket scientists to be responsible
for the first entry of the United States into orbit. Instead, the
public spotlight was directed toward Project Vanguard: rocket
boosters designed to lift the first artificial satellite into space

under the direction of the Naval Research Laboratory, a corporate research outfit viewed as the civilian counterpart to von Braun's Army base. But there was more. Not only would the U.S. enter space on the backs of an ostensibly civilian rocket, but it would do so solely in support of politically disinterested scientific research for the benefit of all humankind. In order to give substance to this lie, the Vanguard rocket program was publicized as the embodiment of a U.S. commitment to celebrate the widely anticipated International Geophysical Year in 1957. On July 28, 1955, James Hagerty, the White House press secretary, announced that "the President has approved plans by this country for going ahead with the launching of small, earth-circling satellites as part of the United States participation in the International Geophysical Year."

Of course, there was no mention of the fact that the same rocket that launched a satellite into orbit could also deliver a nuclear warhead to the Soviet Union, or that the satellite itself could gather intelligence on rival states. Ostensibly, the only thing the American space program would do is to "provide scientists of all nations this important and unique opportunity for the advancement of science." Even von Braun himself, in the course of touting his vision for space at various private gatherings, constantly harped on the civilian applications of rockets. Though he was forced on one occasion to admit that "it would be rather ridiculous to say that space has no military significance," he always left his audiences with a rousing sense of the sublime. Rocketry, he told an audience in Washington, D.C. in 1952, will facilitate "a great deal of advancement for mankind." To one adoring crowd, he claimed that "human progress is the stake," while to another that "curiosity alone is sufficient motivation." But whether it was for military or civilian applications, von Braun was absolutely clear on one point: the United States was motivated, "as always, by a desire for peace and knowledge." The Soviet Union, however, was "motivated by a dream of empire as old as the Czars and Caesars."

Wernher von Braun was a charismatic man, but even he could not convince the powers-that-be to greenlight his rockets. If the United States was to be first in space, it must be a civilian rocket designed for scientific research, not the successor to the

Nazi V-2. The only way von Braun's Redstone rockets would be approved for launch was if the Soviets beat the Americans to space *and* the civilian counterpart to von Braun failed to even the score. And that is exactly what happened. In October 1957, with the Vanguard program still unable to test a successful rocket, the Soviets stunned the world by launching the first artificial satellite, *Sputnik*, into orbit. Just as the U.S. did in its public pronouncements, the Soviets also claimed vindication of its ideology in the progress of its scientists, declaring that "the freed and conscious labor of the people of the new socialist society turns even the most daring of mankind's dreams into reality." Von Braun begged for permission to launch his rocket, insisting that Redstone could have beaten the Soviets long ago. Instead, the civilian Vanguard program was slated for launch. In the course of two short months, two Vanguard rockets failed to reach orbit. The American press derisively referred to them as "Kaputnik" and "Flopnik," while the Soviet leader Nikita Khrushchev proposed that UN aid for underdeveloped countries be made available to the United States.

After two humiliating civilian failures, von Braun's Army team was finally set loose. In January 1958, his Jupiter-C rocket—a third generation successor to the Nazi V-2—put the first U.S. satellite into orbit. The disingenuous separation of civilian and military research outfits has continued ever since. Just seven months after Wernher von Braun finally got his day in the sun, the National Aeronautics and Space Administration (NASA) became operational. But it did not replace its military counterparts on the U.S. payroll. Instead, two distinct space research programs operated parallel to one another: the first to act as a benign and very public civilian face of altruistic scientific progress, the second to prepare for a real-life "star wars" out of the public limelight. As a result, the race to the Moon was consistently entrusted to the benevolent scientists at NASA, who made sure the first words out of the mouth of the first man on the moon were politically correct: "That's one small step for man, one giant leap for mankind."

As we have seen over the course of the past seven chapters, adventurous scholars and daring scientists have been uttering such carefully rehearsed half-truths for centuries. From 1982 to 1991, the U.S. space shuttle program launched forty missions into space. Of these, nine—nearly one out of every four launches—were commandeered by the Department of Defense for military purposes, including seven that remain classified to this day. What did these missions do up there? No one knows. But we can be fairly certain that it was not in the interests of the progress of all humankind. The public face of science, exploration, and archaeology has always been a benign one. But behind the scenes, those who get their hands dirty know exactly what is at stake: wealth and power. In February 1958, just one month after the U.S. joined the Soviets in space, the RAND Corporation reflected on the political implications of the newly inaugurated space age. Unfortunately, it concluded, in a memorable turn of phrase, there was no "escape velocity" that transcended the political rivalries of humankind.

For nearly three centuries now, art and science have promised to put us in touch with the sublime. But art and science are the brainchild of humans, who remain forever mired in the mundane.

Continue the journey at indianajonesinhistory.com:
- EPISODE XIX: Espionage
- EPISODE XX: Nazis and Jews
- EPISODE XXI: The Space Age

CHAPTER EIGHT

Hollywood vs. History

In my first semester of graduate school, every student in my program was required to choose a research topic. It had to be related in some way to modern Chinese history, our chosen course of study. I didn't know much about China back then, but I did know this: if I chose a boring topic, my life would be miserable. So I came up with a plan. I would try to think of the most exciting thing in the world, then look for its historical counterpart in China. My little brainstorm lasted less than thirty seconds, for the answer was obvious: Indiana Jones. To a white, twenty-something-year-old male from American suburbia, few things were more exciting in life than the thought of the man with the bullwhip. To watch the films was to experience a rush of boyish adrenaline every time. Somehow, I was determined to carry that adrenaline over into my research. On the assumption that there were no Chinese counterparts to Indiana Jones, I posed the only question that seemed likely to yield an answer: How did the Chinese react to the foreign archaeologists who took antiquities from their lands?

The answer to that question proved far more complex than I ever could have imagined. I was so stunned by what I discovered in China that I decided to read everything I could about Western expeditions in the rest of the world, in order to see how they compared to the situation in China. This book is the result. (A second, more specialized book focusing entirely on China and the Silk Road is in the works.) A funny thing happened along the way, though. The more I learned about Indiana Jones in history, the less I enjoyed Indiana Jones in Hollywood. In fact, the last time I watched the films, in preparation for writing this chapter, I could barely get through all of them. The boyhood magic had vanished; the adrenaline was gone. Why? Had I watched them one too many times over the years? Had I lost touch with the boyish spark of my youth? Were they never really all that good in the first place? Or had Indiana Jones in history simply proven to be more interesting to me than Indiana Jones in Hollywood?

I suspect it is the last one. In fact, most historians, over the course of their careers, must pay a similar price. The bargain, I think, is more than fair: let us call it the compensations of history. In exchange for the painful loss of the unreflective auras of our youth, the historian discovers a truth far stranger—and, more often than not, more satisfying—than any fiction. What I want to do in this chapter is something that historians rarely do. After spending the past seven chapters systematically replacing the cultural myth with the historical reality, I want to revisit the myth one last time. My goal is to identify where the myth ends and history begins, and put to rest once and for all the nebulous question of the historical accuracy of the Indiana Jones film franchise. At last, it is time to untangle Hollywood from history.

Let us begin with a question that is easy to answer. Where did the inspiration for the Indiana Jones film premise come from? As with most of the issues raised in this chapter, our first and primary source for this question comes in the form of the transcript for a 1978 brainstorming session held in Los Angeles three years before the release of *Raiders of the Lost Ark* (1981). In this one-hundred-and-twenty-five page document, we hear George Lucas, Steven Spielberg, and Larry Kasdan—the co-creator, director, and screenwriter of the first film—discuss in great detail a number of plot elements and character development ideas that would eventually make it into all four films of the franchise. The majority of the talking is done by Lucas, with occasional input from Spielberg and much less from Kasdan. A brief but valuable appendix highlights the additional thoughts and concerns of Kasdan, co-writer Phil Kaufman, and Deborah Fine, who is credited with "research" in the end credits.

In a classic example of cultural recycling, the bulk of the avowed inspiration for the films came from earlier Hollywood productions. One of the first things Lucas admits is that his idea should be "done like the Republic serials. As a thirties serial. Which is where a lot of the stuff comes from anyway." By "Republic serial," Lucas is alluding to Republic Pictures, a film studio most active in the 1930s, 40s, and 50s that specialized in Westerns, B movies, and short serialized mysteries or action stories that played out in consecutive weekly installments, like a comic book. In discussing the character of Indiana Jones, Lucas and Spielberg constantly invoke particular aspects of the on-screen personas of leading Hollywood actors: John Wayne, Clark Gable, Sean Connery, and Clint Eastwood, to name just a few. Not once in one hundred and twenty-five pages of transcribed text does the name of a single real-life archaeologist appear. They also make reference to specific movies or books whose plot, style, or mood they wish to borrow from: *The Maltese Falcon*, *The Land of the Pharaohs*, *Casablanca*, *Treasure of the Sierra Madre*, *King Kong*, *Three Days of the Condor*, and *Lord of the Rings*, among others. Fictional character templates for certain traits of the hero included James Bond, Sherlock Holmes, and Clark Kent.

But Lucas wanted to push the envelope in a new direction. At one point, Lucas tells Spielberg that "you've been describing this to people as a science fiction film, which is good" (Spielberg refutes this; Lucas says "It's in *Rolling Stone*"). Elsewhere they admit on three separate occasions that they are essentially re-creating "one of those rides at Disneyland," more specifically "a real, horror ride." Also mentioned is *Ripley's Believe It or Not*. Collectively, what we are seeing here is a significant debt to pre-existing Hollywood productions; fantasy, science fiction, and detective novels; and mainstream popular culture. Missing from this list is anything resembling history. Though this will likely come as a surprise to many casual fans—it was certainly news to me—it actually makes perfect sense. Lucas and Spielberg were not making a documentary; they were crafting an entertaining story to sell to the general public. As such, it should come as little surprise to find that the overwhelming majority of their inspiration came from other successful entertainment products of their day, those with a tried and proven track record of appealing to a Western mainstream audience.

Interestingly enough, however, Lucas himself seems to have thought he was incorporating respectable historical input into his story. Throughout the brainstorming session, we are regaled with repeated allusions to "Phil's research," a reference to co-writer Phil Kaufman. Lucas describes Kaufman's research as historical in nature. "There's a history of it," he says. "This is, again, where the research comes in. Phil knew more about this than I did, and his notes are very sketchy." What does all this research concern? Mostly the accumulated lore surrounding the Ark of the Covenant—the religious artifact around which the plot of *Raiders of the Lost Ark* revolves—and a supposed Nazi obsession with the occult. Lucas claims to have "more research" on how Adolf Hitler, in "1936 or whatever, was a fanatic for this kind of stuff, occult craziness. We have another book where he was looking for the spear that killed Jesus, which was in a museum in Czechoslovakia. Well, he was a fanatic for finding this sort of occult stuff."

The books Lucas and Kaufman are referring to are Erich von Däniken's *Chariot of the Gods? Unsolved Mysteries of the Past* (1968) and Trevor Ravenscroft's *The Spear of Destiny: The Occult Power Behind the Spear Which Pierced the Side of Christ* (1973). If the titles alone sound like they come from the minds of slick conspiracy theorists, it is because they do. Von Däniken promoted the idea that most early civilizations were inspired by human contact with more advanced extraterrestrial life forms, an idea taken up in *Kingdom of the Crystal Skull*. With regard to *Raiders of the Lost Ark*, we should note von Däniken's theory of how the Ark served as a form of radio communication between the Jews and their god. Ravenscroft, acting as a posthumous amanuensis for a dead Nazi author—I kid you not—tells a spurious tale of Hitler's fascination with the occult and the power of various Judeo-Christian artifacts. From the perspective of a professional historian, it would be too polite to characterize the contents of either book as anything more than utter nonsense. And yet both books made their authors rich men, with von Däniken's *Chariot of the Gods* even climbing the *New York Times* "bestseller list." Various sequels eventually totaled over seventy million copies in sales, not to mention numerous documentaries and television specials.

As with the other cultural influences on Lucas noted above, it is this penchant for proven commercial success—rather than proven historical veracity—which appears to have exerted the greater appeal for the filmmakers. In a single breath during the brainstorming session, Lucas seamlessly merges the content of these two "history" books: "We'll just say that Hitler has been trying to find this [the spear], which is history, and he's also trying to find this Ark." At any rate, it is unclear to what extent Lucas actually digested the content of von Däniken's book. At one point in the conversation, Lucas goes so far as to confuse von Däniken the real-life author with von Däniken the fictional villain: "... in the end they convince him to do it because they say this Professor Erich von Däniken, or whatever, this German version of himself is the one who found it." Spielberg also appears to blur the line between fact and fiction, on one occasion suggesting that a "real slimy German character" would have the name of "Himmler or something like that"—without seeming to realize that Heinrich Himmler, the head of the Ahnenerbe discussed in chapter 7, was a real Nazi leader (not to mention the single most plausible historical villain for Indiana Jones).

In the appended meeting involving Kaufman, Kasdan, and Fine, we learn more about the thin historical basis for the films. After Kaufman reveals his list of "historical" sources for the main plot—*The Spear of Destiny*, the Bible, a television special on the Dead Sea Scrolls, a single entry in the Encyclopedia Britannica (later "corrected" to "Americana"), and a mysterious article on the Ark written by his mononucleosis doctor twenty years earlier—screenwriter Larry Kasdan appears unimpressed. "So basically, it was your doctor, and his article and von Däniken, and the Bible, and nothing else that we know anything about." Deborah Fine (credited with "research" in the casting list) then chimes in with a more blunt assessment, referring to the film's basic plot premise as "fairly hokey." Not only that, but it is based upon speculation that lacks "any serious excavations or attempts by archaeologists to really find it." Kaufman, now on the defensive, silences his critics with the most revealing phrase of all: "You want it to be fun."

That we do, indeed. We are not here to pass judgment on the creators of the Indiana Jones film franchise for failing to adhere to the standards of the historian, which none of them trained or claimed to be. We simply want to make it clear that there is little to no respectable historical input for any of the major plotlines in the series. In other words, the Indiana Jones films owe their greatest debt to Egyptomania, not Egyptology. This simply confirms the futility of any attempt to claim that the character of Indiana Jones was based on this or that archaeologist in history, or that any of the plot lines from the four films in the franchise were inspired in any way by actual excavations or expeditions. True to the priorities of someone working in the entertainment business, the topics about which Lucas and Spielberg appear to possess the most historical knowledge—and concern for historical accuracy— relate to the types of props they intend to make use of. As such, both men reveal an impressive familiarity with World War II fighter plane models, the availability of submarines, and what sort of device Indiana Jones could use to jump out of a 1930s airplane. Lucas may not have been overly concerned about the reliability of Kaufman's mononucleosis doctor, but he was certainly "worried they didn't have life rafts then."

The Indiana Jones film franchise is great fun, but it is more closely related to science fiction, Disneyland rides, James Bond, and crackpot conspiracy theories than it is to history. But surely there is some semblance of history somewhere. There are Nazis in two of the four films and Soviet KGB agents in another, and everyone knows those guys existed. In fact, there is a good deal of history that we can take away from all four films—though little of this appears to reflect the deliberate intentions of the filmmakers. Rather, there are a handful of interesting convergences that seem to suggest an unconscious regurgitation of vague but mostly accurate historical knowledge, as refracted through multiple cultural and media prisms.

Let us begin with what the filmmakers got right. Indiana Jones is a successful American archaeologist active in the decades just before World War II. Originally referred to by Lucas as "Indiana Smith," the character was supposed to be "very Americana square," said to be born in the state of Indiana.

(Kasdan: "What does she call him, Indy?" Lucas: "That's what I was thinking.") In other words, Indiana Jones is the very embodiment of hometown America. This is in perfect accord with we saw in in chapters 5 and 6. Though relative latecomers to the game of archaeology, the Americans poured their money and leadership into the field in the decades after World War I. In the wake of the war, Europe was devastated, and support for foreign expeditions and museum acquisitions dried up overnight. Into the vacuum stepped the Rockefellers and Carnegies, those great American philanthropists who made their fortunes during the Gilded Age. Whether in China or the Middle East, it was Americans who led the way: men like James Breasted and Langdon Warner. Even when Europeans such as Aurel Stein or Ernst Herzfeld still went out into the field, they often did so under the employ and oversight of American universities and museums. The filmmakers even select a plausible *alma mater* for Dr. Jones: the University of Chicago, which was the home of James Breasted and his Oriental Institute.

Another area where the films are on firm ground is in the choice of a French villain, René Belloq, for *Raiders of the Lost Ark*. Though almost certainly an incidental choice—many other candidates of different nationalities were discussed—the selection of a French rival opposite an American archaeologist in the Middle East during the 1920s and 30s is historically felicitous, nonetheless. As we learned in chapters 4 and 6, French scholars were the administrators of choice for nearly every Middle Eastern state desirous of establishing its own antiquities service. And though it is clear to the historian that these French directors were loyal to the governments that employed them—and not to France—this fact was not always clear to the British and American archaeologists who occasionally locked horns with them. Recall how James Breasted, after witnessing the obstruction of Howard Carter at the tomb of King Tut in the mid-1920s under the direction of Pierre Lacau, the director of the Egyptian Antiquities Service, immediately suspected an international French conspiracy against Anglo-American interests. It seems that the filmmakers, in choosing to pit an American archaeologist against a Frenchman in the interwar Middle East, inadvertently hit the historical nail on the head.

Unfortunately, nearly everything else about the choice of locale and era for *Raiders of the Lost Ark* and *The Last Crusade* does not pass muster. In the commercially savvy estimation of Lucas, the Nazis made for great villains and the Middle East provided a suitably "exotic" backdrop. But neither makes much sense from a historian's perspective. From an early date, it is clear that Lucas was wedded to Cairo as the principle urban backdrop. "It's in Cairo," he says during the brainstorm, "but it doesn't have to be. I only use that because it's one of those thirties cities. In the research it will probably be an Israeli city." We should give Lucas some credit here for his candid acknowledgement of the profound gap between filming and historical priorities. But even "Israel" would have been just as unlikely a site for the story he wanted to tell as Egypt. As we saw in chapter 6, the interwar Middle East was split almost entirely among three political actors: the British, French, and independent states. "Israel" didn't even exist yet—it was still the British "mandate" of Palestine. For its part, Egypt was independent but still heavily influenced by French and British interests, the former through the Antiquities Service and the latter as advisors to the king. Not only that, but thousands of British troops were stationed there. In other words, the 1930s was a time when the Nazis would not have been able to set one foot inside Egypt or Palestine unless the French and British had wanted them to.

It should also go without saying that even if the Nazis somehow could have organized a dig in Egypt during this time, the Egyptian authorities never would have allowed them the freedom of movement and lack of oversight that they seem to enjoy in the film. Ever since the tussle between Carter and Cairo over King Tut's tomb in 1923–24, no foreign archaeologist could do anything in Egypt without constant local oversight and stringent restrictions. This observation applies equally to most other Middle Eastern countries at the time. The situation in Turkey was more or less identical to that of Egypt. Syria and Jordan were French and British mandates, respectively, and off-limits to the Germans. Iran was independent but still largely beholden to French and American interests. Iraq, formerly a British mandate but by the time of the first film a newly independent state, might have made for a plausible backdrop if not for continued British and American influence. In short, the 1930s was simply too late a decade for any German excavations or expeditions to make much headway anywhere in the Middle East. It was difficult enough for the Americans, British, and French. But the Germans, only recently stripped of all their overseas assets after their defeat in World War I, would have searched in vain for a peaceful Middle Eastern foothold. In fact, we know that this is precisely what happened: in chapter 7, we saw the Ahnenerbe expedition to various Middle Eastern countries chased away at every turn.

There are some interesting exceptions. In *The Last Crusade*, for instance, the climactic denouement, in which Jones finds the Holy Grail just outside the modern-day city of Iskenderun (in present-day Turkey), is said to occur within the Republic of Hatay. Someone on the set must have done their research, for this tiny republic, wedged between Turkey and Syria, actually existed, albeit briefly: 1938–39, timed perfectly to overlap with the narrative of the film. Would the Nazis have been able to gain entrance to this country? Probably not, seeing how the chief political influences in the republic were advisors from proudly independent Turkey and French-controlled Syria. Another fascinating—and far more plausible—candidate would have been the Italian colonies of North Africa. The Germans and Italians were on friendly terms, and Libya, just to the west of Egypt, had been an Italian colony since 1912. By 1936, the year of the first film, Italy had also taken over Ethiopia, with its wealth of Abrahamic religions. (Interestingly enough, Lucas briefly floated the idea of an Italian villain opposite Jones, only to shoot down his own idea: "No. Italians are too crazy.") Of course, shifting the action just a few years ahead to the outbreak of World War II would have given the filmmakers a host of new options: all of Vichy France's colonies along the north African coast, Italian (and later German) conquests in the Balkans and Greece, and sixty miles of north-western Egyptian desert briefly captured during the Italian (and later German) invasion of Egypt.

Unfortunately for the history buff, Lucas insisted on gun-toting Nazis in the Near East in the years just prior to

World War II. As we have just seen, this is a set of criteria difficult to fulfill anywhere outside of the Italian colonies of Libya and Ethiopia. He also wanted an artifact drawn from the Judeo-Christian tradition, something he and his target audience could identify with. (Here we see the enduring influence of biblical archaeology and Western avatars discussed in chapter 3.) Again, Libya and Ethiopia could conceivably fill this role. But alas, the Nazis cannot. Contrary to the claims put forth in the quack histories of Trevor Ravenscroft and Erich von Däniken, Nazi leaders were not unusually obsessed with either the occult or the spiritually infused baubles of Judeo-Christian material culture. The mysterious rites and jargon of the secret society clubs joined by many Nazi members were scarcely any different from similar fraternal orders found throughout the world, including Britain and the United States.

With respect to Judaism and Christianity, the Nazis were either hostile or ambivalent, but rarely welcoming. Judaism is the religion of the Jews, and we all know how the Nazis felt about the Jews. It would have made little sense for them to covet—much less believe in—the power of the Ark, which represented a covenant between no one other than the Jews and their god. As for the Christians, they viewed Jesus as their savior, and Jesus was also a Jew, one who preached love and equality for all human beings. Not only that, but all the Abrahamic religions originated in the Middle East, far away from the preferred sites of Nazi racial genesis. As we saw in chapter 7, the two poles of Nazi affection for the past are illustrated through the cultural preferences of Hitler and Himmler. Hitler was an unabashed admirer of Greco-Roman antiquity, a bias held by a majority of European elites since Napoleon. (Of course, his Greeks and Romans were Aryans in Mediterranean guise.) He had little interest in the Nordic obsessions of Himmler, whose Ahnenerbe missions attempted to recover the "lost" Scandinavian lore of the least "diluted" of Aryan peoples. Either way, neither agenda had room for Christians or Jews, or their magical relics. If anything, they would have been more likely to destroy the Ark or Holy Grail than to preserve them.

Another recurrent choice of locale in the films is Peru. The iconic opening scene in *Raiders of the Lost Ark*, in which Jones retrieves a golden idol and outruns an oversized boulder, is set in 1936 somewhere in the jungles of Peru. The fourth film, *Kingdom of the Crystal Skull*, returns to Peru and its Amazon hinterlands for a significant portion of the action. In this latter film, Jones is not only said to go to Peru, but more specifically to the former Incan town of Cuzco. Recall from chapter 3 that this was also the launch point for Hiram Bingham and his expeditions to Machu Picchu in 1911–12. The choice of such a well-known site is unlikely to be a coincidence. In the brainstorming session, Lucas told Spielberg and Kasdan that "the film starts in the jungle. South America, someplace. We get one of these great scenes with the pack animals going up the mist-covered hills. Very exotic mist-filled jungles and mountains." He just as easily could have been describing one of the 250 eerily similar photographs of the hike to Machu Picchu published by Bingham in the April 1913 issue of *National Geographic*.

Superficial convergences notwithstanding, Bingham did his dirty work in Peru a full quarter of a century before Indiana Jones is said to have outrun the boulder in *Raiders of the Lost Ark*, and a whopping half century before his more extended, CGI-infused visit in *Kingdom of the Crystal Skull*. But even in 1911–12, Bingham was unable to obtain permission from the Peruvian government to remove artifacts in perpetuity. In fact, he was forced to sign a secret clause permitting Peru to later demand from Yale University the return of the skeletons and other objects Bingham had removed from Machu Picchu. In this, Peru was not unique among Latin American countries of that era. Therefore, despite the undeniable visual appeal of an archaeological expedition ascending the mist-enshrouded peaks of Peru—one imagines Lucas to have been influenced by similar scenes in Werner Herzog's *Aguirre, the Wrath of God* (1972)—such a scene would have been unlikely to unfurl against the temporal backdrop of 1936 (and certainly not that of 1957). Once again, the filmmakers have chosen a historical time frame far too late to accommodate the archaeological free-for-all in which they expect their hero to engage.

Elsewhere, however, the filmmakers appear to have done a bit more homework, at least with regard to historical back-drops. Say what you will about the demeaning portrayals of half-naked natives in *Temple of Doom* and *Kingdom of the Crystal Skull*, at least the geopolitics are (mostly) right. In 1935, the year Indiana Jones stumbles into a northern Indian village terrorized by an underground cult, many of the princely states along the Himalayan foothills did maintain the same sort of quasi-autonomy from the British Raj that is depicted in the film. And there was once an underground network of Thuggee cult members who indulged in murder, robbery, and the worship of a destructive god, though they were long gone by the 1930s. Beyond these simple facts of history, though, the rest of *Temple of Doom* is pure fantasy. As for the *Kingdom of the Crystal Skull*, the filmmakers could hardly miss the mark: the only plausible framework for a film set in the 1950s is the Cold War, which naturally invites themes derived from the exploration of space, nuclear weapons, and Soviet spies (though, as mentioned above, the choice of Cuzco and the Amazon jungle as the setting for an archaeological rivalry between two foreign expeditions is still implausible).

One major theme that runs through the film franchise is the willingness of Indiana Jones to lend his knowledge of foreign languages and ancient civilizations to the U.S. government. This relationship is most readily portrayed in *Raiders of the Lost Ark* and *Kingdom of the Crystal Skull*. In the former, Jones is approached by Army intelligence agents, who ask for his help in finding the Ark before the Nazis do. In the latter, it is revealed that Jones worked for the CIA in Berlin during the Cold War and was tapped as a consultant to examine an unidentified alien corpse for the U.S. military in 1947. With the exception of the alien and unlikelihood of scholars taking the place of in-house, trained CIA operatives in the 1950s—after the post-WWII "divorce"—much of this is an accurate reflection of the work archaeologists and other scholars frequently did on behalf of their governments (see chapter 7). The competing and often contradictory priorities of the relationship are summed up perfectly in one of Spielberg's contributions to the brainstorm: "His assignment is to recover the Ark, but if you see a submarine base, blow it up."

The films even get the imbalance of knowledge between the two sides correct: in *Raiders of the Lost Ark*, the Army officers know virtually nothing of the history of the Ark, and it is up to Jones, who is said to "know more about it than they do," to educate them. "I'm not a spy," Lucas says while mimicking Jones' lines during the brainstorm, "I'm an archaeologist. Why don't you send one of your guys over there to do that?" Because, the Army men reply, their guys "don't know an Ark from a bathtub." Embedded within these lines is the realization that Jones bristles at the idea of being a spy; in other words, someone who prostitutes scientific knowledge for overt political ends. In the film, it is only when Jones later convinces himself of a larger, more noble cause that he accepts the mission. "That thing [the Ark] represents everything we got into archaeology for in the first place," he tells Marcus Brody, a friend and museum director. Of course, as we saw in chapter 7, Mayan archaeologist Sylvanus Morley likely would have regarded his collaboration with the Office of Naval Intelligence in a similar light. He wasn't a spy, he would have said, but rather a patriotic scholar on the "right" side of the war, with important archaeological work done on the side.

The question of Jones' professional morality and ethics is one that Lucas, Spielberg, and Kasdan wrestled with constantly during the creative process. In fact, the feel-good line of dialogue quoted above—"That thing represents everything we got into archaeology for in the first place"—appears only in the final cut of the film. For most of the brainstorming session and early drafts of the script, Indiana Jones was envisioned as a much less savory character. Lucas introduces him to Spielberg and Kasdan as an "outlaw archaeologist" or "bounty hunter of antiquities," someone who "got involved in going in and getting antiquities" and managed to turn it into "a very lucrative profession." At another point he's described as a "grave robber for hire." But once the filmmakers begin to explore the moral implications of these characterizations, they quickly run into problems. The first issue derives from the realization that they want Jones to be somebody "who really knows his job. He's really good at what he does." Otherwise, it wouldn't be a lucrative profession. But how did Jones get so good at finding antiquities? The only plausible answer: he has an academic background. "He is an archaeologist and an anthropologist," Lucas declares. "A Ph.D. He's a doctor. He's a college professor." Later, Lucas again reinforces this point: "We've established that he's a college professor. It doesn't have to be done in a strong way. It starts out in a museum. They just call him doctor this and doctor that."

The realization that Indiana Jones can only be a successful archaeologist—albeit an "outlaw" one—if he has a Ph.D. quickly gives rise to a second problem, one alluded to in the line quoted above. That is, he became an expert on antiquities through his association with universities, but to whom does he sell the antiquities once he retrieves them? Again, the only plausible answer: museums. "He gets his money from the museum," Lucas informs his colleagues. "You understand a little more about him as a professor and all that other bullshit. It also really sets up the fact that he's a bounty hunter and he works for museums." Lucas doesn't yet appear to be troubled by the implications of all the ideas he's thrown into the mix, referring to them as "all that other bullshit." But it doesn't take long before all three filmmakers begin to unpack the tensions involved. In one breath, Lucas, in trying to imagine how his hero might embark upon such a mission, seems to hit upon the legitimizing role of museums almost without realizing it. "We think maybe it's on the underground market, or in a private collection. We'd like to have it. Actually it belongs to us. We're the National Museum of Cairo or something." There it is: only a national museum can serve to justify the removal of artifacts from their original location to another one, as discussed in chapter 1. In other words, Lucas, perhaps unwittingly, has finally discovered the moral discourse of "science," "preservation," and "education" as the only legitimate pretexts for an archaeological adventure.

Now we see the ethics of Indiana Jones begin to change. The filmmakers still want him to be the good guy, but they don't want him to play by the rules. There are certain rules, however, that cannot be broken without turning him into the bad guy. Instead of merely robbing graves for gold, Jones is now said to "swipe it back" in a way that is "sort of legal." What is "sort of legal"? According to Lucas, "it's not like he steals things from collectors and then gives them to other collectors. What he does is steal things from private collectors who have them illegally, and gives them back to the national museums and stuff." In other words, Lucas now understands that only a museum can claim to represent the interests of science, preservation, and education, in a way that private collectors cannot. But he still wants to think of Jones as someone who "steals" things, most likely in an effort to maintain the specter of adventure and danger. Now, however, he realizes that these two ideas are incompatible: in the world of art and archaeology, Jones simply cannot be the good guy if he "steals" things. In the original brainstorm, Lucas immediately corrects his previous statement. "He's not a totally corrupt person, where he'll steal. But if it's sort of fair game, then he comes in."

It is obvious by this point that Lucas is desperately trying to preserve some aspect of roguish intrigue without undermining the likeability of his main character. Eventually, however, the contradictions become too evident to ignore. Kasdan is the first to confront the issue, wondering how "an archaeologist who's spent years studying this" and has "some kind of awe and respect for virgin tombs" can be turned to the dark side. "What's his stance on this? Does it bother him to go in and..." Before Kasdan can expose the gap in logic, Lucas cuts him off. "Basically he's very cynical about the whole thing," Lucas interrupts. "Maybe he thinks that most archaeologists are full of shit, and that somebody's going to rip this stuff off anyway. Better that he rips it off and gets it to a museum where people can study it, and rip it off right." What a wonderful phrase: "rip it off right." It is also an oxymoron. Though Lucas wanted Indiana Jones to be "a very believable character," he quickly realized that an archaeologist who does not consort with universities and museums is not a believable character. But once Jones is associated with these institutions, the moral discourse of science, preservation, and education that justifies their existence also ties Lucas' hands in ways he could not have foreseen.

These issues are not resolved in the brainstorm session. Museums and colleges notwithstanding, Lucas still tries to push the limits of how much immoral behavior Jones can absorb without making him into the bad guy. Again, Kasdan is the one who appears most befuddled by Lucas' repeated attempts to drag Indiana Jones through the mud, only to redeem him time and time again. "I'm a little confused about Indiana at this point," Kasdan says, after Lucas highlights another random moral awakening in Jones. "I thought he'd do anything for this pendant." Lucas does another about face. "But he still has to have some moral scruples. He has to be a person we can look up to. We're doing a role model for little kids, so we have to be careful. We need someone who's honest, trusting, and true." It was later left to Kasdan, the screenwriter, to work out the final ratio of Indy's morality. In one of the early scripts for *Raiders of the Lost Ark*, Kasdan describes Jones' home as "English Tudor, upper middle class home. Quite toney; well beyond the financial reach of an honest college professor." Inside, "the lush tone continues here in Art Deco and shiny marble," with a beautiful woman dressed in silks and sipping champagne lounging on the furniture. When the men from Army intelligence come to interview Jones, his friend Marcus Brody reassures him: "Don't worry, it's not about your business."

All this is removed from the final cut of the film. In their place, most references to Jones' seedier side are delivered in more subtle and comical ways. His lush English Tudor house is now a modest brick abode, well within the reach of an honest college professor, with shiny marble nowhere in evidence. Brody, the director of the imaginary "National Museum" in Washington, D.C., tells Jones that the museum will buy the jewels he's brought back from Peru, "no questions asked." When Jones offers to fill him in on the details of his morally dubious escapades, Brody's response is designed to elicit a knowing chuckle from the viewer: "I'm sure everything you do for the museum conforms to the International Treaty for the Protection of Antiquities." The men from the Army are given similar dialogue when they try to characterize Jones' work. "Ah, how does one say it? Obtainer of rare antiquities." Jones mutters an evasive response: "There's only one way to say it."

Any doubts about Indy's ethical orientation introduced by these humorous scenes, however, are negated by Jones' subsequent confession that the search for the Ark "represents everything we got into archaeology for in the first place." He is also thrilled to learn that the Ark will be given to Brody's museum upon completion of the mission. The edgy morality of Lucas' early brainstorming sessions is not entirely white-washed, however. A memorable scene in a Cairo tea house serves as the occasion for René Belloq, the French mercenary working on behalf of the Nazis, to tell Jones that the two of them had both "fallen from the pure faith" and were "not so different" from one other. Again, though, the filmmakers quickly undermine the force of these comments by having Jones draw a sharp line in the sand between the two men, by suggesting that only one of them (Belloq) must venture into the "sewer" to find friends of similar moral caliber. (An additional sixty minutes spent punching Nazis completes Indy's redemption.)

The second film, *Temple of Doom*, marks a departure from the first film in its decision to eschew any and all references to Jones' professional ethics, for better or for worse. The only two "artifacts" in the film—a collection of magical stones and an urn with the ashes of Nurhaci, the first Manchu emperor of the Qing Dynasty—are not the sort of objects desired by museums, which themselves disappear from the script. The decision to abandon these legitimizing institutions resulted in a much darker storyline. Children are abused and enslaved, men and women are sacrificed, hearts are ripped out of chests, and the viewer searches in vain for a higher good capable of redeeming such a hellish world. Though still a financially successful romp around the yard, *Temple of Doom* left both critics and audience members aghast, and not in a feel-good sort of way.

Not surprisingly then, the third film, *The Last Crusade*, returned to the formula of the first, but this time freed from the hazy morality of *Raiders of the Lost Ark*. Just minutes into the movie, both a younger and older version of Indiana Jones give voice to his newly minted trademark line: "That belongs in a museum!" It takes no more than fifteen minutes of reel time before a variant of this line is uttered on three separate occasions. In place of the considerable sum of cash he was paid by the Army for the recovery of the Ark in the first film, here Jones receives nothing more than an "honorarium" for his contributions to Brody's museum. And when a wealthy collector of Holy Grail paraphernalia attempts to induce Jones to embark on a new mission with the promise of personal gain (eternal life), Jones turns him down flat. It is only when he learns that his father's life is in danger—a higher good if ever there was one—that Indy accepts the assignment. Later, the Austrian villainess Elsa tries to draw moral equivalency between her own unscrupulous actions and those of Jones. "We both wanted the Grail. I would have done anything to get it. You would have done the same." Not surprisingly, Indy takes the moral high ground. "I'm sorry you think so."

With Jones' moral integrity now retroactively established from his earliest days clear into middle age, the fourth film, *Kingdom of the Crystal Skull*, ventures back into the subtle humor of the first film. Early in the story, when Jones first meets his son Mutt, he learns that Mutt's mother once told her son that "if anyone can find the skull," it is his father, "like you're some type of grave robber or something." In response, Jones insists on his professional bona fides. "I'm a tenured professor of archaeology," he says sternly. Later, at an archaeological site in Peru, Mutt reads aloud the sign that greets them: "Grave robbers will be shot." Though Lucas once envisioned Jones as a "grave robber for hire," such labels now only serve as the butt for deadpan humor. "Good thing we're not grave robbers," Jones replies. Finally, inside an underground tomb complex, Jones happens upon a magnificent dagger sheathed inside the vest of a corpse. As he begins to place the dagger in his own coat pocket, Mutt glares at him in disbelief. "Don't want to keep borrowing yours all the time," Indy says in self-defense, fumbling to return the knife. "I was gonna put it back."

If he puts it back, then Indiana Jones is a practitioner of disinterested science. If he doesn't, he is a grave robber. Try as he did, Lucas simply could not fudge the line between these two poles of morality. In the world of museums, archaeology, and art, there are rules, and not even Lucas can break them. In the end, the final composite image of Indiana Jones is that of a competent scientist with a colorful past. He gets into tough scrapes and challenging situations, but always does the right thing in the end. As Lucas hoped, kids can still look up to him. What is fascinating is how the filmmakers, without any apparent exposure to the history of museums and archaeological expeditions, managed nonetheless to arrive at the same conclusions reached by the caretakers of Pompeii and the Louvre more than two centuries earlier: the good guys give artifacts to museums, where they can be studied, preserved, and used to educate the general public. By contrast, the bad guys, driven by greed, vanity, and personal ambition, keep everything in private collections, without regard to the altruistic interests of science, preservation, or education. Though real-life archaeologists and museums may operate within a vast gray area, a major Hollywood action flick meant to provide escapist entertainment for the masses cannot do the same.

If Lucas, Spielberg, and Kasdan could unconsciously weave their cinematic narrative around the noble but largely unspoken discourse of disinterested science, what other sort of subconscious cultural input might have managed to find its way into their Indiana Jones films? As it turns out, quite a lot. Not surprisingly, nearly all of this inadvertent cultural feedback can trace its intellectual lineage back to the foundational discourse of science. Of course, we already know that Jones is presented as a competent practitioner of science. What we have yet to encounter, however, are the strategies deployed by the filmmakers (again, almost certainly unknowingly) to define just what exactly science is. Simply put, the definition of a scientist in the films is not presented through positive explication, by showcasing Jones as a practitioner of the scientific method in cultural isolation. Rather, it is defined through an implicitly judgmental demonstration of contrasting cultural opposites. In other words, the audience comes to understand Indy's degree of scientific competence primarily through reference to the scientific shortcomings of people who are not presented as scientists.

Who are these not-scientists? In both the brainstorming session and the films, they tend to be the dark-skinned natives of exotic lands. Lucas' original idea for Indiana Jones was that he be an "archaeological exorcist," who is "an expert in the occult." Note that he is not a *believer* in the occult, but rather an *expert* in the occult. Lucas himself highlights the distinction. "People will walk through this particular temple and they will die twenty-four hours later," he says. "Nobody knows why. The curse of Mabutu is on that place. Well, he looks at it and sees that there's a fissure in the thing and there's a deadly gas that's coming out of the ground. Because he's an intelligent professor, he knows his science and he can sort of deduce a hoax." Who created this hoax? Why, the "natives," of course. In describing his idea for the iconic first scene of *Raiders of the Lost Ark*, Lucas tells Spielberg and Kasdan that "all the natives get restless and start to split. One of the guys goes to him and says, 'The natives are leaving, they're not going to go any further.' It's the curse of the Buddha, or whatever. He says they can probably get there from here without them." How does he get there without the help of the cowardly natives? With the aid of a crude map drawn by Jones himself, one that provides "enough informa-tion ... where I think I can deduce my way through it."

Be it the curse of Mabutu or the Buddha, the final version of this scene, filmed largely in accord with the sentiments expressed in the brainstorm session, perfectly illustrates how Indiana Jones comes to be defined for the audience as a man of science. Science is defined not in terms of what it is, but by what it isn't: superstitious natives who believe in the occult. Time and again, whenever a character in one of the films intro-duces a fantastic tale of wonder and woe, Jones responds with equal parts skepticism and cynicism. For he is a scientist, and a scientist must regard such tales as little more than "bedtime stories." This being Hollywood, of course, Jones the scientist is never given the last laugh: in each film, at least one "wondrous curiosity," to borrow the Egyptomania phrase, turns out to possess real supernatural powers. Even this partial vindica-tion is undermined by the filmmakers' decision to draw from the Judeo-Christian tradition and extraterrestrial interfer-ence for the selection of three of the franchise's four wondrous curiosity allotments: the Ark, Holy Grail, and crystal skull. In fact, the "Sankara Stones" in *The Temple of Doom* are the only artifacts associated with a non-Western society that are shown to have the "superstitious" powers once relegated to the realm of Professor Jones' "bedtime stories." Tellingly, however, the Sankara Stones are also the only wondrous curiosity of the film franchise to be used solely for sinister purposes, with no apparent redemptive qualities. To put it another way (again borrowing the lexicon of Egyptomania), the Western and alien artifacts turn out to be "wondrous curiosities," while the lone non-Western artifact is portrayed as a "monstrous curiosity."

The implicit, judgmental contrasts between the confident Western man of science and the passive Oriental beholden to superstition and ignorance continued throughout the creative process, from choice of villain to geographic backdrop. In the brainstorm, ideas for various Asian characters are often predicated upon the imagined inscrutability of their faces and minds. At one point, Lucas says that one trait of a potential Oriental villain would be that "you can never tell what they're thinking." In trying to explain the motivations of another character, Lucas makes reference to "the crazy Oriental mind. How do we know how it works. They always wait until the last minute or something." Spielberg, however, eventually shoots down the idea of an Asian rival for Indiana Jones, though not for admirable reasons. "I think he should be German because there's something nonviolent about the Oriental villain. Certainly he can ... be good with swords and everything, but there's something a little more ominous about a real German." These descriptions of Asians as less "violent" and a "real German" as more "ominous" are scarcely veiled code words for ideas about masculinity, which the Orientals are imagined to lack and the Germans to possess. Again, though the filmmakers had no apparent exposure either to the history of archaeological expeditions or to Western depictions of the non-Western world more generally, they nonetheless manage to replicate elements of the discourse of Oriental stagnation, femininity, and decadence produced during that era.

Nowhere are these hidden biases and stereotypes more evident than in the franchise's treatment of expendable dark-skinned characters from distant lands. In their earliest discussions, Lucas and Spielberg reveal the guiding assumptions destined to appear in one form or another in the finished films. In trying to imagine what sort of locals might accompany Indiana Jones into the jungle temple to recover the golden idol in *Raiders of the Lost Ark*, Lucas and Spielberg produced the following exchange:

> **Lucas**: We had it where there's a couple native bearers, whatever, and sort of a couple of Mexican, well, not Mexican... Let's put it...

Spielberg: They're like Mayan.

Lucas: They're the third world local sleazos. Whether they're Mexicans or Arabs or whatever.

Spielberg: They carry the boxes over their heads. They fall off cliffs.

Lucas: The sleazos with the thin moustaches. Those are the peon laborers.

The lives of these "third world local sleazos" are not worth much. They provide labor for the white man, they "fall off cliffs," and they die, but the audience is not supposed to be overly concerned about their fate. A famously unscripted scene that made it into the final cut of the film has Jones facing off against a master Arab swordsmen in Cairo. After the swordsman makes an elaborate display of his martial prowess, Jones simply takes out his revolver and shoots him. Though most viewers laugh at this scene in spite of themselves, the laughter conceals two subliminal messages. The first is that traditional Oriental masculinity is no match for a Western scientist armed with more sophisticated weaponry. The second is that homicide is funny when the character is expendable. If the Arab swordsman mattered to the story in any way at all, this scene would not be funny. It would be repellant.

Only the non-Western characters get cast into such roles. As long as the audience laughs at them, it hardly matters who lives or dies. "They're also with another Arab side kick," Lucas says at one point, "who also got thrown back in the thing. A little comic relief." Elsewhere, in a disturbing preview of the young Asian boy "Short Round" in *Temple of Doom*—whom the filmmakers don't even bother to give a proper name—Lucas proposes a "buffoon character" to be cast as an "Arab kid," who is "just talking endlessly and you never understand what he's saying." Hoping to flesh this role out just a bit, Spielberg adds that "maybe he slows down once in a while to say something stupid. When he talks fast you just don't care." Since no one is supposed to fret over these marginal characters, their actual identities were inconsequential: Mexican, Mayan, Arabs, "whatever." Even a monkey could play the part. In *Raiders of the Lost Ark*, there is a monkey dressed up like the local inhabitants of Cairo, one who is just as expendable as they are (he dies from eating a poisoned date intended for Jones). This monkey was the subject of extended discussion in the brainstorm, much of it cringe-worthy even by the standards of the day. "Can it wear a turban?" Spielberg asks. "It should be dressed up." A few moments later, Spielberg makes the association with the marginalized Arab characters even more explicit. "The monkey should be dressed up as a little Arab." Lucas loved the idea. "I like the idea of not only having a turban, but also a little backpack."

Not that there were no major roles for non-Western protagonists. In *Raiders of the Lost Ark* and *The Last Crusade*, Indy's jovial Arab friend Sallah—referred to as "Sabu" in the brainstorm—pops in and out of the storyline. His appearances, however, are always sudden and unexplained. This was deliberate. According to Spielberg, "Sabu could get out of it and show up later. We don't have to follow his story." Again, Lucas agreed. "We can use him wherever we need him. They can just bump into him, 'Sabu, what are you doing here?'" Yes, says Spielberg, "I like it when a character just reappears." Perhaps so, but this narrative technique is not applied to any of the chief Western protagonists. Even when they simply appear out of nowhere, their presence always makes sense within the storyline. Only the non-Western natives, be they "sleazos," monkeys, or friends, can be used without regard for narrative logic or concern. For everyone else, the story has to make sense, or the show cannot go on.

A similarly cavalier attitude appears to have applied to the choice of location as well. The details of different cities and countries are relevant only insofar as they convey a suitably exotic and dangerous atmosphere. Lucas told Spielberg and Kasdan that he had tried "to move him around the world a little bit to see if we can't get a little Oriental influence into it just for the fun of it." But just what exactly is "Oriental influence," and why is it fun? Well, according to Lucas, in a place like Egypt, "you meet all these interesting characters and every once in a while somebody throws a knife at him, or he beats somebody up, or somebody beats him up, typical Middle Eastern stuff." On another occasion, Lucas predicts that "as soon as he gets there, there are knives coming out of the walls, these slimy characters are following him, all that stuff happens in those places in the thirties." Such a state of anarchy would also allow their hero to remove antiquities with impunity. In Egypt, Lucas imagines a scenario in which "the museum does commission somebody to go into the pyramids and you know, whatever they find, sort of get out without the Egyptian government knowing, because they were in the process of turmoil and nobody's going to know anyway and there's not going to be any official protest, so just do it." It should be obvious by now that neither of these conditions applied to Egypt at any point during the 1930s (or for a century prior, for that matter).

But the Far East could work just as well as the Middle East. In a preview of the opening scene of *The Temple of Doom*, Lucas proposed "a tiny piece in Hong Kong where people are constantly trying to knife him in the back and shoot poison darts into his ears." Hong Kong later becomes Shanghai. "We want to send the guy to Shanghai first just for the environment. Have a little bit of adventure there before he goes to Nepal, before he ends up in Cairo." For Lucas, all that mattered about China was that it was exotic. "The only reason we're talking about the Orient is that it's exotic. He's going to leave Washington and go to three exotic places. He'll go to the Orient with the crowded streets and dragon ladies." In addition to crowded streets and dragon ladies, Spielberg also took care to remind Lucas of Oriental barbarity. "We have to have a beheading," Spielberg adds. "We have to start this scene with a mass beheading. We don't have to show it. If you were really bad, it took three minutes to cut your head off."

Regardless of the details, the most important thing for Lucas and Spielberg was that Indiana Jones spend as little time as possible at home. "Keep him out of the States," Spielberg warned. "We don't want to do one shot in this country." Though this sentiment was later amended to include brief scenes at a New England college and Washington D.C., the message was clear: expeditions were what civilized people did in uncivilized lands. This was the message imparted by the racist cartoon published by the *Saturday Evening Post* in 1937 (see chapter 6), and it is also the message communicated by the over-the-top gross-out banquet in the Indian palace

in *Temple of Doom*: the Maharajah's guests are served writh-
ing baby snake appetizers, eyeball soup, toasted beetles, and
monkey brain dessert. The dark-skinned natives with turbans
on their heads devour every dish with gusto, as does a British
official apparently reconciled to local tastes. Only Jones and
his companions decline to follow their lead.

How are we to make sense of all these racially and culturally
tinged unpleasantries? Are we now obliged to tar the Indiana
Jones film franchise with the damning label of "politically
incorrect"? Or is there any way to account for what appears to
be a consistent trend of casual racism and ethnic stereotypes?
I believe that the historical concept of ethnic and cultural
"Western avatars" can go a long ways in explaining—if not
always excusing—those aspects of the films that appear
most troubling for present-day audiences. As we learned in
chapter 3, "Consuming Indiana Jones," ever since the middle
of the nineteenth century, popular narratives of exploration,
expeditions, and excavations designed for print consumption
invariably highlighted white protagonists with whom audiences back home could identify. If they could identify with
these protagonists on an ethnic and cultural basis—i.e., skin
color, religion, language—then they would prove willing to
pay for the privilege of walking vicariously in their shoes. Once
this business model proved successful, it formed the basis for
endless incarnations of white Anglo-Saxon heroes tramping
through exotic lands filled with dark-skinned peoples.

We first encountered this business model with the manufactured *New York Herald* expedition to find the missing
missionary David Livingstone in the 1870s. The media catchphrase produced by this publicity stunt, "Dr. Livingstone,
I presume?" is only funny to an audience who recognizes the
incongruence of speaking in polite "civilized" terms amid
dark-skinned and scantily clad natives. Though Stanley and
Livingstone were the first profitable ethnic and cultural
avatars of the Western world, they were by no means the last.
We saw how anxious Hiram Bingham was in 1911 when he
found "Lizarraga 1902" etched into the walls of Machu Picchu,
only to be calmed by the discovery that Lizarraga was not
white—thus making Bingham the "discoverer" of the "lost

city of the Incas" for his targeted audience back home. And let us not forget Howard Carter's paradoxical turn of phrase while excavating the tomb of Tutankhamun: "alone, save for my native workmen." If the goal was to create an adventurous narrative of exploration and discovery by vicarious Western avatars for profitable consumption back home, then the presence of native workmen did not change the fact that the white man was, for all intents and purposes, "alone."

The job of the Hollywood filmmaker is to entertain. The job of the historian is to educate. These two priorities often conflict with one another, but this need not be the case. The Indiana Jones film franchise is great fun, but it could be even more fun—and age more gracefully—if the facts of history were reflected more prominently in its plot and characters. The growing prominence of formerly marginalized voices in the public sphere has convinced many people of the need to diversify the cast of mostly white protagonists in Hollywood productions. But the lessons of history had already taught us the folly of portraying Western scholars as the undisputed movers and shakers of the archaeological world by the time the Indiana Jones films were said to have taken place. In fact, as early as the 1870s, there were fully trained and competent Ottoman counterparts to the historical Indiana Jones. Arabs, Indians, and Chinese need not only serve as caricatured villains: long before Indy went after the Ark, the Chinese had already sent out their own expeditions to distant lands, in direct competition with Western rivals. The movies need not—and should not—be filled only with white protagonists. There are major legitimate roles for people with different shades of skin color.

An epic story is waiting to be told here, one that would better stand the test of time. But it requires the combined talents of both entertainers and educators. By joining forces, Hollywood could smooth out the warts of the historian (too boring), and historians could smooth out the warts of Hollywood (too lazy). For just as truth is stranger than fiction, Indiana Jones in history is far stranger—and more representative—than the Indiana Jones we have all consumed to date.

And, I dare say, a good deal more fun.

List of Illustrations

FRONT COVER. Fac-simile des Monumens Coloriés de l'Egypte
SOURCE: *Description de l'Égypte, ou, Recueil de observations et des recherches qui ont été faites en Égypte pendant l'éxpédition de l'armée française*, Vol. 1: *Antiquitiés: Descriptions* (Paris: De l'Imprimerie Impériale and l'Imprimerie Royale, 1809–1822).

BACK COVER. Mode in Which the Young Memnon's Head Was Removed
SOURCE: G. Belzoni, *Six New Plates Illustrative of the Researches and Operations of G. Belzoni in Egypt and Nubia* (London: John Murray, 1822), Plate II.

FIGURE 1.1. Charles of Bourbon, King of Naples and Sicily
SOURCE: *Le pitture antiche d'Ercolano e contorni incise con qualche spiegazione.* Tomo primo (Napoli: Nella Regia Stamperia, 1757).

FIGURE 1.2. Art as Propaganda
SOURCE: Salomon Kleiner, *Representation au naturel des chateaux de Weissenstein au dessus de Pommersfeld, et de celui de Geubach appartenans a la Maison des Comtes de Schönborn avec les Jardins, les Ecuries, les Menageries, et autres dependances* (Augsbourg, 1728), Plate 18.

FIGURE 1.3. Ole Worm's *Wunderkammer*
SOURCE: Wikimedia Commons. Public domain.

FIGURE 1.4. Excavating Pompeii
SOURCE: William Hamilton, *Campi Phlegraei: Observations on the Volcanos of the Two Sicilies As They Have Been Communicated to the Royal Society of London*, Vol. 2: *Plates* (Naples, 1776), Plate XLI.

FIGURE 1.5. From Pompeii to the Louvre
CARTOGRAPHY: Debbie Newell.

FIGURE 1.6. Science to the Rescue
SOURCE: Roger de Piles, *Cours de peinture par principes* (Paris, 1708), p. 497.

FIGURE 1.7. The Grand Gallery of the Louvre
SOURCE: Hubert Robert, *Projet d'aménagement de la Grande Galerie du Louvre* (1796).

FIGURE 1.8. The Imperialist Louvre
SOURCE: Pierre-Gabriel Berthault, *Entrée Triomphale des Monuments des Sciences et Arts en France* (Paris, 1802).

FIGURE 2.1. Thomas Bruce, 7th Earl of Elgin
SOURCE: G.P. Harding, "Thomas Bruce 7th Earl of Elgin." New York Public Library Digital Collections.

FIGURE 2.2. View of the Parthenon from the Acropolis
SOURCE: Edward Dodwell, *Views in Greece, from Drawings* (London: Rodwell and Martin, 1821).

FIGURE 2.3. The Elgin Marbles
SOURCE: Wikimedia Commons. Photograph by Adam Carr.

FIGURE 2.4. Lord Elgin and the Great Belzoni
CARTOGRAPHY: Debbie Newell.

FIGURE 2.5. Muhammad Ali, the *pasha* of Egypt
SOURCE: Auguste Couder, *Mehemet Ali Viceroy of Egypt* (1841).

FIGURE 2.6. Giovanni Belzoni in Muslim Garb
SOURCE: G. Belzoni, *Narrative of the Operations and Recent Discoveries in Egypt and Nubia* (London: John Murray, 1820).

FIGURE 2.7. The Removal of the Memnon Head from Luxor
SOURCE: G. Belzoni, *Six New Plates Illustrative of the Researches and Operations of G. Belzoni in Egypt and Nubia* (London: John Murray, 1822), Plate II.

FIGURE 3.1. The Animal Gods of Ancient Egypt
SOURCE: Ippolito Rosellini, *I monumenti dell' Egitto e della Nubia disegnati dalla spedizione scientifico-letteraria toscana in Egitto* (Pisa: Capurro, 1832).

FIGURE 3.2. Egyptomania in London
SOURCE: Edwin Roffe et al., *The Sydenham Crystal Palace Expositor: With Engravings on Steel and Wood* (London: James S. Virtue, 1854), p. 13.

FIGURE 3.3. From Barbarism to (Western) Civilization
SOURCE: James Henry Breasted, *Ancient Times: A History of the Early World* (Boston: Ginn and Company, 1914), p. 54.

FIGURE 3.4. Merry Christmas from the Pharaohs
SOURCE: "A Happy Christmas." New York Public Library Digital Collections.

FIGURE 3.5. Consuming Indiana Jones, 1821–1912
CARTOGRAPHY: Debbie Newell.

FIGURE 3.6. A Parody of a Parody of a Parody
SOURCE: Photograph by Cindy Jacobs.

FIGURE 3.7. Stanley Meets Livingstone
SOURCE: Library of Congress.

FIGURE 3.8. Avocados from Peru
SOURCE: Copyright and courtesy Peruvian Avocado Commission.

FIGURE 4.1. Moses vs. Pharaoh
SOURCE: New York Public Library Digital Collections.

FIGURE 4.2. An Obelisk in Central Park
SOURCE: Library of Congress.

FIGURE 4.3. Auguste Mariette, Director of the Egyptian Antiquities Service
SOURCE: Wikimedia Commons. Public domain.

FIGURE 4.4. Reorienting the Orient, 1846–1877
SOURCE: Cartography by Debbie Newell. IMAGES: Heinrich Schliemann, *Troy and Its Remains* (London: John Murray, 1875), p. 335; Library of Congress; Auguste Mariette-Bey et al., *Album du musée de Boulaq* (Cairo: Mourès, 1872), Plate 37.

FIGURE 4.5. Heinrich Schliemann, Promoter of Troy
SOURCE: Library of Congress.

FIGURE 4.6. Hiram Powers' *The Greek Slave*
SOURCE: "The Greek Slave." New York Public Library Digital Collections.

FIGURE 4.7. Excavating Troy
SOURCE: Heinrich Schliemann, *Troy and Its Remains* (London: John Murray, 1875), p. 259.

FIGURE 4.8. Hasan al-Banna, Founder of the Muslim Brotherhood
SOURCE: Wikimedia Commons. Public domain.

FIGURE 5.1. The U.S. Ninth Infantry in Beijing
SOURCE: Library of Congress.

FIGURE 5.2. Chinese Bronzes
SOURCE: Wikimedia Commons. Photograph by John Thomson.

FIGURE 5.3. A Gandharan Fresco in Xinjiang
SOURCE: M. Aurel Stein, *Ruins of Desert Cathay: Personal Narrative of Explorations in Central Asia and Westernmost China*, vol. 1 (London: Macmillan, 1912), between pp. 478–79.

FIGURE 5.4. Aurel Stein in Xinjiang
SOURCE: M. Aurel Stein, *Ruins of Desert Cathay: Personal Narrative of Explorations in Central Asia and Westernmost China*, vol. 2 (London: Macmillan, 1912), between pp. 416–17.

FIGURE 5.5. The Treasures of China
CARTOGRAPHY: Debbie Newell.

FIGURE 5.6. The Secret Cave "Library" at Dunhuang
SOURCE: Wikimedia Commons. Public domain.

FIGURE 5.7. The Longmen Grottoes
SOURCE: Édouard Chavannes, *Mission archéologique dans la Chine septentrionale. Planches* (Paris: Imprimerie Nationale, 1909), Plate 353.

FIGURE 5.8. Aisin Gioro Puyi, Last Emperor of China
SOURCE: Library of Congress.

FIGURE 6.1. Role Reversal in the *Saturday Evening Post*
SOURCE: David Huffine, *Saturday Evening Post*, November 20, 1937. Cartoon © SEPS licensed by Curtis Licensing, Indianapolis, IN. All rights reserved.

FIGURE 6.2. The Earl of Carnarvon
SOURCE: Wikimedia Commons. Photograph by Harry Burton. Public domain.

FIGURE 6.3. Howard Carter Inspects King Tut
SOURCE: Library of Congress.

FIGURE 6.4. James Henry Breasted, American Egyptologist
SOURCE: Wikimedia Commons. Public domain.

FIGURE 6.5. The Interwar Middle East, 1920–1935
CARTOGRAPHY: Debbie Newell. IMAGE: Wikimedia Commons. Public domain.

FIGURE 6.6. Obstruction in China
CARTOGRAPHY: Debbie Newell. Images: Library of Congress; Wikimedia Commons. Public domain.

FIGURE 6.7. Sino-Swedish Expedition Commemorative Stamp
SOURCE: Courtesy of Paul G. Pickowicz.

FIGURE 6.8. Marc Aurel Stein
SOURCE: Wikimedia Commons. Public domain.

FIGURE 7.1. Sylvanus Morley's Mugshot for the Office of Naval Intelligence
SOURCE: National Archives and Records Administration.

FIGURE 7.2. Scholars at War
CARTOGRAPHY: Debbie Newell. Image: Archives of the YIVO Institute for Jewish Research.

FIGURE 7.3. Nazi Art Seizures
SOURCE: Bundesarchiv, Bild 101I-729-0001-23 / Meister / CC-BY-SA 3.0.

FIGURE 7.4. The Ahnenerbe Expedition to Tibet, 1938–39
SOURCE: Bundesarchiv, Bild 135-KA-10-072 / CC-BY-SA 3.0.

FIGURE 7.5. Nazi Anthropometry
SOURCE: Bundesarchiv, Bild 135-KB-15-083 / Krause, Ernst /
CC-BY-SA 3.0

FIGURE 7.6. Szajkowski's Revenge
SOURCE: Archives of the YIVO Institute for Jewish Research.

FIGURE 7.7. The V-2 Rocket
SOURCE: Wikimedia Commons. Public domain.

FIGURE 7.8. Ex-Nazi Wernher von Braun
SOURCE: Bundesarchiv, Bild 146-1978-Anh.024-03 / CC-BY-SA
3.0.

Bibliography

This book is a work of scholarly synthesis. It combines the preliminary results of my own research on the politics of archaeological expeditions in northwestern China with my interpretation of the work of many other excellent scholars who have done research on related topics in different times and places. Readers who are interested in learning more about any of the material presented in the preceding chapters are advised to consult the following list of works. Though I am graciously indebted to every one of the scholars listed here, I alone am responsible for the implications and conclusions I have drawn from their research. (Indeed, several of the authors listed below would surely object to the direction in which I have taken their scholarship.) Not included are collections of primary sources, archival collections, or secondary scholarship in non-English languages, most of which relate to the material on China, Xinjiang, and Aurel Stein. Readers interested in these latter topics are advised to await my forthcoming book, *The Compensations of Plunder: How China Lost Its Treasures*.

Chapter 1: That Belongs in a Museum

Delbourgo, James. 2017. *Collecting the World: Hans Sloane and the Origins of the British Museum*. Cambridge, Mass.: Harvard University Press.

McClellan, Andrew. 1994. *Inventing the Louvre: Art, Politics, and the Origins of the Modern Museum in Eighteenth-Century Paris*. Berkeley: University of California Press.

Miller, Peter N., and François Louis, eds. *Antiquarianism and Intellectual Life in Europe and China, 1500–1800*. Ann Arbor: University of Michigan Press, 2011.

Moser, Stephanie. 2006. *Wondrous Curiosities: Ancient Egypt at the British Museum.* Chicago: University of Chicago Press.

Norman, Geraldine. 1998. *The Hermitage: The Biography of a Great Museum.* New York: Fromm International.

Parslow, Christopher Charles. 1995. *Rediscovering Antiquity: Karl Weber and the Excavation of Herculaneum, Pompeii, and Stabiae.* Cambridge: Cambridge University Press.

Tomkins, Calvin. 1989. *Merchants and Masterpieces: The Story of the Metropolitan Museum of Art.* New York: Henry Holt & Co.

Walker, William S. 2013. *A Living Exhibition: The Smithsonian and the Transformation of the Universal Museum.* Amherst, Mass.: University of Massachusetts Press.

Chapter 2: The Compensations of Plunder

Colla, Elliott. 2007. *Conflicted Antiquities: Egyptology, Egyptomania, Egyptian Modernity.* Durham, NC: Duke University Press.

Fitz Gibbon, Kate. 2006. "The Elgin Marbles: A Summary." In *Who Owns the Past? Cultural Policy, Cultural Property, and the Law.* Ed. Kate Fitz Gibbon. New Brunswick: Rutgers University Press, 109–19.

Hume, Ivor Noël. 2011. *Belzoni: The Giant Archaeologists Love to Hate.* Charlottesville, Virg.: University of Virginia Press.

Jasanoff, Maya. 2006. *Edge of Empire: Lives, Culture, and Conquest in the East, 1750–1850.* New York: Vintage.

Maddison, Ben. 2015. *Class and Colonialism in Antarctic Exploration, 1750–1920.* London: Routledge.

Quirke, Stephen. 2010. *Hidden Hands: Egyptian Workforces in Petrie Excavation Archives, 1880–1924.* London: Duckworth.

Reid, Donald Malcolm. 2002. *Whose Pharaohs? Archaeology, Museums, and Egyptian National Identity from Napoleon to World War I.* Berkeley: University of California Press.

St. Clair, William. 1998. *Lord Elgin and the Marbles: The Controversial History of the Parthenon Sculptures.* Oxford: Oxford University Press.

Chapter 3: Consuming Indiana Jones

Cline, Eric H. 2009. *Biblical Archaeology: A Very Short Introduction*. Oxford: Oxford University Press.

Colla, Elliott. 2007. *Conflicted Antiquities: Egyptology, Egyptomania, Egyptian Modernity*. Durham, NC: Duke University Press.

Evans, R. Tripp. 2004. *Romancing the Maya: Mexican Antiquity in the American Imagination, 1820–1915*. Austin, Tex.: University of Texas Press.

Heaney, Christopher. 2010. *Cradle of Gold: The Story of Hiram Bingham, A Real-Life Indiana Jones, and the Search for Machu Picchu*. New York: Palgrave Macmillan.

James, T.G.H. 2008. *Howard Carter: The Path to Tutankhamun*. London: I.B. Tauris.

Mairs, Rachel, and Maya Muratov. 2015. *Archaeologists, Tourists, Interpreters: Exploring Egypt and the Near East in the Late 19th-Early 20th Centuries*. London: Bloomsbury.

Moser, Stephanie. 2006. *Wondrous Curiosities: Ancient Egypt at the British Museum*. Chicago: University of Chicago Press.

Pearce, Susan M. 2000. "Giovanni Battista Belzoni's Exhibition of the Reconstructed Tomb of Pharaoh Seti I in 1821." *Journal of the History of Collections* 12, no. 1: 109–25.

Pettitt, Clare. 2007. *Dr Livingstone, I Presume? Missionaries, Journalists, Explorers, and Empire*. Cambridge, Mass.: Harvard University Press.

Ray, John. 2007. *The Rosetta Stone and the Rebirth of Ancient Egypt*. Cambridge, Mass.: Harvard University Press.

Reid, Donald Malcolm. 2002. *Whose Pharaohs? Archaeology, Museums, and Egyptian National Identity from Napoleon to World War I*. Berkeley: University of California Press.

Wu, Tim. 2016. *The Attention Merchants: The Epic Scramble to Get Inside Our Heads*. New York: Knopf.

Chapter 4: The Age of Discontent

Allen, Susan Heuck. 1999. *Finding the Walls of Troy: Frank Calvert and Heinrich Schliemann at Hisarlik*. Berkeley: University of California Press.

Çelik, Zeynep. 2016. *About Antiquities: Politics of Archaeology in the Ottoman Empire*. Austin, Tex.: University of Texas Press.

Colla, Elliott. 2007. *Conflicted Antiquities: Egyptology, Egyptomania, Egyptian Modernity*. Durham, NC: Duke University Press.

Reid, Donald Malcolm. 2002. *Whose Pharaohs? Archaeology, Museums, and Egyptian National Identity from Napoleon to World War I*. Berkeley: University of California Press.

Shaw, Wendy M.K. 2003. *Possessors and Possessed: Museums, Archaeology, and the Visualization of History in the Late Ottoman Empire*. Berkeley: University of California Press.

Wendell, Charles. 1978. *Five Tracts of Hasan al-Banna (1909–1949): A Selection from the Majmu'at rasail al-Imam al-Shahid Hasan al-Banna*. Berkeley: University of California Press.

Chapter 5: The Treasures of China

Ebrey, Patricia Buckley. 2008. *Accumulating Culture: The Collections of Emperor Huizong*. Seattle: University of Washington Press.

Elliott, Jeannette Shambaugh, with David Shambaugh. 2005. *The Odyssey of China's Imperial Art Treasures*. Seattle: University of Washington Press.

Galambos, Imre. 2012. "A Forgotten Chinese Translation of the Preliminary Report of Aurel Stein's First Expedition." In *Dunhuang Studies: Prospects and Problems for the Coming Second Century of Research*. Ed. Irina Popova and Liu Yi. St. Petersburg: Russian Academy of Sciences, 55–58.

Hevia, James. 2007. "Looting and Its Discontents: Moral Discourse and the Plunder of Beijing, 1900–1901." In *The Boxers, China, and the World*. Ed. Robert Bickers and R. G. Tiedemann. New York: Rowman & Littlefield, 93–113.

Jacobs, Justin M. 2012. "Cultural Thieves or Political Liabilities? How Chinese Officials Viewed Foreign Archaeologists in Xinjiang, 1893–1914." *The Silk Road* 10: 117–122.

———. 2016. "The Compensations of Plunder: Why Chinese Officials Aided and Abetted Foreign Explorers in Xinjiang." Paper presented at the Association for Asian Studies Annual Conference, Seattle.

———. 2016. *Xinjiang and the Modern Chinese State.* Seattle: University of Washington Press.

Kish, George. 1984. *To the Heart of Asia: The Life of Sven Hedin.* Ann Arbor: University of Michigan Press.

Li, Chu-tsing. 1958. "Recent History of the Palace Collection." *Archives of the Chinese Art Society of America* 12: 61–75.

Lu, Tracey L-D. 2014. *Museums in China: Power, Politics and Identities.* New York: Routledge.

Meyer, Karl E., and Shareen Blair Brysac. 2015. *The China Collectors: America's Century-Long Hunt for Asian Art Treasures.* New York: Palgrave Macmillan.

Netting, Lara Jaishree. 2013. *A Perpetual Fire: John C. Ferguson and His Quest for Chinese Art and Culture.* Hong Kong: Hong Kong University Press.

Walker, Annabel. 1995. *Aurel Stein: Pioneer of the Silk Road.* London: John Murray.

Chapter 6: Confronting Indiana Jones

Colla, Elliott. 2007. *Conflicted Antiquities: Egyptology, Egyptomania, Egyptian Modernity.* Durham, NC: Duke University Press.

Gallenkamp, Charles. 2001. *Dragon Hunter: Roy Chapman Andrews and the Central Asiatic Expeditions.* New York: Viking.

Goode, James F. 2007. *Negotiating for the Past: Archaeology, Nationalism, and Diplomacy in the Middle East, 1919–1941.* Austin, Tex.: University of Texas Press.

Jacobs, Justin M. 2010. "Confronting Indiana Jones: Chinese Nationalism, Historical Imperialism, and the Criminalization of Aurel Stein and the Raiders of Dunhuang, 1899–1944." In *China on the Margins*. Ed. Sherman Cochran and Paul G. Pickowicz. Ithaca, NY: Cornell University Press, 65–90.

––––. 2013. "Langdon Warner at Dunhuang: What Really Happened?" *The Silk Road* 11: 1–11.

––––. 2014. "Nationalist China's 'Great Game': Leveraging Foreign Explorers in Xinjiang, 1927–1935." *Journal of Asian Studies* 73, no. 1 (February): 43–64.

––––. 2014. "Huang Wenbi: Pioneer of Chinese Archaeology in Xinjiang." *The Silk Road* 12: 122–31.

James, T.G.H. 2008. *Howard Carter: The Path to Tutankhamun.* London: I.B. Tauris.

Reid, Donald Malcolm. 2015. *Contesting Antiquity in Egypt: Archaeologies, Museums, and the Struggle for Identities from World War I to Nasser.* Cairo: The American University in Cairo Press.

Chapter 7: Scholars at War

Allen, Susan Heuck. 2011. *Classical Spies: American Archaeologists with the OSS in World War II Greece.* Ann Arbor: University of Michigan Press.

Galambos, Imre. 2011. "An English Boy in Chinese Turkestan: The Story of Orlando Hobbs." *Studia Orientalia Slovaca* 10, no. 1: 81–98.

Harris, Charles H., and Louis R. Sadler. 2003. *The Archaeologist Was a Spy: Sylvanus G. Morley and the Office of Naval Intelligence.* Albuquerque: University of New Mexico Press.

Harris, Sheldon H. 2002. *Factories of Death: Japanese Biological Warfare, 1932–45 and the American Cover-Up.* Routledge.

Leff, Lisa Moses. 2015. *The Archive Thief: The Man Who Salvaged French Jewish History in the Wake of the Holocaust.* Oxford: Oxford University Press.

McDougall, Walter A. 1985. *The Heavens and the Earth: A Political History of the Space Age.* Baltimore: The John Hopkins University Press.

Nicholas, Lynn H. 1994. *The Rape of Europa: The Fate of Europe's Treasures in the Third Reich and the Second World War.* New York: Alfred A. Knopf.

Pringle, Heather. 2006. *The Master Plan: Himmler's Scholars and the Holocaust.* New York: Hyperion.

Winks, Robin W. 1987. *Cloak and Gown: Scholars in the Secret War, 1939–1961.* New York: William Morrow.

Acknowledgments

The idea for this book grew out of a course I teach at my home institution of American University. Thus the first debt I must acknowledge is to the many intelligent and engaging students since 2013 who have taken my "Indiana Jones in History" courses at AU, both in seminar and lecture format. In particular, I would like to thank Neil MacIntosh, Dan Kilbridge, Kaitlyn Ross, Kate Pashby, and Laith Shakir, five of the brightest and most enthusiastic students I have had the pleasure of teaching. It was Dan and Kaitlyn who first suggested that my marathon lectures might provide useful fodder for an interesting book, while Kate and Laith continually shared valuable sources and insights from their own research. I also appreciate the enthusiasm and encouragement for this project expressed at an early date by my colleagues Max Paul Friedman, Pamela Nadell, Lisa Leff, Eric Lohr, and Peter Kuznick. It is not every day that one finds such eminent academics who are willing to embrace a book with "Indiana Jones" in its title. It is also with much gratitude that I acknowledge the generous financial support provided by American University's CAS Mellon Faculty Development Fund, without which I would not have been able to defray many of the research expenses associated with this project.

No one is more directly responsible for the existence of this book than Bob McLain, my editor. At a time when few publishers seemed interested in taking on this project, Bob jumped in with a great deal of enthusiasm, efficiency, and trust. Of great value to the refinement of my presentation of the material herein was a series of invitations from Beverly Amsterdam to lecture on "Indiana Jones in History" to attentive audiences at Live and Learn Bethesda. Also helpful was advice from Rebecca Roberts and Robert Sacheli at the Smithsonian Associates

Program, along with Rebecca Basu at American University, on how to move beyond my academic ramblings and distill the essential message of this project into thirty seconds or less. I am also indebted to Maggie Greene, who graciously read early drafts of the first two chapters and continues to offer valuable feedback and encouragement on this intellectual obsession of mine. Paul Behringer graciously shared a key finding from his own promising dissertation research. Doug Esser has gone out of his way to support this project and offer insightful advice. I have striven to replicate the cheeky humor and rigorous standards of Ernie in every page. My parents, Jan and Candy, read through the entire manuscript with a keen eye for typos and offered timely encouragement.

As with all my work, the eight beautiful maps that appear in this book were drawn by expert cartographer and fellow Seattle native Debbie Newell. Unlike all my other work, the broad geographical scope and sweeping timeframe covered by this book have made it impossible to rely solely on the insights of my own research and that of other scholars in my field (i.e., modern Chinese history). A full list of the many excellent scholars whose work I have consulted in the development of my course lectures, this book, and the documentary is available in the bibliography.

The last word goes to my wife, Cindy. Her constant companionship and youthful spark are what makes this lifelong journey worth the while—and a great deal more fun.

About the Author

Justin M. Jacobs is associate professor of history at American University. He received his Ph.D. in modern Chinese history from the University of California, San Diego, in 2011. His obsession with Indiana Jones stems from a hopeless nostalgia for the halcyon days of his youth, when he backpacked among grizzlies in Yellowstone, hiked around Mt. Rainier, scuba dived in Thailand, swam in the Mekong, and slept in alpine yurts in Xinjiang, all without an ounce of back or knee pain. He is now a thoroughly domesticated and boring father of two who makes his home in the Maryland suburbs of Washington, D.C.